A History of
Fisk University,
1865-1946

A History of Fisk University, 1865-1946

JOE M. RICHARDSON

THE UNIVERSITY OF ALABAMA PRESS

Library of Congress Cataloging in Publication Data

Richardson, Joe Martin.
   A history of Fisk University, 1865-1946.

   Bibliography: p.
   Includes index.
   1. Fisk University, Nashville—History. I. Title.
LC2851.F52R5   378.768'55   79-9736
ISBN 0-8173-0015-5

0-8173-1207-2 (pbk: alk. paper)

IN MEMORY OF
JESSE M. RICHARDSON
AND
WEYMOUTH TYREE JORDAN

Contents

Illustrations

Preface

Fisk University has been a leading black educational institution for more than a century. An attempt has been made to trace its evolution and development from 1866 when it was little more than a primary school to the 1930s and 1940s when it became a center of culture and scholarship; from 1871 when it was necessary to send out the Fisk Jubilee Singers to earn operating expenses to the 1940s when it had a several-million-dollar endowment; and from 1866 when black children eagerly sought any education whites gave them to 1925 when students joined alumni to oust a white president whom they considered dictatorial.

The problems of private universities, compounded by being black, have been discussed. For years it was necessary for Fisk to go on annual "begging" campaigns to balance its meager budget. The impact Fisk made on its students and the community has been assessed, as have the major contributions made to scholarship by the university faculty. In short, this is a study of Fisk's evolution, impact, and significance from 1865 to 1946.

Many people assisted in the preparation of this book. I appreciate the courtesies extended to me by the staffs of the Tennessee State Library and Archives, Florida State University Library, the Library of Congress, the National Archives, the University of Mississippi Library, Yale University Library, and the Fisk University Library. I am especially grateful for the cooperation of the following members of the Fisk Library staff: Eurydice W. Smith, Jessie C. Smith, Sue P. Chandler, Helen Bridgeforth, Earnestine Potts, Beth M. House, and Ann Allen Shockley.

The late Arna Bontemps first piqued my curiosity about Fisk University history and encouraged my initial efforts. W. Dickerson Donnelly and Mrs. Grace Harlin placed the records of the Alumni Office at my disposal, and Mrs. Harlin cheerfully spent many hours tracking down alumni. Professor Louis Harlan generously stole time from a busy schedule to guide me to the proper portions of the massive Booker T. Washington Collection. I am also under obligation to Mrs. Grace Nail Johnson for her permission to use the James Weldon Johnson papers.

I remain indebted to those who read the manuscript and suggested improvements: James P. Jones, William W. Rogers, John Hope Franklin, Maxine D. Jones, August Meier, and Patricia Richardson. None of them necessarily agree with my analysis and conclusions. Such errors as appear are solely my responsibility.

A History of
Fisk University,
1865-1946

1

Laying the Foundation

THE HISTORY OF BLACK PEOPLE SINCE EMANCIPATION IN THE UNITED States has been a dramatic struggle against social and economic adversity. Nearly four million slaves were suddenly removed from a condition of total dependence and were "thrown upon their own resources to fight the battle for existence." They were forced to adjust to a radically changed position and make a place for themselves in a "kaleidoscopic civilization" that was growing more complicated with each passing year.[1] The former bondsmen were ill prepared for their new status. Life as slaves had provided little or no exposure to formal learning, and the newly liberated freedmen's responsibility for their own well-being and livelihood necessitated education. Fortunately, a majority of blacks were eager for knowledge. One historian has said that "the zeal with which the ex-slaves sought the benefits of literary education is unparalleled in history...."[2]

In many instances there was an almost sacred nature to the freedman's attitude toward education. "In learning to read he was eating of the fruit so long forbidden to him, and he was entering a mystery which seemed almost holy." A Union army chaplain overheard a black servant congratulating himself on having completed a lesson: "'John Green,'" the servant said, "'you have it. You can read. JOHN GREEN, YOU ARE A MAN!'"[3] In the first flush of freedom, grandparents and grandchildren thronged to crude schoolhouses to secure "the magic of reading and writing."[4] Their demand for training crowded every facility. Families pinched with hunger asked more eagerly for learning than for food. Gray-haired men bent over spelling books with small children. A visitor to Tennessee in the fall of 1865 found nearly all the freedmen, adult and young alike, expressing "a very strong desire" to be educated.[5] In Clinton, Tennessee, blacks employed a white teacher to hold classes in the local Methodist church but white disapproval forced abandonment of the building. Within two weeks the undaunted freedmen had purchased an acre of land and, with axes as tools, erected a primitive but neat log schoolhouse.[6]

The freedmen's ardent aspirations for learning were not surprising. The feeling of inferiority forced upon them by slavery "fathered an intense desire to rise out of their condition by means of education."[7] Throughout his lifetime the slave had seen white power and influence connected with education. If it could enhance the position of the white man, he reasoned, why could it not do the same for him? It seemed that in having education, which for so long had been forbidden, blacks found an assurance of their freedom and "a pledge of its perpetuity." Education was looked upon as "possessing talismanic power." When Northern teachers went South to instruct the freedmen, they found devoted and responsive pupils.[8]

At the beginning of the Civil War a few Northerners, especially abolitionists, showed an interest in educating blacks. Sympathetic Union soldiers and chaplains taught slaves who congregated at their camps, and their work was soon supplemented by representatives of various Northern aid societies. By 1865 approximately seventy-five thousand black pupils were being trained by zealous teachers in areas occupied by Union armies. The crusade for emancipation was transformed into enthusiasm for black education.[9] Among the scores who went South to teach the freedmen were three men: John Ogden, Erastus M. Cravath, and Edward P. Smith. These men became the prime movers in founding one of the outstanding black universities in the United States.

Ogden, who served as a lieutenant in the Second Wisconsin Cavalry during the war, had been captured by the Confederates in Tennessee and spent several months in a prison camp. While in the army he had demonstrated an interest in black troops, trying to secure a command in a black regiment shortly before his capture. Because of his interest in the freedmen and his previous experience as principal of the Minnesota State Normal School, he was appointed superintendent of education for the Freedmen's Bureau in Tennessee. In 1865 he took office with headquarters in Nashville.[10]

Cravath also had the proper background for his important work in black education. Born of an abolitionist family in Homer, New York, he was sent to New York Central College, which was founded by abolitionists. He came in contact with slaves and slavery at his father's house, which was an underground railroad station for escaping fugitives. In 1851 the Cravath family moved to Oberlin, Ohio, where young Cravath entered Oberlin College, a hotbed of antislavery agitation. After graduating from Oberlin in 1857 and completing the school's course in the theological seminary, Cravath became pastor of the Berlin Heights, Ohio, Congregational Church. In December 1863 he resigned his pastorate to become chaplain of the 101st Regiment of Ohio Volunteers. Impressed with the needs of the former bondsmen during the war, he decided to devote his life to educational work in the South. When he was mustered out in Nashville in June 1865, Cravath accepted the position of field secretary of the American Missionary Association, which was one of the most important benevolent societies engaged in the education of blacks.[11]

In 1865 the Reverend Edward P. Smith assumed the work of district secretary of the newly created Middle West Department of the American Missionary Association at Cincinnati. He and Cravath were directed by the association to establish a school for freedmen in Nashville. After a brief survey of the area they decided the city was a focal point warranting more than the anticipated elementary school.

Nashville in 1860 was a small city with a population of 16,988, of which only 3,945 were blacks, but Cravath and Smith were convinced that its central location would enable a school to service both the border states and the deep South. They also seemed to concur with a visitor who claimed Nashville was "a nostril" through which the state had "long breathed the Northern air of free institutions." Cravath and Smith went immediately to confer with Superintendent of Education Ogden, who had already established numerous "promising" Freedmen's Bureau schools in the vicinity. Ogden quickly agreed that Nashville was suitable for at least a normal school for blacks and promised Freedmen's Bureau aid for the enterprise. A search was begun for land on which to build the school.[12]

From the beginning the three men encountered difficulty. Suitable plots of land for sale suddenly became unavailable when owners discovered the land would be utilized to educate freedmen. Land that could be bought was in the wrong location or too expensive. Earlier enthusiasm was turning into discouragement when Smith and Cravath discovered that the Union hospital west of the Chattanooga depot was to be given up by the government. The hospital complex was situated on a block of land about 310 feet by 320 feet and held almost twenty buildings in the midst of the heaviest concentration of freedmen in the city. No area, Smith and Cravath believed, could be better for immediate school purposes. Moreover, its location would soon make such a school the acknowledged headquarters of the missionary and educational work in Tennessee.

However, their optimism was soon slightly dampened. Officers of the American Missionary Association favored the plan to establish a college for freedmen, but there were no funds for acquiring the privately owned land on which the hospital buildings were located. The purchase price was $16,000 with 25 percent down and the remainder to be paid in three annual installments. Ogden, Cravath, and Smith refused to be thwarted by lack of funds. They pledged personal notes to raise $4,000, and a black university was born.[13] The American Missionary Association and the Western Freedmen's Aid Commission paid the second and fourth installments and eventually reimbursed the original buyers. The third payment of $4,000 was made by the Freedmen's Bureau.

The land had been purchased but the hospital buildings still belonged to the government. With the active assistance of General Clinton B. Fisk, assistant commissioner of the Freedmen's Bureau for Tennessee and Kentucky, the buildings were acquired for the school. Because of General Fisk's assistance in securing the buildings and his continued interest—he eventually gave the institution approximately $30,000—the school was named for him.

The aims of the Fisk School—sometimes known as Fisk Free Colored School—were commendable and lofty—and thought by some to be impractical. The founders proposed to provide a free school of grades from primary to normal based upon a "broad Christian foundation." Fisk was further designed to supply the desperate need for properly qualified black teachers. But the founders had no intention of stopping with a normal school. They hoped that Fisk would ultimately become a first-class college that would give blacks the opportunities and advantages of education so long enjoyed by white people.

The aim in founding Fisk and similar schools, as famous Fisk alumnus W. E. B. DuBois said, was to maintain the standards of lower training by giving leaders and teachers the best possible instruction, and more important, to furnish blacks with "adequate standards of human culture and lofty ideals of life." It was not sufficient, DuBois stated, to train black teachers in technical normal methods; they must also, so far as possible, be broadminded, cultured men and women, who would scatter civilization among a people whose ignorance was not simply of the alphabet, but of life itself.[14]

Fisk School was opened on 9 January 1866 with appropriate ceremonies. Distinguished visitors spoke to a large crowd of teachers and pupils from the various local black schools.[15] After a prayer by the Reverend R. H. Allen of the Second Presbyterian Church, Nashville, and music by the local army band, the Reverend Erastus M. Cravath briefly stated the aims of the school. It was to be free, equal to the best in the country, and manned by outstanding teachers. The school would be permanent and would be kept open at least eight months of the year if Northern friends kept their financial pledges. The superintendent of the white city schools, Dr. J. B. Lindsley, discussed the importance of popular education for all races. He rejoiced that Fisk provided the nucleus for the spread of truth and knowledge and looked forward to the day when the advantages, now confined to the few thousand freedmen in Nashville, would be enjoyed by all blacks in Tennessee.[16]

General Fisk expressed gratitude for the opportunity of being "godfather at the baptism of a new and *free* school." Offering advice as to conduct toward whites, he asked the students to avoid criticism and censure. Remember the past only for the terrible lessons it teaches, the former slaves were told, and go among whites with "the hope that this land may become a Christian land, where God is Lord." Among other speeches was one by Nelson Walker, a black barber, who told the audi-

FISK UNIVERSITY, 1866 (*Courtesy of the Fisk University Library's Special Collections*)

ence to seize the opportunity presented for instruction because without an education blacks would never become "a people."[17]

Good wishes were also presented by Tennessee politicians. Senator William Bosson of White County commented on the generosity and interest shown by Northern friends. Nowhere was there a more noble enterprise than assisting a people just emerged from slavery and now taking their place "among human beings as freedmen," he said. William G. Brownlow, a former Unionist and now the controversial governor of Tennessee, voiced approval of all that had been said and all that was proposed for Fisk. He admonished Fisk students to attend school, learn to read the Bible, and then "learn to love and practice it." By way of caution the governor struck the one discordant note in the opening exercises. He advised freedmen to be "mild and temperate" in habits, spirit, and conduct toward white people. As a friend of the institution and desiring its prosperity, he counseled teachers to be "exceedingly prudent and cautious" to avoid giving offense to the white majority. Without federal troops, Brownlow stated, black pupils would not be permitted to occupy the school room "a week, not a week."[18]

Official recognition from Tennessee politicians was gratifying, but, as Governor Brownlow's speech indicated, they by no means mirrored the attitude of all Tennessee whites. None of the speakers had mentioned white Southern financial support—only the benevolent spirit of the North. A large number of whites were unhappy about emancipation and had no intention of granting blacks equality in education or anything else. Judge James O. Shackelford of the Tennessee Supreme Court reflected the views of many Tennesseans when he claimed in February 1865 that the Negro was "inferior," no power on earth could make him equal to the Anglo-Saxon, and he would be governed by white men.[19] Another politician referred to "the everlasting *nigger*—that dark fountain from which has flowed all our woes." Many Democrats spoke in even stronger language.

The founders of Fisk were seemingly unconcerned about white hostility. They could see no reason to anticipate any serious disturbances in judiciously managed schools, but events soon proved them wrong. Many whites simply would not tolerate black schools. They refused to rent land for such purposes or provide houses for teachers of such institutions. In central Tennessee a man was tied to a stake and whipped with forty lashes for teaching eight boys to read. Two schoolhouses were burned in Gallatin, Tennessee, in 1865. When a school was opened in Springfield, "fellows of the baser sort" broke up the benches, knocked down the door, and gave the instructor "such broad hints of visiting him with their wrath, that he shook off the dust of his feet against them and left." In 1868 a Fisk student who went to Woodbury to organize a school left after local blacks warned him he would be "Kukluxed" if he remained. Two

Fisk students teaching for the summer were whipped and driven from their schools in 1869.[20] During the Memphis race riot in May 1866, twelve schoolhouses were burned.

In 1868 a school at Mount Pleasant was broken up and the teachers ordered to leave town. Instructors at Somerville and Saulsbury were beaten and abused by disguised men. Schoolhouses at Carthage, Wartrace, Memphis, Gallatin, and several other places were burned. Teachers were frightened away by warnings from the Ku Klux Klan. One hundred Klansmen rode down Church Street in Nashville on 5 March 1868 to terrify blacks and Republicans.[21]

It was under these conditions that Fisk School opened. The immediate postwar years were bitter and fearful ones for the former slaves—a time of intimidation, bigotry, lynchings, and murders—but both teachers and students were optimistic. It was also a time of hope. A practical application of democracy was what blacks and their friends desired, and education seemed to be the best way to prepare the freedmen for their new role in society.

When Fisk opened, students came by the hundreds. Almost two hundred were enrolled immediately and by February there were five hundred scholars in day school and one hundred in a night class. On May 1 there was an enrollment of nine hundred pupils, and the number increased to an average daily attendance of one thousand for 1866. In the words of Booker T. Washington, "those were wonderful days, directly after the war! . . . Suddenly, as if at the sound of a trumpet, a whole race that had been slumbering for centuries . . . awoke and started off one morning to school."[22]

Not all the pupils were children. One teacher had a class of pupils ranging in age from seven to seventy, all reading at the same level. Parents and children, husbands and wives—all were trying to learn. There was one student over seventy years old who was just learning his letters. His ambition was to learn to read so he could study the Bible for himself. Although his eyes were dim he made commendable progress because his zeal was great. A drayman while out of class, the old man carried his books with him to study during odd moments of leisure time. A former slave over fifty years old, Lizzie Wilson, had made such progress in reading as to surprise someone unaccustomed to the intense desire of "these poor people," a teacher reported. The adults usually attended night school after working all day.[23]

Naturally most of the 1,000 students were in primary work, learning the alphabet or struggling to master the most elementary words in the *First Reader,* but even in the first month at least 106 of the 190 could read. Forty students were doing mental arithmetic, 9 written arithmetic, and 20 were studying geography. By March, 229 students could read and write, 52 were pondering arithmetic, 28 were studying geography, and 50 were writing. Progress was rapid. The monthly school report for April listed only 100 students still working with the alphabet. More than 600 were spelling, 655 were reading, 198 were writing, 226 were in arithmetic class, 104 were studying geography, and 20 were doing battle with English grammar. Two Latin recitations were offered to an undetermined, but certainly small, number of pupils.[24]

Whites, North and South, were frequently amazed by the blacks' rapid progress in education, since they were generally skeptical of the former bondsmen's ability. A Fisk teacher received a letter from a Northern friend pointing out the futility of teaching freedmen—they were little better than heathen, he was told. As late as 1889 the U.S. commissioner of education felt obligated to include some statements from white Southerners that blacks were capable of being educated.[25] Even some of the first Fisk teachers doubted the extent to which blacks were educable. One instructor compared the teachers to early navigators sent out on new seas of discovery. "Would we come to the charmed circle beyond which the Negro mind could not go? We would try," he said, "and when we came to the fatal place we would stop, no sooner." They never reached the stopping place.[26]

The astonishing improvement of black pupils could be understood only if their extraordinary thirst for knowledge was recognized. Many observers thought the intense desire to learn would lessen after a short time, but teachers reported that the sometimes frantic pursuit of learning continued unabated. Education seemed to be some kind of magic, a panacea to cure all ills. Educators in all Southern states commented on the freedmen's almost mystical attitude toward schooling. Some thought there was a religious nature to the blacks' view of learning. In 1862 a Sea Island teacher described a funeral where children standing near the open grave, school books in hand, repeatedly sang their alphabet song. This was, the teacher concluded, evidence that blacks looked upon their lessons as a religious exercise.[27] This attitude toward education declined but interest did not and progress continued.[28]

Dedicated instructors were another reason why the freedmen moved ahead in education. Most of the teachers were on a crusade, sacrificing a more pleasant life, sometimes better paying jobs, and frequently their health to work with former slaves. Inspired with enthusiasm and high purpose, these teachers performed an incalculable service to the South and to blacks. Having faith in the possibilities of the freedmen, they believed opportunities for the highest human development should be open to them. One writer said their motive was in no sense utilitarian; it was purely Christian. To them, blacks were essentially white people with darker skins. Any differences were accidental, not vital, the result of circumstance, not race. Their dedication and belief in the future of blacks spurred the pupils on.[29] The early teachers at Fisk were sent by the American Missionary Association and considered themselves more missionaries than teachers.

The American Missionary Association was not organized primarily for freedmen's aid, but it was in a position to answer the call of destitute blacks on the outbreak of the Civil War. Organized on 3 September 1846 as a protest against the relative silence of other missionary societies concerning slavery, the association had carried on nondenominational work attempting to convince Southerners of the evils of slavery. When the first slaves were freed, the association led the way in systematic relief and education. It sent missionaries to Fortress Monroe, Virginia, as early as September 1861, and the work increased until by 1866 it employed over 350 persons in school and church work among freedmen. The American Missionary Association was the first and most notable of the great missionary societies for the training of Southern blacks. In addition to Fisk, it established Hampton Institute, Berea College, Atlanta University, Talladega College, Tougaloo University, and Straight University (now Dillard). The history of the association is that of patient and persevering efforts of hundreds of persons who gave themselves and their means to aid a people struggling upward from slavery.[30]

The man selected to supervise the association's missionary teachers at Fisk was John Ogden, who resigned as superintendent of education of the Freedmen's Bureau to accept the position of Fisk's principal. Ogden was primarily interested in training teachers who could go out and instruct thousands of others. Most of the other early teachers remained at Fisk only a short time and left no lasting impression, but they did commendable work while there. In April 1866 there were ten instructors assisting Principal Ogden.[31]

Nearly all the instructors had duties in addition to teaching. To provide a free school for the recently emancipated was not enough; numerous people still needed food and clothing. In 1865 Nashville blacks organized a provident association managed exclusively by themselves to provide relief for the poor, regardless of color, but poverty limited their organization's work.[32] Teachers canvassed the city, trying to determine those most in need of relief. Food packages and especially clothing were distributed. Mrs. Charles Crosby dispensed eighty-four packages of clothing to the destitute one day in May. Multitudes came to the doors of the teacher-missionaries for help. In April 1866 Ogden received in one shipment eleven boxes, two casks, three barrels and two bales of clothing valued at $3,000 from various aid societies. On another occasion twenty boxes and three barrels of clothing arrived from England. But the gifts were never sufficient. The clothing was sold to those who had some money and given to the impoverished.[33] Some books were sent to Fisk by charitable associations, but not enough. Fisk students reputedly gathered the rusty handcuffs from the city's former slave mart and sold them as scrap metal to earn money to purchase books.[34]

Religious work was even more important to the faculty than relief. In the words of Cravath, "It is better that some suffer for food and clothing than that so many suffer for light and truth." The missionaries who went South to teach were imbued with the Puritan tradition. They were religious men and women first and teachers second. They maintained strict rules for the students and endeavored to prevent any immoral or even frivolous conduct. Compulsory chapel services and prayer meetings were held regularly.

Conversion of new students was confidently expected and sought more eagerly than progress in learning. The principal's reports announced with greater thankfulness the number of souls saved than the material gifts received. In early 1868 Ogden wrote that nearly every pupil of responsible age "is now either a professor of religion, or seeking it." Twelve or fifteen conversions had occurred within the week and the work was still increasing.[35] The monthly school report in October 1870 listed enrollment and average attendance but also boasted that fifteen prayer meetings and four open-air meetings had been held. Twenty-five teachers and students were doing missionary work at school and in the city. There had been six conversions that month. All of the female pupils were "professed disciples," but a few of the men were "yet seeking." It had been most delightful work, reported a teacher. Family prayers had been "a heaven begun on earth." "O to make this school a fountain of good influence, of piety, of burning devotion for Christ," he added. "I believe it will be made so."[36] To many of the teachers there was no division between religion and education. One of the primary objectives of the school, according to Principal Ogden, was to illustrate that conversion was the proper door into both the kingdom of science and the kingdom of heaven. Science and religion were made to go hand in hand, he said, and the two joined were the heaven-appointed means of "uplifting humanity to its proper standing and dignity."

The American Missionary Association not only approved Fisk's missionary activities but at its 1867 annual meeting resolved that education should be thoroughly religious and none but evangelical teachers should be sent to the South. For many years Fisk remained religiously oriented. Faculty meetings were always opened with a prayer, and services were held daily. In 1869 the faculty voted to hold short prayer meetings after the usual prayers at night.[37] According to Henrietta Matson, who remained a great religious force on campus for years, the additional prayers were answered. In 1870 Fisk was "visited by a very great revival." At the first prayer meeting of the year the "spirit of God was so manifestly present that sinners were deeply convicted and many of them cried aloud for mercy." It became common, she said, for students and faculty to gather for prayers after study hours. Conversions continued to occur from day to day and within three weeks a majority of students "professed a hope in Christ." This was just one of many "revivals" in which Miss Matson participated.[38]

Missionary activity was not limited to Fisk students. In 1870 six neighborhood prayer meetings were held weekly in the city by Fisk personnel. Professor Henry S. Bennett superintended the Tennessee Penitentiary Sunday School, and other members of the faculty worked with the prisoners. Meetings were held at random by individuals any time the need arose.[39]

The religious work was usually nonsectarian. The American Missionary Association had been nondenominational but soon after the war it became largely Congregational. There was some fear that Congregationalism would gain an upper hand in the school. Ogden, a Methodist, favored the establishment of a Union church. He intended to steer Fisk clear of any ecclesiastical complications—to teach Christ and Christianity, but not sectarianism. Levi Coffin, an outstanding figure in the underground railroad, warned Ogden to beware of "Friend Cravath," who as field secretary of the association exerted considerable influence on Fisk policy. Cravath, Coffin claimed, was so full of Congregationalism he needed "careful watching lest he should try to run this machine on Congregational wheels and finally make a sectarian machine of it." The Fisk faculty solved the problem in June 1868 by organizing the independent Union Church of Nashville. Individuals could retain their own religious tenets and church connection, while at the same time uniting to strengthen the religious influence at Fisk.[40] Numerous ministers of all protestant denominations were produced at Fisk.

Fisk's benevolent activities and religious emphasis did not allay white suspicions. Schools in Tennessee and throughout the South continued to be destroyed, and white teachers were ostracized and abused. Fisk experienced less difficulty than many other places. Though the faculty was not accepted by local white society, there was seldom physical mistreatment. The same could not be said for students. Children were abused on the way to school. Miss E. A. Easter sometimes acted as a guard to protect her students from stoning. One teacher applied to the city for a guard to defend pupils going to and from home. In March 1866 Ogden requested the Freedmen's Bureau to restrain the mobs of boys, black and white, who collected near the school throwing rocks and other missiles at each other, endangering peaceful citizens. Fisk pupils, complained Ogden, were almost daily assailed on their way to and from campus, and were cut and bruised to an alarming degree.[41] General Fisk gave orders to arrest and punish such offenders, regardless of color. These outbreaks were symptomatic of the condition of blacks in Tennessee and in most of the South. Governor Brownlow seemed to think little could be done. If Christ came to Davidson County, Tennessee, Brownlow stated, with shoulder straps and stars on his shoulders, with a military staff of apostles, he could not give satisfaction to rebels of the area.[42] Fisk students would long be subjected to discrimination and sometimes abuse by white people.

Despite difficulties, 1866 proved to be a good year for Fisk. Although there was considerable hostility, some whites had grudgingly accepted the idea of black education and were beginning to recognize the freedmen's ability. In November Governor Brownlow recommended black suffrage, in part because the ex-slaves had displayed a greater aptitude for learning than expected.[43] Moreover, the first demand of Fisk School was to provide its pupils with enough learning so that they could teach, and this goal was accomplished through several students in the summer of 1866. When classes ended on June 15 Cravath was convinced the school had been successful and had made a favorable impression not only in Nashville but also throughout the state.[44]

2

From School to College

DURING 1866 ONLY THE MOST ELEMENTARY SUBJECTS WERE TAUGHT AT Fisk School, but the dream of a normal school and college was not lost. Since its inception Ogden had argued that Fisk should be in the "business of making teachers," leaving elementary education to others.[1] Then in the spring of 1867 a Tennessee school law provided for free, segregated, common schools. Though this separation of races was vigorously attacked by Ogden as an attempt "to pander to wicked prejudices," it made the training of black teachers even more imperative.[2] Southern whites were reluctant to teach in black schools and white missionaries could not supply the anticipated demand. When in the fall of 1867 Nashville opened free public schools for all races, thereby relieving Fisk of many of its elementary pupils, the goal of normal and higher education was advanced.

In keeping with Ogden's desire for a black college in Nashville, Fisk School was incorporated on 22 August 1867 as Fisk University. Ogden, Joseph H. Barnum, W. W. Mallory, John Lawrence, and John Ruhm were the incorporators.[3] The purpose of the corporation as stated in the charter was the education and training of young men and women of all races. Trustees were authorized to confer all such degrees and honors as were granted by universities in the United States. This was a masterly statement of human expectation and optimism, since Fisk did not yet have students even of normal grade. A board of trustees of not less than three or more than nine was to be organized.[4] The school would remain under the control of the American Missionary Association.

College work could not be immediately offered but a normal department was organized at the beginning of the 1867 school term. The first class of twelve was accepted in November 1867, and a second one was enrolled in January 1868. A month later Ogden, a normal school expert, claimed that the original class was doing as well or better than any class he had ever seen. The second group was doing nearly as well. Dr. Barnas Sears, general agent for the Peabody Fund and former president of Brown University, was sufficiently impressed after visiting Fisk to appropriate $800 in scholarships for sixteen of the most promising students.[5] Two years later Sears, who had visited both white and black schools, declared that Fisk was the best normal school he had seen in the South.

The course of study in the normal class did not, as white opponents charged, consist entirely of Latin and Greek.[6] Reading, arithmetic, geography, and penmanship were studied in the first two terms of the beginning year. During the third term, students worked with reading and sentence analysis, arithmetic, English grammar and composition, and elementary algebra. The second year included the previous subjects in addition to botany and natural history. Geometry, history of the United States, teaching theory, natural philosophy, chemistry, physiology, and natural science were taught in the final year. In addition to "the most rigid and searching class drills" in the above subjects, there was a daily study of the science of education and art of teaching. Furthermore, normal students (to acquire skill in teaching and managing schools of various grades) taught one-half hour each day in the model school under the principal's direction. The model school, organized for this specific purpose, contained about sixty pupils studying reading, arithmetic, and geography.[7]

In 1869 the Tennessee superintendent of public instruction, John Eaton, Jr., was inspired by a Fisk visit. "The proficiency of those examined," Eaton stated, "was gratifying" and indicated the wisdom of efforts made to prepare competent teachers. John M. Langston, the black general inspector for Freedmen's Bureau schools, was no less pleased after attending spring examinations. Classes in the model school were examined by students in the normal department. These teacher-pupils exhibited good teaching talent, Langston said, and the scholars showed "much capacity" and gave evidence of having been "well drilled . . . with great advantage." Examinations in the normal and high school were conducted by teachers of the university and were "in every way highly satisfactory and creditable to the scholars as well as their instructors." Langston was especially impressed with the "remarkable degree of proficiency" exhibited in algebra, bookkeeping, arithmetic, English grammar, and Latin.[8]

By 1869 twelve students had gone out from the normal school to teach and were doing splendidly. These teachers, the American Missionary Association thought, were more effective than white instructors from the North. They had "the readiest access to their own race" and could "do a work for them" no other teachers could accomplish.[9] Of course the normal school students were only a small portion of those from Fisk who taught. Numerous students operated schools in the spring and summer. The number of pupils taught by Fiskites in the first few summers after the university's opening is estimated at ten thousand, although some estimates indicate this number was met in one year. Frequently these student-teachers could impart only the most basic knowledge, but even that was thankfully accepted. Fisk teachers were found in almost every Southern state.

The establishment of the normal department was accompanied by a reorganization of the entire school. In 1869 Fisk consisted of a normal and high school, model school, theology department, a very practical commercial department, and the college. In addition, special courses in vocal and instrumental music were offered. The normal and high school had about 120 pupils, three-fourths of whom were preparing to teach. The model school included three grades and served as a training laboratory for older pupils. Although it was never large, the theology department was organized to accommodate those who expected to enter the ministry of any evangelical denomination.

The college department, including a three-year preparatory course, was fully organized in 1869, but there were no students until four were accepted in 1871. The number increased to eight in 1872 and nine in 1873. For years the college was the smallest department at Fisk. The number of students was small, but their program of studies was rigid. A skeptical visitor witnessed an examination of the college students in 1875. The freshmen were tested on Virgil's *Aeneid,* geometry, and botany. Sophomores stood an examination in Latin, Greek, and botany. The visitor concluded that blacks were capable of mastering the most difficult studies and of highest attainment in the best colleges.[10]

The curriculum in the college and the college preparatory classes was similar to that in a majority of the contemporary liberal arts schools. The freshmen studied Latin, Greek, and mathematics. Greek, Latin, French, mathematics, and natural science were taught to the sophomores. The juniors labored over the same courses with additional work in German, natural philosophy, history, English, and astronomy. Mental and moral science and political science were added for the seniors.[11] The college prep pupils studied Latin, Greek, English, arithmetic, world history, and algebra. All students received a lesson in the Bible once a week.[12]

In conjunction with the regular studies, essays, debates, declamations, and original addresses were required at stated times. The Union Literary Society, organized on 31 January 1868, provided practice in the above activities for approximately fifty of the better male students.[13] The society's object was self-improvement of its members in general knowledge, parliamentary usage, and the art of conducting deliberative bodies. Some of the subjects debated were: Should there be a national university? Should women receive preference as teachers in public schools? and, Was Cortes justified in the conquest of Mexico? Speeches were made and essays read on such topics as: Would the Negro in the South ever be on a plane of equality with the white man? Were the Puritans justified in banishing Roger Williams? and, Should judges be appointed or elected?

Most of the Fisk college students received their earlier training at Fisk, since there were few schools for blacks above the most elementary level.

Some localities in Tennessee were reluctant to pay school taxes, reputedly because blacks as well as whites would benefit. By 1872 only 29 of
93 counties had levied a special tax for schools. One Fisk student attended school in a log cabin so well ventilated, he said, one could throw a
cat between the logs and never touch a hair. It was admirably suited for
the study of astronomy, he thought, for one could see "the glory of God
reflected in the heavens" through the roof. But the instructors and
facilities were inadequate to prepare students for further training. Such
schools generally operated only about three months out of twelve. For
this reason Fisk continued to maintain lower departments. In 1872 there
were 94 pupils in primary grades, 87 in intermediate, 35 in the normal
school, 33 in the college preparatory course, and only 8 in college.[14]

The reorganization of the school also included the establishment of
the boarding department or "home." Since most of the pupils in the
primary grades were quite young and many students were from outside
the city, some kind of boarding arrangement was needed. In early 1867
a building was set aside to accommodate thirty young women. Two
female teachers lived with the girls and helped them with their studies
after school hours. Dining and living in common with the teachers
seemed to have such a good influence on the pupils that the idea of a
"home" began to be considered. A majority of instructors favored a
common dining hall where the influence of the faculty could be brought
to bear on pupils. In this way, the faculty believed, the pupils could be
acculturated and acquire manners, habits, and "general Christian training" that could be received in no other way.[15]

Teachers and students boarding on campus were organized into a
family or "home." A system of detailed labor was arranged, each pupil
having certain duties in the home each day. This work was intended to
help pay expenses and also to train students in matters of housekeeping
and economy. The teachers—and most observers—thought the home a
success. A reporter for *Harper's Weekly* said the "most beneficial effects"
resulted from the arrangement. Bringing the pupils under the "social,
refining and elevating" influence of a Christian family had "surpassed
the most sanguine expectations" even of those who introduced the plan.
Students were charged $2.75 per week for living in the home. This sum,
which paid for room rent and all other necessities, seemed to be cheap.
Still, since a majority of students were unable to pay, the strictest economy had to be observed. Students believed that money was saved on
food. In later years an alumnus said the thing which most impressed him
about going to Fisk was the "scarcity of the supper." Those who complained about the food were bluntly told if they wanted to grumble they
should pay their bills first.[16]

Since a major reason for organizing the home was to improve morals
and manners as well as the mind, rigid regulations were uncompromis-

ingly enforced. Boarders were compelled to observe neatness and order both in person and their rooms. They rose promptly at the ringing of the first bell and studied from 5:30 to 7:00 in the morning; lights were put out at 10:00 P.M. Each student on campus was expected to attend chapel every morning and Wednesday afternoon, and regular services on Sunday. Visits to rooms of other students were prohibited during study hours (5:30 to 7:00 A.M., 8:30 to 12:00 noon, 1:00 to 4:00 P.M., and 6:30 to 9:00 P.M.). Males and females were not allowed to visit each other or friends in their private rooms under any circumstances. All interviews had to be public and in the presence of a teacher. Tobacco in any form, ardent spirits, and games of chance were strictly forbidden at all times and places while the student was connected with Fisk. To teach economy and prevent needless expenditure, pupils were required to deposit all their money with the treasurer upon entrance.[17] Violation of rules could lead to immediate expulsion, but sometimes less drastic punishment was used. In 1869 a student was brought before the faculty for leaving campus contrary to orders. It was recommended that he be "switched vigorously." On the same day an adventurous young man accused of taking "undue liberties" with a female pupil (undue liberty could be as minor as touching her hand) was sentenced to be reprimanded before all students in chapel.[18]

Most students had neither the time nor inclination to violate many of the regulations. A number of them were in their late teens or older and considered themselves fortunate to be able to attend Fisk. Thus most of them attempted to take advantage of the opportunity. The privations that students inflicted upon themselves in order to remain in school were incredible to observers.[19] Board and room were less than three dollars a week and tuition for primary students was only one dollar per month. Tuition in the high and normal school and college was only twelve dollars a year, but even that was high when the average wage for a farm laborer was from eight to fifteen dollars a month. Some of the city pupils in the winter of 1868 were forced to miss school because it was too cold to walk barefoot. Nashville supported a soup-house where cornbread and soup were served once daily. Some of the day-pupils lived on that one meal.[20]

Staying in school was a desperate struggle. Numerous Fisk students taught sometime during the year to pay their expenses, but frequently at the end of the session they discovered they could not collect their wages for months, if at all. In 1873 almost one-half of the student body, 110 of 256, taught from five to six months.[21] Pitiful letters were written by parents begging officials to wait while they struggled to scrape up enough money for their children's board and tuition. An aunt wrote in 1868 trying to get her niece in school. She could attend for only a short time, the aunt said, because of lack of money. The father, a laborer, had a wife and four children whom he had purchased shortly before emancipation. He was trying to give the oldest daughter as much education as his scanty means would allow so she could be useful to herself and society. In 1871 a boy wrote the Fisk treasurer that he could not return to school because his mother was ill and could not tend the crops alone. Another pupil left school in 1874 because he lacked proper clothing. Sterling Brown's case is just one illustration of the difficulty students experienced in staying in school. Brown was born a slave at Post Oak Springs, Tennessee, in 1856. After emancipation he worked on a farm until 1867, when he entered Fisk, attended for a short time, then dropped out to earn enough money to return. Ten years after his first enrollment he was still a student. In the ten years he had managed to be in school about twenty-six months.[22]

The school gave financial aid to as many students as possible. Teachers raised money from their friends, home communities, and churches. The Freedmen's Bureau seldom provided aid for individuals, but in 1868 it furnished transportation to the university for twenty normal students. Black churches frequently sponsored a local student, sometimes several if possible. More important was the Peabody Fund, which supported both blacks and whites throughout the South. It provided $800 for students from the normal school in 1868 and renewed the sum annually for several years. Peabody aid was granted to students in their last year of the normal course. Recipients obligated themselves to teach at least two years, and no one was to be aided with more than $50 or more than one year.[23]

Financial problems were not the only ones encountered by Fisk students. They were never able to forget for long that many white Southerners considered them second-class citizens. Each wave of violence affected the school and the morale of the pupils. The knowledge that a student was subject to maltreatment at any time whether he was a college student of good standing or a criminal was not conducive to the student's stability and best effort. In July 1868 over four hundred members of the Ku Klux Klan hanged a man at Franklin and threatened the black schoolmaster. Two Fisk students opened a school in Dresden, Tennessee, in July 1869. On the night of September 2 they were taken from their boarding house by armed, masked men, forcibly escorted to a nearby woods, and "there severely whipped and under pain of death compelled to discontinue teaching. . . ." Klan activity around Nashville in 1869 kept some students out of school. "School will probably begin *small*," a Fisk instructor wrote in August 1874. There was great excitement, he mentioned, over the question of civil rights resulting in much bloodshed.[24]

Despite numerous difficulties Fisk students continued to advance. Examinations in 1871 showed that standards of scholarship were rapidly improving. Even skeptical local whites were convinced. Fisk's reputation for well-trained students resulted in its graduates usually securing good positions as teachers. Superintendents of education in several states were so impressed with them ·that Fiskites virtually monopolized several school systems. The demand was greater than Fisk was able to supply. A few white children even availed themselves of the opportunity to attend Fisk, at least one of whom later taught with "marked distinction."[25]

Although the number of students declined after 1867, the addition of a normal school and college department necessitated a faculty increase. By 1869 thirteen were associated with Fisk, all of them missionary-type teachers dedicated to uplifting the former slaves. Dedication was necessary to tolerate their living conditions. The furnishings and equipment were Spartan in their plainness. A teacher who arrived in 1869 was shocked to see her room; furnishings consisted of a hospital cot, a washstand, a table, a small wardrobe, and "a very small, very unmanageable stove." Of all the missionary beds she had slept in, another instructor said, the one in Nashville was the hardest. In addition to classroom duties, teachers had to do considerable housework. It was not until 1870 that the faculty voted to exempt women from splitting kindling and carrying coal to build fires in the public sitting room.[26]

Salaries were poor and often in arrears. In late October 1870 a teacher wrote asking for salary due her on October 1. She apologized for requesting her back pay, but it was cold and she was without shoes. In December 1874 another instructor asked for her salary for October and November. If she could get a few dollars for Christmas, she promised to petition for no more until the end of the spring term. Her salary was fifteen dollars per month. Though wages were quite low, the situation was not as bad as it appeared, since in the early years the American Missionary Association furnished the teachers' room and board.

Poor health, caused in part by overwork and poor food, was a common complaint of the faculty. All of the staff ate at a common mess with the students. The bread was horrible, meat sometimes tainted, and insects were frequently cooked in the food, according to one instructor. Though this teacher undoubtedly exaggerated about the food, health was a constant problem. It was necessary to be physically as well as spiritually strong to teach at Fisk. When an American Missionary Association official recommended a teacher for Fisk who was good but "always weakly," the steward asked that she not be sent. "We have too many weak lungs and sour stomachs now for the good of the cause," he said. From 1866 through 1875 letter after letter told of someone who was ill with chills and fever or nervous exhaustion, or who was suffering simply from overwork.[27] These hardy souls could seemingly tolerate almost anything except each other. They quarreled and bickered among themselves like petty children.

The sacrifice, constant privations, overwork, and social ostracism perhaps made necessary some method of emotional release. That method seemed to be fighting with each other. Quarreling was common, but in 1868–1869 it threatened to disrupt the school.

Much of the resentment was directed at Principal Ogden and his wife, who was matron of the boarding department without pay. She and Ogden considered her work satisfactory, but other teachers complained. George L. White, treasurer of Fisk and Cravath's brother-in-law, claimed that dismissal of Ogden was the only way to solve Fisk's problems. White was a strong-willed man who did not take kindly to opposition, and his relationship to Cravath placed him in a powerful position. White's only complaint against the Ogdens seemed to have been operation of the boarding department. There were others of those serious-minded people, however, who thought Ogden too flippant for his position. One wrote a letter to American Missionary Association officials condemning Ogden, saying, "is it right for a Supt. to *chuck* young ladies under the chin—and especially for a man who wooed and won his present wife while a school girl. . . . What can the religious influence of such a man be?"[28] There was no place for frivolity or even a sense of humor at Fisk.

The faculty squabble was ended momentarily when Ogden resigned in 1870 to accept a similar post at the Ohio State Normal School. He claimed that circumstances of his family demanded a change. The official association explanation was that Ogden, a normal school advocate, was not in sympathy with the desire to develop Fisk into a university. The evidence is not very convincing. It is more likely that Ogden was forced out by White. While at Fisk, Ogden did good work and most of the credit for the school's early success is due him. The community's confidence was temporarily shaken by his departure. He was not particularly popular with local whites—no one who taught blacks was—but they respected Ogden's ability and sincerity.[29]

Ogden was replaced by Adam K. Spence, who gave up a professorship of foreign languages at the University of Michigan to go to Fisk. Born in Aberdeenshire, Scotland, in 1831, and brought to the United States in 1833, Spence attended Olivet College, Oberlin, and the University of Michigan, receiving the Bachelor of Arts degree from the latter in 1858. He was immediately made instructor in Greek at his alma mater and remained there until 1870. He was recruited to Fisk to build the college department and is properly credited with the initiation and development of collegiate work. Scholarly, deeply religious, and solemn, he was the opposite of the gayer Ogden. A student warned her boyfriend, who had become a college teacher, never to become like Professor Spence. "Deliver me from such as he," she said. "I do not want to be afraid to laugh." At first Spence was not convinced that blacks were equal in ability to whites, but he believed they should be given a chance to prove themselves. He was fond of telling local citizens: if the Negro is inferior to whites, give him a superior training; and if he is superior, give him inferior training; but if equal, give him the same. A strong advocate of civil rights, he sometimes sat in the galleries at Nashville theaters because the management refused to seat Fisk students elsewhere. He retained the position of principal until 1875 when Erastus Milo Cravath became president of Fisk. Spence continued to serve as professor of Greek until 1900.[30]

Spence headed a faculty of approximately fifteen members, at least four of whom were destined to leave their imprint on Fisk. Helen C. Morgan, an 1866 graduate of Oberlin, joined the Fisk staff in 1869 and remained for thirty-eight years as professor of Latin. She was one of the first women in the country to attain the rank of full professor at a coeducational institution. Dedicated to Fisk and black education, she refused to leave for a higher salary at Vassar.

The Reverend Henry S. Bennett served as professor of theology and as Fisk pastor from 1867 to 1894. Born of Quaker parents, in Brownsville, Pennsylvania, on 16 April 1838, Bennett later became a member of the Presbyterian church. He was graduated from Oberlin in 1860 and the theological seminary there in 1863. While at Fisk he traveled around the South, establishing new schools; he was Sunday school superintendent of the Tennessee state prison and spent much time training black ministers. He was one of the very few early instructors at Fisk who was not always terribly solemn. His cheerfulness, like Ogden's, must have distressed a few of his mournful, long-faced, hell-fearing colleagues.[31]

Another important instructor during the formative years of Fisk was Spence's brother-in-law, Frederick A. Chase. Chase was born near King Ferry, New York, on 29 January 1833, and was educated at Union College in Schenectady, New York, the Homer Academy, in Cortland, New York, the University of Michigan, and Auburn Theological Seminary at Auburn, New York. After briefly serving as a pastor, Chase decided to become a teacher and accepted the presidency of the Lyons Collegiate Institute in Lyons (now Clinton), Iowa, where he remained until 1872 when he joined the Fisk faculty. He is remembered primarily for establishing the science department at Fisk. Chase Hall was named in honor of Professor Chase and his thirty-one years' service to the school.[32]

The critical and frustrating position of treasurer was held by George L. White. White was born in Cadiz, New York, in 1838. After attending public schools until age fourteen, he became a teacher. When the Civil War broke out he turned to soldiering, fighting in the battles of Gettysburg and Chancellorsville. Having been a "most faithful staff-officer" of General Clinton B. Fisk during the war, White was appointed by Fisk as an agent of the Freedmen's Bureau in Nashville. While a bureau agent he began to teach vocal music at Fisk and later joined the staff as treasurer and teacher of music and penmanship. He proved to be an effective treasurer, but made many enemies in the process. Spence accused him of being a schemer, ambitious for himself, a man of no education, gruff and impolite. He had favorites on the staff whom he delighted in honoring while others he treated very coolly. Spence, who thought White was the controlling power at Fisk, threatened to resign in 1872 because of their differences.[33]

The quarreling was not restricted to White and Spence; everyone seemed eager to join the fray. Again the major problem was the common dining hall. Dozens of letters were sent to the association's headquarters complaining of the food. An unsightly squabble developed with almost every member of the faculty either making charges or issuing denials. White tried to arrange for the faculty to have better food and to eat alone, saying that he believed "half our quarrels and troubles arise from sour stomachs." Even after White left Fisk, the bickering continued. Spence looked forward to the 1874 school year with "gloomy foreboding." The faculty, he said, spent their time "biting and devouring" each other. The situation became so severe that the corresponding secretary of the American Missionary Association was sent to make an inquiry. He found that all were Christian men and all thought they were right, which made a solution difficult. He recommended the selection of a strong, wise, prudent man—firm but conciliatory, decided yet kind—to take up the position of president. This report was probably one reason why Cravath was elected president in 1875.[34]

The shattered nerves and short tempers, caused in part by overwork, undernourishment, social ostracism, and lack of privacy, were probably intensified by Fisk's precarious financial situation. Quarrels were frequently caused by economics, and certainly the financial condition would have tried the patience of anyone. From the beginning the institution was near bankruptcy. The missionary association had many other schools to support in addition to Fisk. Tuition was supposed to pay part of the expenses, but hard times and the poor jobs available to blacks made it difficult to collect. Conditions were so critical in 1869 that the faculty voted to dispense with dessert in the dining room except once a week. Teachers preserved blackberries, huckleberries, apples, peaches, and vegetables through the summer to feed boarders during the year. Even in this enterprise nature seemed to be against them since several dry spring seasons made berries scarce.[35]

There was some outside aid, but not nearly enough. The Peabody Fund, as mentioned earlier, applied to only sixteen students. Generous donations occasionally received from the Freedmen's Bureau were primarily for construction. Bureau funds built a two-and-one-half-story girls' dormitory and Howard Chapel in 1869, much to the gratification of Fisk officials, but money for current expenses was desperately

Erastus M. Cravath (*Courtesy of the Fisk University Library's Special Collections*)

needed. Of the $25,000 total eventually received from the Freedmen's Bureau only a fraction could be expended for necessities other than buildings and repairs.[36]

By 1871 circumstances were so critical it seemed the school would fold. The boarding department matron gloomily predicted the institution's downfall. Not even local debts for food and fuel could be paid. Total indebtedness was about $2,000, most of which was due, but there was no money in sight. One day the matron had food enough only for lunch and there was no money in reserve. Spence went to the schoolrooms and collected $10.50 in tuition, which was given to the matron to buy supplies for the evening meal.[37] But no more could be collected and creditors were pressing for payment. The good name of the institution was at stake. The decaying old barracks were virtually beyond repair, making obvious the need for new buildings and a larger campus. Even the most optimistic teachers were preparing to seek employment elsewhere. It was at this juncture that one of the most dramatic stories in the history of education began—a trial tour by the Fisk Jubilee Singers to secure funds for the university.[38]

3

The Jubilee Singers

FISK STUDENTS AND TEACHERS DEMONSTRATED CONSIDERABLE INTEREST IN music from the time the school opened. During leisure hours students sang together the songs they had learned as slaves. By happy circumstances George L. White had a special love for music, and though he had never received musical instruction and made no pretensions as a vocalist, he had a knack for getting good singing from his pupils. While a Freedmen's Bureau agent in Nashville he was invited to teach singing at Fisk. He later became treasurer of Fisk after the university was chartered, but he continued his work with music.

White was so delighted with the students' progress that he arranged a public concert in Nashville in the summer of 1867. The successful program resulted in a local editorial urging white support for Fisk.[1] Other concerts were given in Tennessee cities with favorable results, including one for members of the National Teachers Association, meeting in Nashville.

White had used the singers primarily to advertise the school, but after repeated successes he began seriously to consider choosing the best singers and utilizing them to earn badly needed money. Only a few people agreed with him, including John Lawrence, a local Fisk trustee, who said a singing tour of Fisk students would be a "pioneer band of genuine Ethiopian Minstrels without the burnt cork." He felt it necessary to add, "I am writing you seriously." Few others besides White took such recommendations earnestly. In early 1871 White wrote Cravath (who was then field secretary of the American Missionary Association) suggesting a tour in the North. "Nothing of *the kind*," he said, "was ever put before the public North." A talented company, as had accidentally gathered at Fisk, could not easily be found, he added. If they should break up, their equals could not be collected with a year's searching. A successful concert was presented in May at Gallatin, Tennessee. Whites were surprised and the blacks were delighted. Still American Missionary Association officials were unconvinced of the advantages of a Northern tour.[2]

Local university trustees decided to undertake the project without the support of the association. In June 1871 they resolved to retain twelve singers, drill them through the summer, and make arrangements to send them on a tour of the North during the following year to raise funds.

Board was to be furnished the students during the summer, and if the way opened for concerts they were to be engaged for a year with expenses of clothing and travel provided. If the proposed concerts were successful, the singers were promised the further compensation of entire support in Fisk for the succeeding year. Meanwhile White continued to plead to the association for backing. Cravath, who finally came to favor a tour, was unable to persuade the association to assume responsibility. It was too expensive and success too uncertain. Cravath would not assume liability for the plan on his own. White wrote General Fisk asking for a loan of $300 to get his singers to the North. Fisk refused, fearing it would bring failure and disgrace upon the institution. Still determined, White replied he was trusting "in God and not in General Fisk."[3]

In early September 1871 the singers went on an eight-day trial tour in Tennessee and Georgia which cleared $47.95 above expenses. With this small encouragement, White, on 6 October 1871, took all but one dollar of institution funds plus what he could borrow and set out on his mission. The university was on the verge of collapse. There was food for one week. Fisk's welfare seemingly lay in the hands of a small band of recently emancipated slaves and an untrained musical director. No one was optimistic. White himself said, "I have less courage than I have ever had before in regard to our future." Hardly anyone expected the singers to collect funds for the school, and there was much uncertainty about whether they could even make their own expenses. As Professor Spence said, "if they fail they get home if they can."[4]

All of the original singers were of humble birth and circumstances. Isaac Dickerson was born a slave at Wytheville, Virginia, on 15 July 1850. After his mother died, when he was five (his father had been sold away previously), he worked as a houseboy. Upon the outbreak of war, Dickerson accompanied his master, a colonel in the Confederate army. He was captured by Union soldiers but soon paroled. After the war he worked as a hotel waiter and school teacher, eventually enrolling at Fisk to improve his meager education.

Born in Lebanon, Tennessee, on 24 February 1853, Maggie Porter knew little of the harsher side of slavery. Her mother was a house servant who was moved to Nashville shortly before the war. Miss Porter began her education under a free black at age twelve and was one of the first students to enter Fisk.

Minnie Tate, the youngest of the company, was born in Nashville in 1857 of free parents. Her mother had been a slave but was freed by her master just before his death. Miss Tate was taught by her mother to read and write before she entered Fisk.

Jennie Jackson was the granddaughter of Andrew Jackson's personal body servant. Her mother was freed before Jennie's birth. Miss Jackson worked as a house servant until she enrolled at Fisk in 1866, where she continued laboring as a servant to pay her way in school.

The oldest member of the troupe was Benjamin Holmes, born on 25 September 1846 or 1848 in Charleston, South Carolina. In 1862 he was sold to a master in Chattanooga. The next year he was pressed into the Union service and became an officer's servant in the Fourteenth Army Corps until March 1864, when he went back to work for his owner at thirty dollars per month. After clerking in a store, working in a barber shop, and teaching school, he entered Fisk in 1868.

Perhaps the most mischievous of the group was Thomas Rutling, who was born in Wilson County, Tennessee, in 1854. His father and brother were both sold away from him before he was two years old. He continued on the plantation until 1865, when he moved to Nashville and soon after went to Fisk. Considering himself a ladies' man, Rutling was in difficulty with the staid teachers a good part of the time. On one occasion he was reprimanded before the entire school for writing romantic notes to a fellow student. Apparently the punishment was ineffective for soon afterwards he signed a confession to a similar offense, promising that with the "help of God and the aid of man I will never be guilty of such a thing again."

Eliza Walker was born a slave six miles out of Nashville in 1857. After the war her father ran an ice house in the city. She entered with the first class at Fisk.

Born in Fayette County, Tennessee, on 19 September 1848, Green Evans was the most widely traveled of the singers. His master moved all over the South to escape the Union army. Finally Evans encountered a Yankee officer in Selma, Alabama, and became his servant for two years. In 1865 he went to Indianapolis as a waiter but the next year returned south to Memphis. After teaching school for a time, Evans entered Fisk in 1868.

Probably the most indispensable member of the company was Ella Sheppard, born in February 1851 in Mississippi. Her father, who operated a livery stable in Nashville, had purchased his freedom for $1,800. Upon hearing that Ella was about to die from lack of care, he bought his daughter for $350. Later they moved to Cincinnati where Miss Sheppard took music lessons. When her father died she went to Gallatin, Tennessee, to teach school. After saving only six dollars she enrolled at Fisk and was fortunate enough to secure a position as assistant music teacher at the school during the summers. In this capacity she helped White drill the singers before the tour. During the first Northern trip, White placed Miss Sheppard in charge of the entire training of voices and the general care of the singing while he attended to the management of the enterprise. One Fisk teacher said of her: "In intellect, in spirit, and in musical attainment she was one of the gifted women of the world." The composition of the troupe changed from time to time, but remarkably it maintained unwavering excellence.[5]

The singers' first stop on the Northern trip was Cincinnati, where two Congregational ministers opened their churches for "praise meetings." The meetings were successful in every way except financially. On Monday the group gave its first concert on the tour at Chillicothe, Ohio, and collected almost fifty dollars. This was the weekend of the great Chicago fire and although the troupe was in debt and out of money, the entire proceeds were donated to the Chicago relief fund. It was also at Chillicothe that the singers first met with indignities, which were frequently repeated throughout the tour. The two leading hotels refused to accommodate them. Finally a hotel manager was found who gave them rooms upon their promise not to dine with white guests.

A return to Cincinnati netted large audiences but little money. A concert in Springfield, Ohio, drew only twenty people, and other meetings were no more auspicious. The singers were becoming more discouraged and fearful. In Akron, Thomas Rutling attempted to accompany himself upon the piano. "In his fright, he played in one key and sang in another—an experiment he found unsuccessful." Finally he rallied and received a "hearty encore" for his effort. Newspapers generally gave sympathetic coverage to the singers; a Cleveland reporter wrote, "no rendition we ever heard went deeper into the heart of an audience, or more perfectly conveyed the sentiments of the lines. . . . The congregation sat as if spellbound until the last faint notes died away." Yet no money accompanied the praise.[6]

Suddenly the outlook brightened. A hearing before a synod of Presbyterian ministers in Springfield brought the singers' cause prominently before Presbyterians. Soon afterwards they were invited to appear before the National Council of Congregational Churches at Oberlin. A member of the council who was present said "that dignified body, taken by surprise, was now melted to tears and now lifted to jubilation." A subsequent collection yielded $130, but, of greater consequence, Fisk's purpose was brought before the representatives of a large part of the constituency of the American Missionary Association. For the first time the association endorsed the singers, and, in addition, provided them with an advance agent.[7] Of even more importance, the singers changed the type of songs used.

At first their programs were composed entirely of what the troupe called "white man's music." They were eager to sing such songs to prove they could do as well as whites. Sometimes in the evening they gathered and hummed and crooned to each other the songs of their fathers, but they had no intention of singing "slave songs" publicly. Had it been suggested, they almost certainly would have rebelled. Slavery was too close to perform such songs for the public. Moreover, the singers were so under the hypnotism of white disparagement of all things distinctly black that they were reluctant to put spirituals on their programs. Occasionally two or three spirituals were sung as encores and always the audience was inspired, but it was only after the singers recognized the intense effect of the songs upon musically enlightened audiences, and after urgent insistence by White, that such music was incorporated in the program. Eventually most of the songs on the program were slave songs. Thus the singers were launched upon their career of "revealing and vindicating the extraordinary folk genius" of blacks as reflected in the spirituals.[8]

Since the slave songs were not yet written down, to remember and teach them to each other required much rehearsing. By doing so, the singers rendered an important service not only to Fisk University and the nation but also to the world. The rise in the popularity of spirituals can be traced largely to their pioneer effort. People began to understand something of the spiritual quality of the contribution blacks had already made and could make to American culture. Though not always accurate, the spirituals showed a remarkable knowledge of the Bible. One critic has ventured to suggest that if the Great Book were destroyed much of it could be reconstructed from the songs. These songs were not "composed" after the manner of ordinary music but sprang into life from the heat of religious fervor and oppression. They were beautiful songs, folk songs in the truest sense, songs created by a people giving voice to an emotional life, a life for which America was responsible. These songs were first made available in 1872 when Theodore F. Seward published *Jubilee Songs: As Sung by the Jubilee Singers of Fisk University.*[9]

It was when they began singing spirituals that the name Jubilee Singers was taken by the troupe. Some title seemed essential since they were being referred to as minstrels or occasionally as "nigger minstrels." After a night of prayer, White decided upon the designation in memory of the Jewish year of Jubilee (Leviticus 25:8-17). The dignity of the name Jubilee Singers—a name destined to become famous throughout the Western world—appealed to the group and such they became.[10]

After a few more days in the Midwest the singers set out for New York. Again hotels refused them rooms so they stayed in private homes. The experience was repeated numerous times. Hotels rejected them while families of highest social prestige welcomed them into their midst. Despite rejection by hotels it was in New York that the Jubilee Singers really caught the imagination of the country. Henry Ward Beecher invited them to sing at the Plymouth Congregational Church in Brooklyn. The appearance was a great success and soon the singers were being received throughout the East with wild enthusiasm. By December there was no longer any question about their ability. As White said, "they have stood the test nobly." They ought, he added, "to be immortal in name."

White was convinced it was only a matter of time until money would come in. The power of music had been proved even to officers of the American Missionary Association.[11]

From New York the singers visited the principal cities of Pennsylvania, New Jersey, and New England. They sang in Boston at the written request of Governor William Claflin, Wendell Phillips, William Lloyd Garrison, Everett Hale, and other important men. Everywhere newspapers commended them and large crowds attended concerts. At New Haven, Connecticut, a recital was scheduled on the same night the popular Beecher was to lecture. There was so little demand for tickets to his lecture that it was postponed; Beecher attended the concert instead and addressed the audience on Fisk's behalf. The last week in Connecticut grossed almost $4,000. Gifts for Fisk poured in daily, including silverware, clocks, gas fixtures, books, and even a valuable gold bracelet. One concert in Tremont Temple in Boston netted $4,234.[12]

Success followed the singers to Washington, D.C. At one concert Vice-President Schuyler Colfax and numerous senators were in attendance. "Parson" Brownlow, now senator from Tennessee, too ill to attend the recital, requested a private performance. Ella Sheppard said he wept like a child as he listened to the humble slave melodies. President Ulysses S. Grant invited the troupe to sing for him at the White House. As they entered, the president arose, received an introduction to and shook hands with each singer. After listening to "Go Down Moses," President Grant chatted with the students, told them he had read much about their tour, and wished them a "glorious success." The singers were then conducted through the White House.

Thomas Rutling claimed the singers went to Washington not to make money but to sing a piece of land out of the hands of Congress. By this time not only were buildings on Fisk campus in decay, but the two-and-one-half-acre campus was obviously becoming too small. The site being considered for a new campus belonged to the government, and a bill concerning its disposal was at that time before the Senate. Although the new buildings were placed elsewhere, the desired land was given to Fisk.[13]

Returning to New England, the singers were eagerly received. Often additional trains had to be run to cities in which the concerts were held. In less than two months they earned approximately $12,000. Furthermore, the singers had rendered a service for Fisk and for blacks. Fisk became the best-known black college in the country, and in the words of one white listener, "the ideas of many with regard to the race seem entirely revolutionized." How could representatives of a race only recently emancipated be so intelligent, sing so beautifully, and have such poise if they were actually inferior?

After closing their first campaign in Poughkeepsie, New York, the

JUBILEE SINGERS. *Left to right:* Mabel Lewis (Imes), Minnie Tate, Green Evans, Ella Sheppard, Jennie Jackson, Maggie Porter, Isaac Dickerson, America Robinson, Thomas Rutling, Benjamin Holmes, Georgia Gordon (*Courtesy of the Fisk University Library's Special Collections*)

Jubilee Singers returned to Nashville on 2 May 1872. Besides paying the school debts and furnishing other support, they brought with them several thousand dollars which purchased the present site of Fisk University. In all they had earned $20,000. Still they had not gained complete acceptance. Passing through Louisville, Kentucky, on the way home, the singers, accompanied by the jeers of numerous whites, were roughly ejected from a railway station waiting room. Even this failed to dampen their good spirits. A railway superintendent placed them in a first-class coach and they returned to Fisk "amid great rejoicing."[14]

The singers were permitted to rest in Nashville for only a week. Invited to participate in the second World's Peace Jubilee at Boston in June 1872, they decided to tour the Midwest on the way. Again they met success. "Well the Jubilee Singers have done themselves credit," Principal Spence heard from his mother in Ann Arbor, Michigan, who reported the city throbbing with excitement. Mrs. Spence said unqualified praise came from every quarter.[15] In their first appearance at the World's Peace Jubilee the singers were hissed, but later they enthralled an audience of forty thousand people when they sang "The Battle Hymn of the Republic" in E-flat.

The singing was to be accompanied by a symphony orchestra, and White decided the song would probably be played in E-flat. In order to be heard the troupe would have to be able to enunciate every word perfectly in a key three half-steps higher than usual. Using his violin, White rehearsed the singers for weeks on the words from C to E-flat. When the day came for the "Battle Hymn" to be sung and well-known musicians faltered and strained in an attempt to rise to the pitch of the orchestra, the Jubilee Singers knew the reward for their many hours of practice. Others were to sing the first two verses and the singers the third. When their predecessors could not sing their part satisfactorily the conductor asked the singers to join on the chorus but they preferred to wait for the third verse. "Then with apparently one voice, pure, clear and distinct," they sang out

"He hath sounded forth the trumpet,
which shall never call retreat."

The audience was electrified. People arose in wild cheering, throwing handkerchiefs in the air and waving. The musicians did likewise. Johann Strauss the younger, the great composer, reputedly waved his violin excitedly. It was a triumph not soon forgotten.[16]

The remainder of the summer was spent in rest and rehearsals at Acton, Massachusetts. In the fall the singers were divided into two groups so they could visit smaller places where it would have been too expensive to go in full company. The fall tour barely paid expenses. In early 1873 the group was reorganized to consist of eleven members.[17]

There followed a successful three-month campaign that netted another $20,000.

Since the Jubilee Singers' fame had traveled to Europe, a visit was planned to England for the early spring. Testimonials from leading ministers and men of rank in the United States brought the singers immediately before English religious and philanthropic societies. Mark Twain wrote friends in England about the coming appearance of the singers. "I heard them sing once," he said, "and I would walk seven miles to hear them sing again. You will recognize that this is strong language for me to use, when you remember that I was never fond of pedestrianism." These ladies and gentlemen, continued Twain, "make eloquent music—and what is as much to the point, they reproduce the true melody of the plantations, and are the only persons I ever heard accomplish this on a public platform. . . . I do not know when anything has moved me as did the plaintive melodies of the Jubilee Singers," he added. Twenty-four years later Twain had not changed his mind. He wrote that the Jubilee Singers' "Music made all other vocal music cheap. . . . It is utterly beautiful, to me; and it moves me infinitely more than any other music can." In the singers and their songs, Twain thought, "America has produced the perfectest flower of the ages." He loved the songs and sang them, not badly, for his family and friends.[18]

After a voyage accompanied by considerable seasickness, the Jubilee Singers received their first hearing in England on 6 May 1873. Lord Shaftesbury had sent invitations to the nobility, members of Parliament, clergymen, editors, and others of influence. The singers were an immediate success. The next day the *Times* (London) music critic quoted testimonials about their ability and added, "We can not say that expectations raised by these praises have been disappointed." Congratulations and invitations came in abundance. The singers accepted an invitation to sing for the duke and duchess of Argyll and their friends. Much to their delight, Queen Victoria drove over to hear them. The queen expressed her gratification; she especially liked "John Brown's Body." The singers, according to Mabel Lewis (Imes) made what was for them a rare faux pas. They turned their back on Queen Victoria, forgetting to bow. Obviously not offended, the queen later had their portrait done by the court painter.[19]

Prime Minister William E. Gladstone also showed interest in the troupe. On three occasions he invited them to his home, the first time to a dinner party in honor of the prince and princess of Wales and the czarina of Russia. The singers chanted the Lord's Prayer before dinner and sang afterwards. They were asked to visit the Gladstone family in North Wales. The singers spent the day with the Gladstones, mingling freely with the family and examining the prime minister's art treasures.

At dinner, servants were dismissed and the Gladstones themselves
served the singers to show how much they and their mission were es-
teemed. Later Gladstone sent a book collection to the Fisk Library.
Another social invitation was accepted to the deanery at Westminster
Abbey.[20]

The singers were especially welcomed by ministers, missionary
societies, and temperance organizations. They never drank alcoholic
beverages, and their performances contained religious songs. One reason for their popularity was the English missionary societies' interest in
Africa. A European scramble for African territory had intensified concern for missionary work on that continent. Many Englishmen believed
that black missionaries would have the greatest success in Africa and
they looked to educated Americans to achieve the desired result. For
years Fisk University and the Jubilee Singers were closely associated in
the English mind with African mission work. Fisk sent its first student
missionaries to Africa in 1878.

The singers were also in demand for evangelical services. When Jennie Jackson sang, "You may bury me in the East, you may bury me in the
West, but I'll hear the trumpet sound in the morning," she held vast
audiences as fixedly as the ministers. The singers were invited to perform at a meeting held by Dwight L. Moody, the famed evangelist who
preached to as many as fifteen thousand people at a time. After one of
the meetings a local minister said: "Their songs are so intense in their
spirituality that strong men bowed in tears...." Such activity gained
them the support of religious societies throughout Great Britain.[21]

A journey through Scotland, Ireland, and Wales was similar to the
English experience. In Edinburgh the singers were invited to dinner
with the lord provost and friends. The town council of Glasgow welcomed them under the patronage of city authorities and introduced
them to city hall. At the Edinburgh dinner a Scottish minister found
himself seated between two girls of the troupe. "More intelligent or
better-mannered companions at table no one could desire," he pro-
nounced. "After such an education as they have received at Fisk University," added the minister, "I was prepared for the intelligence; but I own
that I was not prepared for the quiet, unassuming cultured manner." A
Glasgow newspaper reported that the Jubilee Singers lived up to their
reputation as singers of "great natural power and expression...." They
sang well together "with exquisite precision of time and accent, and with
a simple earnestness which bespeaks the sincerity of their feelings," the
paper announced.[22] Concerts in Scotland sometimes earned $1000 per
night. The reception in Ireland and Wales was equally enthusiastic.

Still all was not happy on the European tour. Miss Susan Gilbert, the
chaperon, became ill and had to rest. Gustavus D. Pike, the business
manager, was sick and Mrs. White became too ill to travel. White, decid-

ing it was his duty to go on with the work, left her in Glasgow. While on the verge of collapse himself, he was called to Glasgow, arriving in time to see his wife die of typhoid fever. White was so incapacitated that he was unable to take a very active part in the singers' campaign. At one time he was totally prostrated with lung hemorrhages.

With so many of the management ill it seemed time to go home. Furthermore, there was some difficulty between a few members of the troupe and White. No one wanted to discuss the problem in correspondence, but there were several comments that White appeared to be in trouble with the singers again. White was a hard taskmaster, and the illness, grief, and weariness of constant touring and work probably caused tempers to be short. Also, some of the singers wished to remain after the tour was over and give concerts on their own, and White disapproved of this plan. Finally a solution was reached and a last great concert was planned for May 12 in London with Lord Shaftesbury presiding. The proceeds of the final performance were the largest received on the tour.

During the European campaign the singers raised nearly $50,000 for the construction of Jubilee Hall on the new campus. In addition they received gifts of books and of special sums for the library and for purchase of "philosophical apparatus." Moreover, they had made Fisk University and Nashville, Tennessee, known throughout Great Britain.[23]

The troupe returned to Nashville on 27 May 1874, and though temporarily disbanded the singers were permitted only a short rest. Soon another foreign tour was planned. The university was growing and required more funds, so in September 1874 the company was reorganized.[24] Since some of the singers had already sacrificed four years of their life and education it was decided to pay them a salary of $800 a year (they had received $500 for the previous foreign tour).

During the winter and spring they toured the North. Though they received a fine reception from Henry Ward Beecher and other ministers, receipts were small. Discriminatory treatment in hotels and restaurants was humiliating, especially after their acceptance abroad. In Columbus, Ohio, some white guests left the dining room at their appearance. After a concert in Trenton, New Jersey, they were constrained to return to Philadelphia because no Trenton hotel would accommodate them. Even in the nation's capital the manager of the Continental House requested that they be seen as little as possible. This humiliation was partially appeased by their meeting the great Frederick Douglass, who attended a concert and invited them to his home, where he sang for them.[25]

In May 1875 a company of eleven members set out for England. Since White's health would not permit him to do the work alone, Theodore F. Seward, a composer who had first written down the Jubilee songs, was secured as an assistant. Erastus M. Cravath followed later to serve as business manager. The group arrived in time to attend the annual meeting of the Freedmen's Aid Society in London on May 31. Fifty years later the music critic for the *London Daily News* recalled hearing the Jubilee Singers at that time. "The opening bars of 'Steal away to Jesus' were sung so softly they seemed to come from nowhere," he remembered. The audience was especially pleased with "John Brown's Body." These songs, he said, were never sung in "Sambo" dialect. They were sung with precision and deep religious fervor.[26] Within an hour of their arrival the singers were invited by Evangelist Moody to sing at his afternoon service at the Haymarket Opera House. Assuming it was their duty, the troupe temporarily turned aside from concerts to help win souls. The company secured quarters in London and labored with Moody for a month, singing to approximately 10,000 to 12,000 people daily. America Robinson, a new member of the troupe, believed Moody was "something of an alarmist." At the end of the month the evangelist rewarded each of the singers with his grateful thanks and an autographed Bible.[27]

Meanwhile the Jubilee Singers had become so popular with Londoners that they had difficulty getting through the crowds after concerts. The audience parted to let them pass, but on both sides they kept asking to shake hands. One woman came and stood near America Robinson, saying she felt it a great honor just to be near her.

The adulation did not prevent the troupe from becoming homesick. Miss Robinson longed for a "good American dinner." One need not go to England for good food, she said. Ella Sheppard found the English people a "stiff set," and "so stupid or ignorant" about Americans and blacks. Though the singers appreciated England's lack of prejudice they were frequently offended by the supercilious attitude toward the United States. The men in the company seemingly spent their rarely found leisure time more pleasantly than the women. Occasionally, according to Miss Robinson, they left some "very sad ladies behind." In Wales, Thomas Rutling, still holding his earlier romantic propensities, "became enamored with the Belle of Builth." She "seemed very sad" when he left.

After a few successful concerts in England the company went again to Scotland. Full houses greeted them everywhere; one concert in Glasgow netted $1,700. They also did religious and social work, holding Sunday school meetings especially for children. At a breakfast for the poor they were appalled. "There were over two thousand of the most wretched looking people I ever saw," Miss Robinson stated. "There is nothing in America to compare with these poor things." Miss Robinson did not even like the weather in Scotland; it rained all the time. The coat of arms of Greenock, she said, was a duck with an umbrella.[28]

From Scotland the singers went to Ireland and were almost overwhelmed with their reception. The Irish seemed even more demonstrative than the English and Scots. In Dublin several thousand persons attended a concert and nearly as many more were refused admission. Newspapers were extremely friendly.[29] The singers continued to travel Great Britain until the summer of 1876, receiving applause from both the nobility and the masses. According to the *Liverpool Daily Courier,* some classical musicians viewed the singers with something akin to contempt, but "the people go in crowds to hear them, and the religious songs call unbidden tears from the eyes of the listeners." During their leisure hours the company entertained, free of charge, the poor and unfortunate, including the inmates of the Royal Albert Asylum.[30]

This constant, whirlwind activity eventually began to affect the troupe's health. Ella Sheppard was almost continuously ill. On one occasion a physician told her she must stop her work and rest in order to recover. Yet she persisted. After receiving word of her mother's death, Julia Jackson became so ill she had to stay behind. Several months later a severe headache followed by a paralytic stroke left one-half of her body powerless. Others were sick and in bad humor, so in the summer of 1876 it was decided to go to Geneva, Switzerland, for rest.[31]

Mishap pursued the company to Geneva. A misunderstanding caused Maggie Porter, probably the best singer, to leave the troupe. When she apologized and offered to return, the others refused to receive her. It was thought the singers would have to be reorganized completely. But in October 1876 White wrote that the "painful circumstances" had been readjusted and "we are *at one* again." Then Isaac Dickerson broke his arm falling off his bicycle. Earlier he had sprained his leg showing "off before some swells" on his machine.[32] Despite troubles, the summer was not a total loss. The troupe obtained a much-needed rest and gave an excellent concert in Geneva. The performance was an experiment to determine whether a trip to the Continent would be financially feasible. The audience could not understand English much less the vernacular of the slave songs. Yet they "applauded, wept or smiled at the same places as an English audience." When asked how they could enjoy the songs without understanding the words, they replied that they could *feel* them. White said the singers had never given a better concert, and such a remark coming from him meant a great deal. "When *he* is satisfied," Ella Sheppard stated, "we know everybody else must be, therefore we felt unusually thankful."[33]

Even with the Geneva success a continental tour seemed hazardous. Whether the songs would retain their power when the meaning of the words was lost remained questionable, and a failure would mean heavy loss. A London concert convinced the managers it was worth a try. G. P. Ittman, Jr., a leading Rotterdam merchant who was in London on business, attended the concert. He was so pleased that after the performance he introduced himself to the singers and urged them to visit Holland. He promised to do all in his power to make them a success. As good as his word, Ittman prepared the way, enlisting the support of influential friends throughout the kingdom. A Dutch composer was found who translated the songs with remarkable effectiveness. Committees were formed in various cities to prepare for the singers' arrival. Nowhere did the singers receive a heartier welcome than in the Netherlands; the attentions they had received at the hands of the great and learned in other countries were quite overshadowed. Baron and Baroness Van Wassenaer de Catwijck entertained them at the Hague. The queen of the Netherlands was present; when the singers were introduced by the American consul, she went forward and spoke to each of them in a cordial manner. She expressed pleasure at their singing and demonstrated her sincerity later by attending a public concert. The company also performed for the king, who gave a generous subscription. Concerts caused even greater excitement in some of the small towns where inhabitants had never seen blacks. After two months of adulation in Holland, the singers returned to England $10,000 richer. They began preparing for a trip to Germany, which they considered the most critical experiment of all.[34]

Events proved that apprehension over a German tour was unjustified. As usual Lord Shaftesbury's letters of commendation had preceded the singers. They immediately received invitations to give concerts, the most significant being from the crown prince to visit "New Palace" in Potsdam. Upon arrival the singers were greeted individually by the prince and princess. After they began singing the troupe was surprised to see the kaiser himself enter. He had come from Berlin to dine and had detained his special train just to hear them. The crown princess wept during the singing of "Nobody Knows the Trouble I See," later apologizing for her "weakness." In a subsequent conversation she told the singers she had been anxious to hear them since Queen Victoria had written her a long letter extolling their virtues. While tea was being served the princess brought her children forward to shake hands with each member of the group. The crown prince asked for a copy of their songs, expressing a desire to sing them with his family.

The first concert, attended by numerous well-known German music critics, was given in "Sing-Akademie" in Berlin. It was a test of strength. If the singers failed to please the critics, a friend told the company, they might as well go home. They passed the test with ease. Newspapers the next day were filled with compliments. One critic suggested that German musicians could learn something from the former slaves. The rest of the trip was anticlimactic.[35]

After eight months in Germany most of the singers wanted to return home. For three years they had been away from school and family. Furthermore, there was illness again. Jennie Jackson, coughing blood for weeks, finally had to leave the troupe in late 1877. Several others had been replaced for one reason or another. White resigned, leaving the ill Ella Sheppard with the musical responsibilities. Financial returns were becoming smaller because both Great Britain and Germany were suffering from depressions. Some of the company remained on the Continent to study; the rest returned thankfully to Fisk in July 1878.[36]

The contribution made by the Jubilee Singers is incalculable. Fisk University's founding is unique since the students themselves played a vital role. The work done by the Jubilee Singers was as important as the labor of missionary societies, philanthropic organizations, and the early teachers. At a time when the school was suffering financial difficulties they went on tour, and at the end of seven years they had given $150,000 to the university. These funds purchased land for a new campus and constructed Jubilee Hall. Fisk University and Nashville became familiar words to hundreds of thousands of Europeans and millions of Americans. The eyes of the public on two continents were turned to Fisk as the source of supply for missionaries and teachers in Africa. In appearing before the queen of England, emperor of Germany, other crowned heads, presidents, and nobility, they showed the world what former slaves were capable of doing.

As the first to popularize and capitalize on slave songs, the singers set the pattern black colleges used for decades to secure white approval and contributions. So popular were the interpretations of the spirituals by the Jubilee Singers that these songs are still sometimes called "jubilees." But most important was their work in preserving the spirituals. "With their superlative rendering of the songs of aspiration and longing, of sorrow and yearning," they sang their way into the consciousness of two continents and charmed the world with the beauty of black music.[37]

4

Era of Construction and Definition: 1875-1900

THE PERIOD 1875 TO 1900 WAS A DIFFICULT ONE FOR BLACKS IN GENERAL and for education in particular. Besides the problems normally experienced by American colleges and universities, Fisk suffered vexations caused by caste and the blacks' position in the United States. The power of "Radical Republicans," a combination of blacks, Northerners, and "scalawags," lasted only a short time. In 1869 ex-Confederates in Tennessee were enfranchised. The "iron clad" oath which Congress had imposed at the beginning of Radical Reconstruction to disqualify ex-Confederates was repealed in 1871. The effect of pardoning Southerners could be seen in the revival of the Democratic party, which, combined with continuing intimidation and violence perpetrated by such organizations as the Ku Klux Klan, soon began to force Republicans out of office. By 1876 Southern Republicans could claim only Florida, South Carolina, and Louisiana. In the next year, when President Rutherford B. Hayes withdrew federal troops from the South, Republican power in the former Confederate states was at an end.

After 1877 white hegemony in the South was accepted by the federal government, thereby leaving blacks no effective defense of their political and civil rights. Northerners apparently had tired of the crusade for blacks. Even many abolitionists had been paternalistic rather than egalitarian toward freedmen. It was easy for such men quickly to become disillusioned with blacks' "lack of progress."

Reconciliation between the North and South, accompanied by a rising antiblack prejudice, was achieved largely at the blacks' expense. The North eventually acquiesced in discriminatory treatment. By the end of the century Northern public opinion generally accepted blacks as inferior and unfit for suffrage. Piece by piece a racial system was effectuated until early in the twentieth century racial subordination, segregation, and disfranchisement were virtually complete in the South.[1] It was under these gradually worsening conditions that Fisk officials had to try to turn Fisk into a university worthy of the name.

Despite steadily deteriorating conditions for blacks in the United States, the years 1875 to 1900 were ones of constant growth at Fisk. There were improvements in the faculty, the college department, facilities, physical plant, and reputation. While the Jubilee Singers were trying to secure funds, the faculty continued to pray, quarrel, and move onward, but they struggled with renewed vigor and faith.

In October 1873 the cornerstone of Fisk University was laid on the new campus. The ceremony was described by a local newspaper as " a notable event" in Nashville history, and one which marked the beginning of "a memorable epoch" in the section's educational history. The new location was a beautiful twenty-five-acre site, formerly Fort Gillam, just outside Nashville.[2] Two years later the new Jubilee Hall, fruit of the Jubilee Singers' concerts, was occupied. It was described as "all that could be desired," both in its architectural appearance and substantial construction, as well as its adaption to the permanent uses of the university. Mrs. Clinton B. Fisk and some friends undertook to furnish the new hall. Before students occupied the building, Professor Spence entered each room and offered a prayer, asking God's blessing upon each room and future tenants.[3]

Jubilee Hall was formally dedicated in an elaborate ceremony on 1 January 1876. Among those present who gave addresses were Tennessee Governor James A. Porter; General Fisk, now president of the Fisk board of trustees; General Oliver O. Howard, former Commissioner of the Freedmen's Bureau; the bishop of the Methodist Church, South; and a number of educators and politicians. Letters were read from Congressman James A. Garfield, L. Q. C. Lamar, Dwight L. Moody, and the U.S. commissioner of education. The concern of such a distinguished group was a tribute to the rapid intellectual progress of the former slaves and the growing reputation of Fisk.[4]

Meanwhile, there had been a much needed change in Fisk's administrative organization. The principal had had little power. Authority lay with the American Missionary Association secretary who visited the school perhaps four times a year. Any controversy between department heads was referred to New York, generally by the most contentious party, and upon that representation (unless others happened to write) the question was usually decided. The lack of local authority was one cause of many faculty squabbles. The problem was solved in 1875 with the appointment of Erastus Milo Cravath as president and professor of mental and moral philosophy. Cravath had been associated with Fisk from the beginning, first as a founder and then as the association secretary. During his term as secretary he had helped establish several other black colleges.[5]

President Cravath was strong-willed and authoritarian. Though his imperiousness at first caused some irritation among the faculty, they were soon working together with less friction than that experienced in former years. Of large vision, of great faith, with positive convictions, the first president left his influence upon hundreds of students. W. E. B. DuBois, who was a student under Cravath, knew him to be "honest and

sincere." More than to any other individual, Booker T. Washington
wrote years later, Fisk was indebted to Cravath for "the character of the
work done and for the atmosphere which surrounds the university."
The wife of one of his successors referred to Cravath as "a wonderful
man, with a wonderful vision" who was "ever before the minds of the
people." He served as president for a critical quarter of a century.[6]

Coupled with the election of Cravath as president was a changed relationship between Fisk and the American Missionary Association. Fisk
property had been held jointly by the association and the Western
Freedmen's Aid Commission. In 1870 the latter quitclaimed its one-half
interest in the land for one dollar and the title merged in the association.
Cravath accepted the presidency on condition that Fisk property held by
the association should be deeded to the university trustees, and that the
trustees should create a faculty with full power and privileges belonging
to a university teaching staff. The association transferred the old university property and the new Jubilee Hall site to the trustees with the pro-
viso that Fisk should be conducted according to association principles.
No person could be elected as trustee of Fisk without the association's
prior approval. Any income from the old property should be used to
satisfy debts incurred by the association for the university. Fisk trustees
assumed all debts and obligations created by the purchase of the new
campus. Though the formal relationship was severed, the American
Missionary Association continued to give support and guidance to Fisk.[7]

Another important event in Fisk history occurred in 1875: The first
college class was graduated. Four students—James Dallas Burrus, John
H. Burrus, Virginia E. Walker, and America W. Robinson—had entered
the freshman class in 1871. All were listed in the graduating class of
1875, though the latter was in Europe with the Jubilee Singers.[8] The
graduates gave speeches that elicited frequent and emphatic applause.
"The ability displayed in the productions of the graduating class was
fully up to the standard of college graduates," an observer wrote. "They
evinced a capacity of research and a facility for expression which proved
that hard study had wrought its legitimate result—accurate culture."
Fisk had taken the students nearly ten years before, with little more than
a knowledge of the alphabet, and had guided them through preparatory
studies, a thorough classical course, and a rigid examination which
earned them each the Bachelor of Arts degree. They were reputedly the
first black students to graduate from a liberal arts college south of the
Mason and Dixon Line. President Cravath spoke "feelingly" of the sac-
rifices made by the pupils and their parents. All had worked in order to
attend school. The two Burruses and their younger brother Preston,
their mother said, had successively worn a single pair of trousers which
she had "turned and patched."[9]

If a school can be judged by the success of its alumni the first four

JAMES DALLAS BURRUS (*Courtesy of the Fisk University Library's Special Collections*)

graduates were excellent recommendations for Fisk. Miss Robinson remained with the Jubilee Singers until 1878, then spent a year on the Continent studying French and German. After a year of study she returned to the United States and devoted her life to teaching. When she received her master's degree in 1890 she was principal of the Macon Public School in Macon, Mississippi.

Virginia E. Walker (later Broughton) went to Memphis where she taught for many years. After engaging in local missionary work with the Women's Baptist Home Mission Society, Miss Walker began to travel about the state in missionary activity when she was not teaching. By 1910 she was secretary of the Women's Baptist Missionary Board and a teacher at Howe Institute in Memphis. Eventually she gave up teaching and became a state missionary for Tennessee.[10]

The careers of the Burrus brothers dramatically demonstrate what some gifted and dedicated individuals could accomplish despite the handicaps under which blacks struggled. Born of a slave mother and their white master, the Burruses paid their way through school by working as waiters and teachers. They were spurred on in their desire for an education by being told that John C. Calhoun had once said: "Show me a negro who can parse a Greek verb or go beyond the first equation in algebra and I'll show you a man." John selected Greek and James studied mathematics.[11]

After graduation James accepted a position as instructor of mathematics and became the first full-time black teacher in the Fisk college department. He remained at Fisk until the fall of 1877 when he entered Dartmouth College to do graduate study in mathematics. Meanwhile John was teaching and engaging in politics. He became principal of a Nashville school but also had time to hold office. In 1876 he was selected by the Republican State Committee as a national convention delegate from Tennessee's Sixth Congressional District. He cast his ballot for Rutherford B. Hayes. After the convention he traveled for a time before accepting the principalship of the Yazoo, Mississippi, city school. When James left Fisk for Dartmouth, his brother John replaced him. In 1879 John stopped teaching to begin an intensive study of law. Admitted to the bar in early 1881, he practiced law in Nashville for a year and then accepted the presidency of Alcorn Agricultural and Mechanical College at Rodney, Mississippi.[12]

While John was studying law, James was concluding his graduate work at Dartmouth. He received an honorary Master of Arts degree in 1879, reportedly the first black to receive such a degree from an accredited college in the United States.[13] After making a survey of the White Mountains in New Hampshire for the United States government and teaching two more years at Fisk, James went to Alcorn Agricultural and Mechanical College as professor of mathematics and superintendent of the college farm. It was largely through James's efforts that John succeeded former Senator Hiram R. Revels as president of Alcorn.[14] Alcorn had been called an agricultural and mechanical college but it was under the Burruses that the "mechanics departments were made realities." They also improved other departments. White legislators in Mississippi had much confidence in them, and working together they "built up this institution into one of the first modern state colleges for Negroes...." Their faculty was procured, not from other A & M schools, but from Fisk.[15]

In 1893, after deciding that if blacks were ever to be independent the race would have to make money, the Burruses left Mississippi and returned to Nashville. John became a farmer and lawyer and James joined his younger brother Preston in the drug business. James also purchased several lots near Fisk and constructed numerous houses for rental and sale.

Much of the Burruses' profits were used to aid Fisk. Any financial campaign found them as contributors. In 1915 James donated seven pieces of property valued at about $7,000. In 1916 the brothers gave Fisk five notes of one hundred dollars each, payable one a year for the next five years. They added 8 percent interest to date of maturity, making a total of $600. James and Preston contributed $112 to a Fisk Endowment Fund in 1917, the year of John's death. In 1922 they presented, in keeping with John's wishes, an eighty-five-acre farm to the school. James in the fall of 1926, gave $1,000 to a campaign to clear the university of debt. But his greatest gift—everything he owned—was made in 1928.

By 1926 James, the only brother still alive, though eighty years old and unwell, was still engaged in the drug and real estate businesses. After suffering a heart attack in the summer of 1928, he drew up a will leaving his property to Fisk. When the president told Burrus what his money could do for the school, tears came into his eyes and he said, "that's what I've lived for." On 5 December 1928, James went to pay a creditor who lived on the outskirts of town. Probably the conductor on the streetcar paid slight attention to the old gray-bearded, blue-eyed man who mounted the car at Thirteenth Avenue and asked to be put off at the end of the line. Burrus took his seat at the rear of the car set apart for blacks, leaned back, and closed his eyes. When the conductor came to rouse him, he was dead. He left to his beloved Fisk University his entire estate, which included about eighty-five houses and stocks and bonds valued at approximately $120,000.

So ran the closing chapter of the human drama of James Burrus and his attempt to prove himself of value to his fellow man by self-denial. He realized "in its fullest measure the social limitations" which blacks faced no matter what their mental accomplishment. But he was not deterred.

James Dallas Burrus had for over three decades driven about Nashville in his buggy collecting rents and running a drugstore, but behind that "motion of life there existed for forty years the increasing purpose of making himself financially secure so that he might serve his race." Not only were the ambitions of the Burruses worthy but they achieved them with integrity, propriety, and intelligence.[16] The Burrus brothers, Virginia Walker, and America Robinson set a standard of achievement that the alumni of Fisk or any other school would have to struggle to equal.

There were no college graduates in 1876 and only two the next year, but the college department grew steadily, though slowly. In 1877 there were fifteen college students and eleven more were added the next year. By 1883 there were thirty-three college pupils and forty-eight in college prep classes. Fifteen Bachelor of Arts degrees were conferred in the spring of 1885. By 1898 the college department had increased to fifty-four students.[17]

The theology department also had a few advanced students, the largest number being nineteen in 1880. Most of the theology students left before completing their course of study, thus the first graduate was Paul Louis LaCour in 1893. LaCour had done part of his work at Harvard before entering Fisk. The theology department was discontinued in 1909 after graduating only sixteen people.[18] In connection with the theology department Fisk trained students for missionary work both in the United States and abroad. There was a strong feeling that Fisk students should uplift their race in Africa as well as in this country. The first missionaries from Fisk went to Africa in 1878 when Albert P. Miller and A. E. Jackson sailed with their wives to the Mendi Mission on the west coast. Before leaving, Miller made a statement about Fisk which eventually became the school motto: "Her sons and daughters are ever on the altar." In 1880 Nathaniel Nurse, who had been sent to Fisk by London friends to be educated for missionary work, joined the Millers and Jacksons at the Mendi Mission. Benjamin F. Ousley, Jr., and his wife, 1881 and 1883 graduates, respectively, were sent in 1884 to Kambani, Inhambane, East Africa.[19] Fisk retained an interest in Africa that gradually broadened to include African history and culture.

The actual scholarship at Fisk during these years was not equal to a first-class university, but it was improving. Standards were sufficiently high to elicit a constant flow of commendatory statements from observers. In 1878 Governor Porter wrote that Fisk was doing "a noble work for Tennessee and the Southern states generally" by furnishing effective teachers and making intelligent citizens of its pupils. After being entertained by a Fisk music program in 1879 the state legislature in a joint resolution lauded the school. The legislators said they were "highly gratified to note the remarkable advancement" made by students in general culture and especially in musical culture; therefore, "Resolved by the General Assembly, That we earnestly commend the Institution to the colored people of the State as one of high aim, thorough in its work and ennobling in its influences."[20]

Fisk was described in 1885 by a local white reporter as "the most important and influential institution of its kind in the United States." An out-of-state guest, impressed by a visit to Fisk, discovered that many white Nashvillians shared his view. A white lawyer expressed his appreciation of the character of Fisk's work by saying, "I wish this miserable prejudice were done away with, or I had the moral courage to rise above it, for I do not know of any other institution in all the South where my children would get as thorough training as at Fisk University."[21]

A New Yorker who visited Fisk in 1883 was almost ecstatic with enthusiasm. "There is so much to say I scarce know where to begin," she wrote, "and I find myself in a tumult of feeling contemplating the great work done there. It is certainly a place of national interest and not less should it be a national pride." She had expected to be pleased but her impression was beyond expectation. The intelligence of the pupils, she stated, opened her eyes "to the development of a race whose intellectual faculty I have never fully appreciated until today." No college in the country, she thought, could "show a more dignified, intelligent and thoroughly gentle and well-bred set of pupils." Already in the 1880s Fisk was considered a place to visit. Important travelers through Nashville nearly always called at Fisk. Among those who visited on campus between 1885 and 1900 were Theodore Roosevelt, Ohio Senator John Sherman, former President Rutherford B. Hayes, Admiral George Dewey, Frederick Douglass, and guests from several foreign countries.[22]

Fisk's increasing fame began to attract students from all parts of the country. W. E. B. DuBois, who went to Fisk from the relatively isolated Great Barrington, Massachusetts, was just one of many pupils from the North and East. Fisk's strong attraction to blacks is not surprising. It aimed from the beginning to become a full-fledged college that could afford its students a course of study similar to that of Northern schools. Students were encouraged to become teachers, physicians, clergymen, and lawyers. The faculty believed that in this way blacks as a race could be most effectively elevated.

After the political gains of Reconstruction disappeared, blacks could be assured of an improved standing only in the field of education. The pursuit of education, therefore, became one of their great preoccupations. Learning was viewed as the greatest single opportunity to escape the increasing proscriptions and indignities being heaped upon them.[23] Moreover, with increased segregation, professional people and leaders were more needed than ever. Fisk was a logical place to go. As a result of persistently adhering to the idea of training leaders of a people, Fisk assumed a strong hold over the "talented tenth" of the race.

That Fisk students considered themselves a part of the talented tenth and as future leaders of their people was evident in the writings in the *Fisk Herald*. Started in 1883, the *Herald* became within a short time a surprisingly good college newspaper. Fiskites were especially strong supporters of civil rights and wanted no part of Booker T. Washington's "Atlanta compromise." W. E. B. DuBois stated, "At Fisk the problem of race was faced openly and essential racial equality asserted and natural inferiority strenuously denied." Through the columns of the *Herald* Fiskites condemned the student who wrote a *Vanderbilt Observer* article abhoring social equality; also criticized were the whites who ejected a black minister from a railway car. In an 1889 article the editor doubted the existence of the much discussed "New South." It certainly retained old ideas, old customs, and old prejudices.

In 1891 the *Herald* aimed a broadside at mob law which had "committed some of the most atrocious, dastardly and diabolical deeds ever known to civilization." "Like unto the savage or the dark and barbarous ages of Europe," the *Herald* stated, "do these blood-thirsty villains roam over the Southern states, bathing the soil with innocent blood . . . perpetrating deeds upon humanity so heinous . . . that the very thought of which thrill the soul with horror." Tennessee, along with her sister states, the *Herald* claimed, had sat by quietly while such crimes were committed. When in 1891 the separate car law, "conceived in prejudice, born in iniquity and executed in injustice" went into effect, the *Herald* called upon the black man to "stand in the strength which God had blessed him and battle for his rights." When the land was covered with lifeless forms of white as well as black citizens, a strong editorial asserted, the South would cease to be a land of class legislation and depression. Only then, it was added, would there be a new South worthy of praise.[24]

Fisk students were not content just to write about equal rights. They worked actively to retain or secure them. At a banquet in Louisville, Kentucky, the Jubilee Singers refused to perform until black members of the audience were permitted to sit where they pleased in the hall. In 1888 about twenty Fiskites were called before a legislative committee on elections on charges of illegal voting. An inquiry revealed that all who voted did so legally and voted a straight Republican ticket. They gave notice that they were a new type. "We are not the Negro from whom the chains of slavery fell a quarter of a century ago," the *Herald* said, "most assuredly not."

Yet Fisk students were by no means serious all of the time. They frequently acted like young people everywhere. In 1881 Oscar Marshall was punished for attending a circus without permission. Circus attendance, voted the faculty, was "demoralizing" in its influence. A young girl was informed by a faculty committee that "her love making and flirting" were disapproved and unless she "discontinued the same" she could not return to school. A three-member faculty committee was appointed in 1877 to "settle the matter" of a report that Toby Frizes had been using tobacco. On another occasion some students who attended a public execution were forced to make a public confession and promises of amendment. The faculty administered discipline with a heavy hand, though Professor Frederick Chase in 1875 introduced a resolution that corporeal punishment be rarely dispensed.[25]

Students were dealt with harshly when they broke regulations, but they received strong faculty support in their advocacy of civil rights. Fisk "had always striven to exemplify racial concord." Professors Chase, Adam K. Spence, and Henry S. Bennett sent their children to Fisk. These white children attended the same classes, participated in the same events, were concerned about the same problems, and retained the same loyalties to the school as other students. Mary E. Spence received both her B.A. and M.A. at Fisk and later became professor of Greek at her alma mater. A historian of the American Missionary Association concluded that Spence more than any other leader in association colleges insisted upon equality for blacks in American life. The only hope for progress, he thought, was the training of unquestionably superior leadership. When a Nashville reporter interviewed Cravath, he "spoke with an increase of warmth over his usually quiet manner" when talking of the injustice of public accommodations. Girls were trained, he said, through "years of difficulties and effort, to reach a stage of refinement and self-respect, to be forced into the company of brutes in a smoking car. . . ." Cravath contended such laws were behind the spirit of the times and "in common justice should be remedied." The Fisk president reacted angrily and quickly when a Nashville ticket agent refused to sell pullman berths to the Jubilee Singers. Cravath telegraphed George Pullman, who rebuked the agent and ordered him to sell tickets to the students. Pullman cars were officially nonsegregated for the next quarter-century.[26] Student integration was prohibited by state laws after the turn of the century but a mixed faculty was retained.

The extent to which a college influences a person cannot be determined, but DuBois, who became one of the country's greatest warriors against racial injustice, breathed the atmosphere described above and certainly it had some effect on him. He was astonished upon his arrival at Fisk to discover that fellow students sometimes carried firearms for protection. During the summer of 1886 DuBois taught at a school in Lebanon, Tennessee; it was a small log hut without doors or windows. He learned about conditions under which blacks lived and how much they needed intelligent leadership. Some white farmers expressed a doubt about whether they liked such a "biggety nigger" as DuBois. At the end of the summer he said he would not take $200 for his experience and would not go through it again for $300.

Personal contact with the Fisk faculty was "inspiring and beneficial" to DuBois. The "excellent and earnest teaching" and absence of distractions enabled him "to re-arrange and re-build" his "program for progress and freedom among Negroes." At Fisk he began his public speaking, and, as editor of the *Fisk Herald*, his writing. DuBois while at Fisk "became an impassioned orator and developed a belligerent attitude toward the color bar." Upon graduation in 1888 he already had more than a general idea of what his life's work should be. Fisk, said DuBois, broadened the scope of his program of life. Later he remembered his years at Fisk as a time of "splendid inspiration." At Harvard the next year he found no better teachers, only teachers better known.[27] Many other less famous students absorbed the same ideas as DuBois. If Fisk alumni had been asked to vote on the correctness of the position of DuBois or Booker T. Washington during their controversy, DuBois would have won easily.

The members of the faculty primarily responsible for creating the atmosphere in which DuBois grew and thrived were Cravath, Spence, Bennett, Chase, and Helen C. Morgan. Though less influential in creating the "Fisk spirit," other teachers advocated the same ideas. These were not misfits teaching at a black school because they were unable to secure positions elsewhere.[28] Any of them could have found better paying and less burdensome jobs. After studying at Fisk, Harvard, and in Germany, DuBois claimed Spence was "a great Greek scholar by any comparison." The others, he thought were also good. Writing years later, DuBois said it made little difference whether one was studying Greek or biology—the significant thing was that he was studying under Adam K. Spence.

Despite the teachers' ability, they continued to suffer from social ostracism, miserable pay, and overwork. On one occasion Miss Morgan taught ten classes daily. Such workers developed an "exaggerated and often morbid sense of responsibility" that held them to their duty "with the courage of a soldier on a perilous outpost, only to be vacated at the risk of disgrace and maintained at the great risk of collapse of health."[29] Their religion gave them some solace: It was naturally expected that one would suffer while doing God's bidding. Their religion was more than spiritual; it meant practical applications of Christ's teachings. This idea played an important role in developing the Fisk spirit. All methods of work were devised for the purpose of making students "strong, earnest, broadminded Christian men and women"—Christian men and women who were to "give their lives to the uplifting and benefiting of their people."[30]

Faculty spirit and organization changed little during the Cravath administration, but the number of faculty did. There was an increase in teachers, especially in the college department. The staff grew from fifteen in 1876 to thirty-five in 1900. A few of the new members were black. As early as 1871 Fisk tried to employ a few black teachers on grounds that claims of equality could not be sustained with a segregated faculty, but they found that qualified blacks were scarce. Most of the black faculty were Fisk graduates, including the Burruses and Ella Sheppard, mentioned previously, plus: Ferdinand Augustus Stewart, B.A. '85, M.D. Harvard '88, who was medical examiner; Harriet F. Kimbro, Normal School '75, principal of the intermediate school; George W. Moore, B.A. '81, B.D. Oberlin College '90, associate professor of theology; and Flora F. Wright '96, music teacher. Moore was also the only black member of the board of trustees, appointed in 1885.[31]

Growth of the college and faculty caused Fisk's financial problems to remain critical. Letters to and from Fisk presidents dramatically indicate the difficulties of financing a private institution. More often than not balancing the budget was a frantic struggle each year. Money earned by the Jubilee Singers went into the new plant and could not be used for current expenses. Blacks could make only small contributions since most of their lives were still circumscribed by the plantation and farm. Furthermore, depression resulting from overexpansion and increased production of cotton settled over the South after 1873, affecting thousands of black farmers.

Fisk's financial condition was so poor that when the Nashville Board of Health ordered the school in 1876 to have the privies cleaned it had to be done on credit. The next year Mrs. A. K. Spence was sent North to collect funds primarily to support students, and in 1878 she and Professor Spence were dispatched to Great Britain to raise money, but the results were disappointing. Endowment receipts, essential to a private school, were about $75 in 1876. By 1900 the endowment had increased to $44,967.44, but this was just a fraction of the amount needed. The total earnings for Fisk in 1888, including tuition, were $5,883. During one crisis salaries were reduced by 20 percent. Some were not subject to the cut because it applied only to those drawing $25 or more a month.[32]

Most of the great philanthropic foundations that aided black education were created after 1900, but some support was received from the Peabody Fund and the John F. Slater Fund. Also there were some bequests. In 1882 Jabez L. Burrell of Oberlin, Ohio, left Fisk an interest in a piece of land that netted $6,000. In 1889 a black Nashville woman left a legacy of $1,000 to establish the Lucian Bedford Scholarship.

Most of Fisk's operating funds had to be raised by the university itself, but solicitors sent from Fisk encountered opposition from the American Missionary Association. Fisk tried mainly to collect from churches, the

NORMAL CLASS, 1898 (*Courtesy of the Fisk University Library's Special Collections*)

same source of association income. The association felt that since it paid part of Fisk's expenses, the school could not properly seek aid from organizations which normally contributed to the association. This policy hindered any successful plan for raising money. Fisk ended the century in debt and with no solution to financial problems in sight.[33]

Despite lack of adequate funds, the Fisk physical plant grew considerably between 1875 and 1900, primarily by gifts. Jubilee Hall, of course, was financed by the singers. In 1882 Livingstone Hall was erected, principally through a $60,000 donation by Mrs. Valeria G. Stone of Malden, Massachusetts. A gymnasium and workshop were constructed in 1889 through gifts. Bennett Hall, built in 1891 at a cost of $25,000, was paid for by the American Missionary Association and the Jubilee Singers. In 1892 a legacy of General Fisk resulted in the construction of Fisk Memorial Chapel. Mrs. Fisk, Miss Mary F. Penfield, and Paul D. Cravath, son of the president, were responsible for the construction of the president's house in 1897. The Daniel Hand Training School was built in 1895 from the income of the Daniel Hand Fund. It was later remodeled for use by the music school.[34]

The deaths of Professor Spence on 24 April 1900 and of President Cravath on 4 September 1900 ended an era in the history of Fisk University. Together they had devoted sixty-five years to the cause of black education. Soon all of the original missionary teachers were gone. But their endeavors had not been in vain. Fisk University boasted a national reputation and distinguished alumni in almost every state of the Union. Some able people had been developed—poor libraries, inadequate facilities, and discrimination notwithstanding. They had overcome the incubus of poverty-stricken homes and educationally limited backgrounds.

By 1900 Fisk had graduated over 400 students from the college, theology, normal, and music departments. Of those still living in 1900 and known to Fisk officials, 8 were college professors, 12 were principals and 45 were teachers in high or normal schools, 34 were principals and 120 instructors in grammar school, 20 were ministers, 9 practiced law, 16 were in professional schools, 13 in business, 9 employed by the United States government, and 45 were housewives. One student had been a college president and two were editors. At least 700 additional Fiskites who had never graduated were engaged in teaching.[35] This record sounds even more impressive when it is realized that only 1 percent of the blacks in the United States—or less than 23,000 persons—were in professional service in 1900.

Fisk alumni were especially well known as teachers. A traveler through the South in the 1880s noticed the influence of Fisk students wherever he visited. He believed Fisk had served as a stimulus to other schools. In 1883 Texas operated nine teacher institutes for blacks throughout the

state, and four of them were conducted by Fiskites. The white superintendent of education in Tunica County, Mississippi, told Professor
Spence in 1878 that he had just employed seven more Fisk students to
teach. As long as he was in office all his teachers would come from Fisk,
he said.

One example will serve to show why Fisk teachers were in such demand. A small black community in southwestern Georgia decided it
needed a school and applied to Fisk for a teacher. The young lady who
answered the call became Sunday school superintendent, janitor, and
moral leader of the community as well as instructor. Noting that some
pupils lived too far from school to commute daily, she rented a building
and housed the young girls. Soon students were so numerous that an
addition was built. It was without door and sashes, but pupils came and
were well taught. Fiskites, regardless of occupation, frequently became
community leaders throughout the South.[36]

5

Head or Hand?

BEFORE THE END OF CRAVATH'S ADMINISTRATION CLASSICAL EDUCATION
for blacks had fallen into disrepute, and industrial training was in vogue.
Booker T. Washington was the high priest of industrial education. Such
education did not originate with Washington; he merely brought to its
climax a trend under way well before his "Atlanta Compromise" speech.
European educational theories of agricultural and mechanical training
enjoyed considerable popularity in the United States by the second quarter of the nineteenth century. During and after the Civil War it became
an extensively used and controversial form of education under the impact of industrialization. It became the subject of the most vigorous
pedagogical battle in the white National Education Association in the
1880s.[1]

Vocational training had also been advocated by educators in black
schools several years before Washington became famous. Many early
missionaries, including American Missionary Association teachers,
taught domestic arts to women and janitorial and repair work to men. In
Virginia, Samuel Chapman Armstrong, who had noted the good results
flowing from craft schools operated by his missionary father in Hawaii,
emerged with the first permanent and successful example of the industrial doctrine at Hampton Institute. The Hampton idea proved quite
popular. In the years following Reconstruction there was an increased
emphasis on economic activity as a means of solving the race problem.
Blacks were deprived of a voice in politics and were untrained for indus-
try. There were complaints that they were given higher education that
was impractical. Knowledge of Latin, Greek, and higher mathematics
would be of little value in guiding a mule down cotton rows or in laying
bricks. Higher education, in fact, was more widely discussed than practiced, but it was believed that by learning trade skills, which would in
turn bring wealth, blacks would gain the respect of whites and thereby be
accorded their rights as Americans.[2] Impetus was given industrial education in the United States in 1882 by the creation of the John F. Slater
Fund.

By 1890 industrial education had been accepted by large numbers of
people throughout the country. Some Northern capitalists supporting
black education seemed less interested in "making men" than in training

workers. Black laborers might even be used as "scabs" to counteract the growing labor unions. Southern whites grasped eagerly at industrial education as a method of satisfying blacks' desire for learning while at the same time keeping them in their "place." Some Northern friends, weary of the black crusade yet unwilling to abandon the former slaves to the mercies of a reactionary South, thought industrial education might be a solution. When Washington gave voice to these ideas in Atlanta in 1895 he quickly emerged as a national leader.[3]

For years a conflict raged among black educators over the respective merits of vocational versus liberal arts education. Washington said the former would provide the black man with the "foundation of a civilization upon which he will grow and prosper." He wrote, "Until there is industrial independence, it is hardly possible to have good living and a pure ballot in the country districts." Washington complained that young men had been taken from farms and taught law, theology, Greek— everything except the subject they most needed, which was farming. Since self-support and industrial independence were the first conditions of uplifting any race, practical training in agriculture, trades, and stock raising should occupy first place in the educational system, Washington claimed. Though too late to cry about previous miseducation it was time for both races to acknowledge the error and "go forth on the course that . . . all must now see to be the right one,—industrial education." It was cruel, Washington said, to increase the wants of a black youth by a liberal education without at the same time increasing his ability to supply these enlarged desires. Furthermore, Washington and friends thought that by becoming capable of producing something the white man needed and by becoming more prosperous than whites, blacks would earn respect and the racial situation would be improved.[4]

W. E. B. DuBois, the spokesman of the opposing forces, championed the cause of higher education for the best black minds—the talented tenth—at schools like Fisk. Moreover, Washington might have been wrong when he insisted that the South was most impressed with blacks who owned property. Southerners may have "liked" the property-owner more, but the white man considered and feared most the educated black. Manual trades were patronizingly rewarded but white opinion considered evidence of intelligence in a black as a sign that he was out of his place. The black could expect toleration as reward for hand labor, persecution and resentment for evidence of mental capacity. The alacrity with which the white South accepted industrial education was enough to make blacks suspicious. There is evidence that the emphasis placed on vocational instruction was due to a general belief in the mental inferiority of the race and a desire to keep them as common laborers.

Even white educators, who should have been the most enlightened, reflected popular opinion. The president of the North Carolina College of Agriculture and Mechanics claimed in 1901 that a radical change was needed in the black educational system. Their colleges of law, medicine, theology, science, literature, and art should be turned into schools for industrial training, he said. The University of Georgia's chancellor was willing to grant a concession: Black schools should be industrial and agricultural but the three R's could be taught. He quoted a Georgia millionaire who had over one thousand black employees as saying, "I want a hand in the field to whom I can send a written inquiry or direction as to his work and who can return to me in writing an intelligent response."[5]

Critics of Washington could also point to the failure of industrial schools to realize their aims. The need, according to Washington, was not so much bricklayers and laundry women as industrial leaders. Apparently industrial schools were not at first too successful in supplying the demand. The American Missionary Association in the early 1900s employed approximately fifty vocational teachers annually, over half of them blacks. The association found the average industrial school graduates inadequate in such capacities because they had received too little academic training.

During this time even when Tuskegee graduates completed the academic as well as the industrial course they had scarcely begun standard secondary work. From the beginning Fisk and Atlanta University graduates formed the backbone of Tuskegee's teaching force. It was Fisk graduates who turned Alcorn A & M in Mississippi into an effective agricultural and mechanical school. The J. K. Brick Industrial School at Enfield, North Carolina, was headed by a Fiskite. He had managed some highly successful feats of rural engineering on the school's eleven hundred acres and had set up engines in the shops which were the wonder of the white neighborhood. When whites asked where he learned to do all these things, he replied, "Oh, studying Greek at Fisk." Not only did industrial schools teach insufficient academic subjects, but the type of vocational training was outdated before it began. Crafts and attitudes taught were "more congenial to the premachine age than the twentieth century."[6]

Placed in their proper perspective there was little reason why the two types of education should have been antagonistic. As Kelly Miller said, numerous earnest advocates of the black cause seemed "to have lost the power of binocular vision" and had become "one-eyed enthusiasts over a narrow feature." The two forms of education, he said, far from being opposites, were supplemental. Higher education applied to the few, vocational education to the many. The former supplied the motive, the latter the method. Certainly industrial education correctly taught to those who had neither the inclination nor ability to take college training would be useful and could improve the blacks' economic status. There was a need for both. Industrial education would be beneficial as long as it was not detrimental to higher education.

The contention that students were being taught useless subjects in college was not borne out by the Fisk experience. Fisk graduates, at least until the Great Depression, had little difficulty in securing good positions, and with increased segregation even more professional people were required. There was an urgent need for more lawyers, physicians, and able teachers. If teaching Greek to blacks seemed foolish to many, was this more foolish than teaching it to whites? The classical course was brought to Fisk because it was taught in most liberal arts schools at the time. As the curriculum was broadened throughout the country it was expanded at Fisk also. Moreover, what the former slave perhaps needed most was lofty ideals. One inducement for providing material needs is the knowledge that life is more than food and shelter.

Washington protested that he was not opposed to advanced training, but sometimes he was not very convincing. In a speech to Fisk students in 1895 he said some people mistakenly thought industrial instruction was antithetical to college training. Not so, said Washington. "Give me a college man everytime," he asserted, "a man with a trained mind to receive industrial training rather than a person with an untrained mind." Such a statement must have been less than reassuring to proponents of higher education.[7]

Unfortunately, narrow-visioned people seemed to predominate. Industrial education swept the South with a corresponding loss of interest in black liberal arts colleges. Within a few years it was almost impossible for schools of Fisk's caliber to get money from philanthropic foundations without Washington's approval. Fisk President George A. Gates discovered in 1910 that Hampton and Tuskegee had "cornered" New York funds for black education in the South. Influential businessmen in the Midwest, a Fisk solicitor reported, knew about Tuskegee and industrial schools but showed little interest in Fisk. Indeed, the popularity enjoyed by industrial education can be partially explained by the influence that Washington exerted over the distribution of Northern funds. Tuskegee, DuBois said, was the capital of the black nation.

Schools devoted to higher education struggled along on the small amounts offered by the charity of a few Northern idealists, or they deliberately, though unenthusiastically, added vocational departments as bait for philanthropists. Even President Theodore Roosevelt placed his stamp of approval on industrial education. In his annual message to Congress in 1906 he said, "Of course the best type of education for the colored man, taken as a whole, is such education as is conferred in schools like Hampton and Tuskegee; where the boys and girls, the young men and women, are trained industrially as well as in the ordinary public school branches." Other men and women who usually had sound judgment accepted Washington's plan without question. Some of the adherents were more radical about industrial education than he was. They failed to reflect on his services to higher education. Washington eventually developed a broader view, and in 1909 he became a member of the Fisk board of trustees and rendered important aid in fund collecting.[8]

Despite the temptation to turn to applied arts and trades, Fisk clung to its original purpose of liberal education for black youth. A few vocational courses were taught from time to time, but never to the injury of the college. As early as 1868 John Ogden rejected an American Missionary Association official's suggestion to offer industrial education at Fisk. He had little faith in agricultural and mechanical schools, Ogden stated, and anyway what was needed in the South was thorough normal training for black teachers. The sooner Fisk struck out in that direction ignoring all the "*conflicting* or minor" issues, he averred, the quicker education would be placed on a solid basis. Though its name has usually been associated with liberal arts for blacks, the American Missionary Association was one of the most influential forces fostering industrial education. Hampton Institute was an association school, and relatively ambitious programs of industrial education were inaugurated at Atlanta University and Tougaloo. Fisk officials always resisted.[9] The students did work and they were taught the dignity of labor. Nearly all students engaged in house cleaning, janitorial service, construction of sidewalks, or other pursuits, but the object was to teach thrift, economics, and to aid students in staying in school.

Never contending that industrial education was unnecessary, Fisk argued only that it should not supplant college training. The *Fisk Herald,* which usually mirrored faculty views, acknowledged in 1883 the need for vocational training, but added, "if this is to be brought about by a loss of popularity on the part of colleges, it will prove a great misfortune." The *Herald* asked for industrial schools for the masses, and colleges and universities for those with literary tastes and political and professional aspirations. Later the newspaper explained the reason for its point of view: In the first place, it said, the black man's relation to the nation was no longer that of ex-slave. He was a part of the body politic, with responsibilities, ambitions, desires, national pride, and love of country like other citizens; therefore, he should receive similar training. Further, the *Herald* asked, ". . . how dare any man or set of men presume to limit us in our intellectual improvement—in the shaping of the highest faculties unto which we have been endowed?"[10]

Determination to maintain higher education did not mean that Fisk would refuse all money for vocational instruction. Although Cravath urged the need of higher education as the best method for training leaders, he accepted $900 from the Slater Fund in 1884 to instruct intermediate girls in household duties and to teach printing. By May, seventy-four students had received some instruction in cooking, nursing, and sewing. Classes met only one hour a week and were for girls of less than college grade. All expenses for such courses were paid by the Slater Fund; no Fisk money was used. Fisk officials saw no reason why the girls should be barred from free training which would make them more efficient wives and mothers, or why Slater money should not be accepted to print the *Herald*.[11]

Industrial education was discussed for the first time in the Fisk catalog in 1885. While distinctively vocational training was not a prominent feature of the school, the catalog stated, all the arrangements of the boarding department were devised with a view of forming correct habits and ideas that would prepare students for the practical duties of life. This had always been true at Fisk. Sewing, nursing, and cooking courses were not a part of the regular curriculum. A student could choose to take them on her own time if she desired.[12] A few years later officials claimed the school had not "deviated in its purpose by the breadth of a hair." They believed in industrial education but elected to leave the work to institutions which had that as their primary aim. It would enter upon industrial work only so far as it was in harmony with higher education. College work was always first.

Less industrial training was given to men than to women. Annually a few students who helped print the *Herald* were instructed in the various types of work done in a job office. In 1886 a Slater Fund representative reported that Fisk was "doing well" with women, but he was discouraged about the lack of industrial training for men. He hoped the latter would be offered more training the next year, but in 1888 he found that a little painting was the only industrial work they were doing.[13] Eventually a workshop was placed in the basement of the gymnasium where instruction was given in woodworking to the common English and college preparatory departments. Even here the women invaded the men's domain. Six women from the normal school entered the class and their "elementary joiner work was quite creditable; they measured as closely and sawed with as much deftness as their brothers." The nature and use of varnishes, paints, stains, and polishes, and cabinetmaking were studied by advanced woodworking students. In 1898 all industrial training was temporarily suspended because of insufficient funds, but in 1902 Fisk again halfheartedly offered domestic science courses. Instruction was committed to Mrs. James G. Merrill, wife of the late President Cravath's successor. Mrs. Merrill worked without salary, attempting to prepare the future homemakers and the teachers for their duties.[14]

By 1900 it seemed to Fisk officials that the pressure to offer industrial education had declined. People were beginning to realize that college training was no less essential for blacks than vocational instruction, President Merrill said. After all, one industrial school had ten Fisk graduates on its staff. In 1900 Washington gave a speech at Fisk in which he endorsed college training. This was a pleasant surprise to many Fiskites, the *Herald* reported, who had come to believe Washington had been "sowing dragon's teeth, in apparently yielding to the Southern sentiment, that the Negro should not be educated beyond an industrial training."[15]

Merrill was soon disabused of his rosy view. In 1903 he made a "strenuous effort" to secure money for the college from the Slater Fund. Every trustee of the Slater Fund north of the Mason and Dixon Line was either written or personally interviewed. Merrill's plea was based on the need for teachers, a demand which Fisk was well equipped to supply. When he thought it prudent he added that industrial schools were not equipped to do such work. The readiness with which both normal and collegiate graduates found useful employment was a "forceful witness" to the foresight of Fisk's founders, Merrill claimed. His request was brought before the Slater board but was not resolved to his satisfaction. Two years later the Slater Fund appropriated $5,000 to Fisk, not for the college, but to add a department of applied sciences. The new department, Merrill said, was so correlated with the existing institution as to maintain its "unalterable" purpose to be a school of higher learning. Fisk, Merrill added, did "not expect to make farmers, carpenters, masons, laundrywomen, dressmakers" of its students but to teach them "the underlying principles of chemistry and physics as applied to modern industry and agriculture." The courses still applied to secondary and normal pupils only.[16]

Although it suffered the financial consequences for a few more years, Fisk adhered to the cause of higher learning. When eventually the balance swung back toward college instruction, the school was in an excellent position to build upon a solid foundation and render even greater service to blacks. Rather than Fisk switching to industrial education, Tuskegee and similar institutions added college departments.

Refusal to yield to the pressure of industrial education advocates did not mean Fisk officials were opposed to change. During the first two decades of the twentieth century there was a gradual modernization; modifications, while not doing violence to the school's original aims, gave it a wider appeal and greater usefulness. Cravath was succeeded as president by the Reverend James G. Merrill, who had joined Fisk in 1898 as dean of faculty and professor of logic and moral science. Merrill was born in Montague, Massachusetts, on 20 August 1840, and was educated at Amherst and Princeton Theological Seminary. After serving as pastor in Congregational churches for several years, he became editor in 1874

ALL THE COLLEGE CLASSES, 1888–1889 (*Courtesy of the Fisk University Library's Special Collections*)

of the *Christian Mirror,* subsequently renamed the *Congregationalist.* He became acting president upon Cravath's death and president in June 1901.[17]

Merrill's motto for Fisk was, "the development of Christian manhood in an education for service," and he believed students could be better prepared for service to the people by broadening the curriculum. In 1902 a summer school for black teachers was inaugurated. Poorly educated teachers were enabled to increase their knowledge of subject matter, while at the same time they were exposed to the newest teaching methods. This was in accordance with the Fisk policy of ministering to the community as well as to its students. In 1906, in an apparent concession to industrial education, several new electives were added for college students. The plan was to add pure sciences, with as much practical application as possible, to supplement the work in classical studies. Though the new courses were to be equal to the classics in disciplinary and cultural value, they were to familiarize students who wished to be industrial and business leaders with the necessary principles. Courses in meteorology, climatology, botany, agricultural chemistry, floriculture, architectural drawing, economic entomology, and thermatology were made available. Students were still required to take the usual college course.[18]

In 1908 Merrill resigned in frustration and was succeeded by George A. Gates. Merrill had no desire to leave, but plagued by the enemy of all Fisk presidents, lack of money, he decided the best interests of the school demanded his departure. "The only real difficulty is the money side," Merrill told the trustees, "and this difficulty is so great that I have come to the conclusion that I have no longer a right to continue in my present position."[19]

Gates went to Fisk after successful administrations as president of Iowa State College, Grinnell, and Pomona College in California. Born in Vermont on 24 January 1851, Gates was graduated from Dartmouth in 1874 and, after two years' study in Germany, from Andover Theological Seminary in 1880. More of a free thinker than previous Fisk officials, Gates was rejected for ordination by the Congregational Church in Littleton, New Hampshire, in 1880 because he was too unorthodox. His belief in the theory of evolution was unacceptable at the time, but he was eventually ordained. Some of the Fisk faculty were concerned about his religion—or lack of it. He was religious, just not evangelical. A professor who worked under Gates at Iowa State said he was "peculiarly adapted to aid in effecting the transition of the earlier type Christian college to that of an educational institution open to all truths, and he became a conspicuous leader in the adjustment of the new education to the new social gospel." While at Iowa State Gates created "the chair of applied Christianity." His purpose was to promote the study of social conditions and the search for methods of Christian application to them. Long before the social gospel became widespread in the United States, the philosophy had been ingrained in Fisk pupils, so Gates entered sympathetic surroundings.[20]

The trustees who expected Fisk under Gates's leadership to enter upon a new period of development were not disappointed. During his brief administration (1909–1912) standards were raised, a new enthusiasm was engendered, and the curriculum was made more flexible. First, the merging of the normal school and college, begun before Gates's arrival, was completed. The normal department had trained scores of effective teachers—the Nashville Board of Education had granted a holiday to all black public schools on the day of Gates's inaugural since 50 percent of the teachers were Fiskites—but the need for a normal school had declined. Students desiring to teach as quickly as possible could still get a normal diploma at the end of the sophomore college year. By the end of 1909 Fisk pupils could select one of three college programs, all leading to the Bachelor of Arts degree: the classical degree, which had changed little; the scientific course, which was especially adapted to industrial school graduates who wanted further training; and the education course for teachers. Gates also added sociology, a subject that came to receive much emphasis in black schools and one for which Fisk became internationally known.[21]

Sociology was a newcomer in the history of education. In 1892 Albion Small went to the University of Chicago to head the first such department in the United States. Fisk was fortunate enough to secure George Edmund Haynes to teach the subject. Haynes received his B.A. at Fisk in 1903, his M.A. at Yale in 1904, and the Ph.D. at Columbia in 1912. While a graduate student at Columbia, Haynes made an extensive study of the economic and social conditions of New York blacks that was later published as *The Negro at Work in New York City*. Interest generated by Haynes's work eventuated in the formation of the National League on Urban Affairs.

Haynes went to Fisk in 1910 to establish a social science department and a training center for social workers. The Department of Social Science cooperated with the Board of Missions of the Methodist Episcopal Church, South, in conducting a settlement house in Nashville. Senior sociology students were required to give four hours of field work at the house. These students ministered to an average of 350 families. Fisk had always emphasized community service, but its fame for training social workers began with Haynes, who became an international expert on racial affairs.

Gates also continued the upgrading of standards. In 1913 Fisk, Howard, Wilberforce, Knoxville College, Virginia Union University, Atlanta University, Morehouse, and Talladega joined to set uniform entrance

SENIOR CLASS, 1909 (*Courtesy of the Fisk University Library's Special Collections*)

requirements and to cooperate in solving mutual problems. This cooperative enterprise led to considerable advance in the standing of black schools.[22]

The raising of standards was accompanied by an increase in the number of college students. In 1905 Fisk's enrollment went over 100 for the first time. By 1913 the total had increased to almost 200, but the college was still outnumbered by secondary pupils.

The progress of the Merrill and Gates administrations was made under the most unfavorable circumstances. Most blacks were still struggling with poverty. Segregation and disfranchisement had not ended terror and violence. Blacks' status had deteriorated rather than improved. Southern opinion became more extreme, and the North became increasingly indifferent to the black man's fate. Thomas Dixon's *The Clansman* and Charles Carroll's *The Negro a Beast,* both violently antiblack, were widely admired. Northern scholarly opinion in biological science supported racist theories of black inferiority. Lynchings and brutal murders occurred all over the South and sometimes in the North. There were 2,500 lynchings in the last sixteen years of the nineteenth century. Over one thousand more blacks were lynched between 1900 and the beginning of World War I. In the early years of the twentieth century there was a rash of riots throughout the country, the most sensational one occurring at Atlanta in September 1906.

Conditions in education were little better. In some areas, black schools, upon every sort of pretext, were being impoverished, if not totally abandoned. Senator Benjamin Tillman of South Carolina received some applause when he said that blacks wore their education like a coat of paint. Scratch the paint and a savage would be revealed beneath the surface, he said. Dr. Charles W. Dabney, president of the University of Tennessee, in 1903 "emphasized very forcibly" the idea that black education should be halted until the Southern white was thoroughly educated. Dr. William Polk of the Cornell medical faculty spoke of blacks as children and said amalgamation was threatening the ruin of the white race. Even the purest stream, he said, succumbed to unchecked contamination. The superintendent of schools in Birmingham, Alabama, claimed it was essential for black children to begin school earlier than the whites because the premature closing of their brain sutures caused an early arrest of brain growth. He claimed that education received by black youths after the age of twelve or fourteen usually had little effect since it was acquired after the higher faculties had become inactive. It remained as a sort of superficial gloss which would easily break under the strain of the lower habits of blacks, he said.[23]

The prevalent attitude toward blacks and their education aggravated Fisk's usual problem of finances. Though no private black school had an adequate endowment, the financing of liberal arts colleges was doubly difficult. Each year it was necessary to beg operating expenses. Students still had trouble paying tuition and American Missionary Association support continued to decline. In 1902 President Merrill wrote of the self-denial of students, of the young man who lived on seven cents a day in order to finance his return to school. More than three-fourths of the male students had no vacation at all during the summer, Merrill said. They worked every possible day to make money for school in the fall. State normal scholarships, distributed by senators, aided a few students, but appropriations for this purpose were cut in the early 1900s. About the only foundation from which Fisk could secure money was the Slater Fund, which insisted its grant be used in the Department of Applied Sciences. Little wonder that Merrill resigned in defeat. By 1912 both Fisk and Atlanta University were in such dire financial straits that a merger was considered. Atlanta trustees twice voted down the plan.[24]

What little success Fisk experienced in money raising in the first twelve years of the twentieth century was due largely to Booker T. Washington and his wife. Washington attended a Fisk college commencement for the first time in 1889 and declared himself "highly pleased" with what he saw and heard. He was especially impressed with the delightful, dynamic Miss Margaret Murray, a member of the graduating class. Miss Murray, who had planned to teach in Texas, found herself instead at Tuskegee as head of the Ladies Department. In 1891 she and Washington were engaged and two years later were married. Mrs. Washington was for years one of her husband's most effective helpers, but she did not forget Fisk. In her first year at Tuskegee she had written: "I do not believe in these all colored schools. I really do not. Something is lacking although I am not able to tell you what it is." Fiskites, she believed, were by far the best workers at Tuskegee.[25] She used her influence as Mrs. Washington to aid her alma mater and Booker, Jr., was sent to Fisk.

Mrs. Washington was most successful in securing a Carnegie library for Fisk. Officials solicited Carnegie for years without much success. Finally in 1908 he gave the school $20,000, in part as a favor to Mrs. Washington, whom he admired. The cornerstone was laid on 22 May 1908 by Secretary of War William Howard Taft. Taft had agreed to speak at the ceremony at the urging of Washington.[26]

Meanwhile, there was a move to make Washington a member of the Fisk board of trustees. His power with the foundations caused him to be a popular choice for that position at many schools—as a trustee of Howard University he was once appointed a "committee of one" to confer with the Carnegie Foundation. In November 1909, Washington was elected to the Fisk board. President Gates deemed it necessary to announce publicly that Washington's selection did not mean, as some feared, that Fisk would be taken over by industrial education. The Tuskegee head, Gates proclaimed, had accepted "to indicate and emphasize his conviction concerning the value of Fisk's work." Still, Washington occasionally found it necessary to rebuke Gates for his strictures on industrial education.[27]

Although Washington rarely attended trustee meetings he took his duties seriously and was a valuable aid in applications for money. He gave Fisk solicitors a list of names to whom they should apply and an endorsement expressing his faith and interest in the school. A personal letter was written to Andrew Carnegie, saying: "Fisk University I consider is doing the best work of any institution in the South in purely college directions for the education of our people. . . . Fisk has the confidence, support and good will of the Southern white people as well as the colored people to a larger degree than is true of any college in the South that I know of." When President Gates and Warren G. Waterman, professor of geology, visited Carnegie about ten days later they were "greatly pleased to see indirect evidences" of Carnegie's high regard for Washington and "to note the remarkable effect" of Washington's letter in gaining them "a very cordial reception." On another occasion Washington asked his wife to write Carnegie, saying a letter from her would have a stronger appeal than one from him. Washington was also a close friend of Carnegie's secretary, James Bertram, who wielded considerable influence upon his employer. On one occasion he sent Bertram an opossum and sweet potatoes for New Year's. Mrs. Bertram wrote, thanking him kindly, but failed to say whether she had eaten the opossum.[28]

At its October 1910 meeting, the Fisk board of trustees determined to inaugurate a campaign to raise not less than $300,000. Harvey L. Simmons, a New York trustee, and Professor Waterman were placed in charge of the operation. They quickly found a lack of interest in Fisk's type of work, but with Washington's aid some progress was made. Theodore Roosevelt, though he emphatically favored industrial education, wrote a letter of endorsement in 1911. Officials attempted to persuade Carnegie to preside at a New York fund-raising dinner, but he declined on account of illness. Mrs. Washington arranged to have a Fisk quartet sing for him in his home, and he got out his checkbook. In June 1911, the General Education Board, established by John D. Rockefeller, agreed to appropriate $60,000 to Fisk provided the school could raise $240,000 more by October 1912. Julius Rosenwald, president of Sears, Roebuck, and Company, was persuaded to visit Fisk and declared himself "greatly pleased" by what he saw. In 1913 he gave Fisk $2,500 with a promise of $10,000 annually for five years to defray current expenses. By June of the same year the General Education Board's conditional gift had been met—an extension of time had been granted—with liberal subscriptions from Carnegie, Rosenwald, J. Pierpont Morgan, Charles

A. Hull, Charles H. Rutan, and others. Fisk alumni had pledged $45,000.[29]

The successful campaign for $300,000 by no means solved Fisk's financial problems. It would be at least two years before it would all be paid in and invested. Over $50,000 was needed immediately to liquidate outstanding indebtedness and for building repairs. Another $50,000 was needed for installation of steam heat, lighting, and a laundry plant. But the successful campaign did allow Fisk to operate in the black for a time. The endowment was increased to a little more than $255,000. And more important, it showed that money could be secured from the great foundations for liberal arts colleges. It was an age of philanthropy. Newly rich Americans were founding and endowing schools all over the country and black education benefited substantially. In the early twentieth century several foundations—the General Education Board, Anna T. Jeanes Foundation, Phelps-Stokes Fund, and the Julius Rosenwald Fund—were created and worked directly to aid black education. In a little more than a decade these organizations would give Fisk a million-dollar endowment.

In the meantime President Gates had resigned. While on his way to New York in February 1912 to meet with the trustees, he was in a train wreck near Huntingdon, Pennsylvania. Several passengers were injured and a few killed. President Gates at first seemed to be one of the least injured. He gave aid to the others but was the last to leave the hospital due to a brain concussion. A return to work at Fisk resulted in complete mental and physical collapse. He took a leave of absence, spending the spring in the North Carolina mountains, but to no avail. During the summer came attacks of mental disturbances so serious as to necessitate his immediate resignation, which was written by Mrs. Gates without his permission or knowledge. He died soon afterwards. Though some of the Fisk faculty disapproved of him—Professor Mary E. Spence said he had some excellent characteristics but "made a mess of things"—Gates's administration was, on the whole, a successful one. The faculty had been concerned primarily about his lack of evangelicalism and the increased liberty granted to students, but he modernized the school and had initiated a successful drive for money. He also won many new friends for Fisk in Tennessee, as well as in the North.[30]

By the end of Gates's administration, Fisk alumni had reason to be proud. Fisk had long since passed beyond the experimental stage. It was a school recognized by educators and others as a significant factor in the promotion of an intelligent democracy in America. Among black colleges Fisk stood prominent with its long list of graduates, many of whom had achieved distinction and had reflected honor upon their race and their school. Black leaders in the pulpit and schoolroom, Chancellor

James H. Kirkland of Vanderbilt thought, had been "trained very largely" at Fisk University. "I know of no other institution," he added, "of like character that has held so constantly to high standards and ideals." Governor Ben W. Hooper of Tennessee claimed Fisk was "doing a great and permanent work" for blacks not only in the South but in the entire nation. But the compliments from Booker T. Washington were probably most gratifying of all. Fisk had been, he said, to an extent, a model for all other schools in the South. It deserved special credit for maintaining its standards under peculiar disadvantages. "Thruout the South, and in other parts of the country," Washington continued, blacks "cherished a feeling of love and even reverence for Fisk University that is not generally understood by the rest of the world. It is a great advantage to a school to have gained that sort of reputation among the people for whom it exists."[31]

But all was not as well at Fisk as Washington had intimated. Washington had earlier warned Gates that the school was losing touch with local people of all races. Indeed, former President Cravath had worked closely with the black community, but, according to the *Nashville Globe*, later presidents had less contact with blacks than those missionary teachers who came soon after the Civil War. President Merrill may have tried too hard to appease whites. Black schools could not survive without white toleration. Merrill wrote the editor of *McClure's* magazine: "I trust that I do not lack the courage to expose my views, but so long as I know that Fisk is doing an uncalculable amount of good, I do not think it wise to jeopardize the existence of my work by an unnecessary exploitation of my private opinions." Merrill was later active in the National Association for the Advancement of Colored People (NAACP), but while at Fisk he kept a low profile.

President Gates later offended the *Nashville Globe* editors and some other blacks when he reputedly invited whites to commencement with assurance that the audience would be segregated. The *Globe* editors, who had been attacking white presidents at Fisk for years and who believed that Fisk should have a black president, may have reflected the view of only a minority of Nashville blacks, but it was obvious that the next president would be watched suspiciously by both the black community and students.[32]

6

Growth with McKenzie

AFTER GATES'S RESIGNATION FISK WAS ADMINISTERED FOR MORE THAN
two years by a committee of faculty and officers.[1] The school had the
potential for important growth and the trustees wanted to be certain
they selected a man for president who could direct Fisk to new heights.
In 1917 a government publication indicated the advantageous position
of Fisk. There was a "striking unanimity" among educators, the study
said, in the belief that Fisk and Howard University were the two institutions in the country which were qualified for further development as
universities. Only three black schools—Fisk, Meharry, and Howard—
had sufficient teaching force, equipment, student body, and income to
deserve the characterization of "college." Fisk had also done notable
work in advanced teacher training, according to the study. The facilities,
ideals, and location of Fisk made possible its development into a true
university. Its location was close to a large black population; the trustees
claimed it lay within a twelve-hour journey of more than four million
blacks.

As late as 1920, of the approximately sixty-five Southern black institutions offering college courses, fifty-four had less than 50 students. Only
five black schools south of Washington, D.C., had as many as 100 students. Fisk, with 327 (422 if the summer quarter was included) pupils,
was the only school with an enrollment over 126. In 1922 more than
one-third of the black students in college were enrolled at Fisk and
Howard.

Although inadequate, Fisk also possessed better facilities than most
schools. The physical plant and other property were valued at approximately $380,000 in 1914. Furthermore, the government publication
continued, Nashville's white colleges, with which Fisk usually maintained
cordial relations, helped develop a "sympathetic appreciation" of the
Southern blacks' problems and "a cooperative relationship with progressive southern people" in the improvement of their condition.[2] The
study of 1917 was subjected to much bitter criticism by blacks, but it was
an important document. In response to its publication there was a vigorous attempt to improve the faculty, standards, and facilities in numerous
schools.

In February 1915, the Fisk board of trustees unanimously elected Dr.

Fayette Avery McKenzie as president.[3] Born on 31 July 1872 in
Montrose, Pennsylvania, McKenzie was graduated Phi Beta Kappa from
Lehigh University in 1895. After serving for two years as a private tutor,
he went to Juniata College in Huntingdon, Pennsylvania, as teacher of
French, German, English history, and economics. Two years later he
moved to Philadelphia's Blight School for Boys, where he taught
modern languages. At the same time he studied sociology, economics, and
history at the University of Pennsylvania. From 1903 to 1905 McKenzie
taught at the Wind River Indian Boarding School on the Shoshoni Indian Reservation in central Wyoming. In 1908 he won his Ph.D. from
the University of Pennsylvania with a dissertation about the American
Indians' relations to the white population. From 1905 to 1914 he taught
at Ohio State University, continuing his work with and research about
the Indians.

Though he had never been associated with black education, McKenzie
had worked with another minority group and seemed to be the person
needed at Fisk. After McKenzie's election to the presidency, W. O.
Thompson, president of Ohio State University, wrote of him: "Now that
he has gone from us I may say that McKenzie had made a very distinct
impression in the university and had made a place for himself in the
esteem and affection of a great many people . . . outside of university
circles and in the city at large. . . . I regret very much to lose him but I
appreciate his promotion." After seeing him in action for a few months,
George Edmund Haynes wrote that the outlook was in every way more
auspicious than at any time during his five years at Fisk. The president
was demonstrating his sympathy with "those high ideals of scholarship
and character" which had been the foundation of the school, Haynes
said.[4]

In his inaugural address McKenzie seemed to reflect the long-
standing aims of the school. "Fifty years of idealization and effort, of
sacrifice and devotion, of conscience and intelligence," he said, "have
made Fisk University the symbol, the corporate realization, of education
and culture for the Negro race in the South." The two great ideals of
Fisk had been and would continue to be, he added, culture and service.
It was also evident from his speech that the Fisk emphasis on religion
would be sustained. President McKenzie deplored the lack of special
religious training for teachers and church leaders. The school should
have, and would have in the future, he vowed, a school of religion. In
addition to the inaugural address there were speeches by five black and
five white men who spoke in "cordial and most interested terms of Fisk
and their desire to cooperate with such a great institution." One observer
believed the inauguration struck a new note which left every person
feeling he was unfaithful to his duty if he were not striving to help blacks
upward. Accompanying social events were, of course, integrated. Several

visitors told Mrs. McKenzie they had never before seen blacks and whites meet socially in such a friendly manner.[5]

McKenzie as president continued two important developments already begun at Fisk: expansion of the curriculum and raising of standards. By 1916 four different college courses were available: science, education, classical, and home economics. The special training for social service had been extended to include religious pedagogy, sociology, recreation, statistics, manual training, and domestic sciences. There were seven teachers in the music department offering classes in vocal and instrumental music. The facilities both in instruments and books were probably the best in any black school. Fisk had taken "the pioneering step" in offering courses in business under the Department of Applied Economics. The Fisk faculty persisted in teaching students to be leaders for their people, but only a minority were taking the old classical course, and even it had become more flexible. By the 1920s Bachelor of Arts candidates had to have at least the following courses: two in expression, two in religion, three in chemistry or physics, one economics, one sociology, two education, three English, three modern languages, two physiology, and two in psychology or ethics. Other subjects offered were: accounting, agriculture, insurance, management, money and banking, business law, art, drama, six courses in journalism, mechanical drawing, and nine courses in sociology. Certainly no one could charge that the curriculum was impractical.[6]

As soon as McKenzie arrived at Fisk he began to talk about scholarship and improving standards. The need for raising standards was obvious. Improperly trained students went out from the many colleges to teach and sent back inadequately prepared pupils to receive below-standard education. Letters from prospective students provide ample evidence of lack of preparation. A young man from Hickman, Kentucky, wrote to "Dear Proffeser" for enlightenment. "I am asking for an information," he said. "I want to begin in medicated course please enform me of the price of a month boarding and rooming inside." Another wrote to "Mr. President and Factures" as follows: "I beg to state that I wants to be come a student of Fisk Univrsity and work my way in Fisk Univiersity and wants to Board where I will be warm I wants to work and pay my way in Fisk." A young teacher from Alabama advertised at Fisk for a husband. "A tall bright well educated boy are preferred or real light Brown skin write at once send your picture," she said. The young woman gave her qualifications as being "partely french highly educated . . . bright with Dark brown Bob hair big brown eyes 5 feet 6 in. high. . . ." Another student, acknowledging a letter of acceptance, admitted that he was "a student of ability, courage and endurance with brain power" and "Good character 100%." He was born, he said, with a great art, "as an author, a great magnificent writer." He added, "I wants you to give me plenty of work on your campus," and in two years "fame and fortune will be mine."[7]

The above letters are pathetic, but not unusual and not surprising. In 1920 there were more high school graduates than college graduates— twenty-eight and twenty-seven respectively—teaching in Tennessee's black secondary schools. With such inadequately prepared teachers trained in poor high schools, nothing else could be expected. Moreover, there were only twenty-two secondary schools for blacks in the entire state. In 1922 a mere sixty black pupils graduated from high school in Tennessee. Students went to Fisk woefully unprepared through no fault of their own. They were victims of the Southern system. When rigid standards were enforced it seemed almost brutal and naturally caused much consternation. In a trustees meeting, an alumnus, Dr. William DeBerry, asked "whether by any chance the application of these standards was being carried out in too 'cold blooded' a manner." The board unanimously endorsed McKenzie's policy of bringing Fisk into line with the highest standards of collegiate education irrespective of color, but still considerable resentment was created.

Such antagonism toward improved standards was, in part, what McKenzie was referring to in 1921 when he wrote that "we are fighting at Fisk with all our energies, and against a good many oppositions" to prove that a black college could operate on the same plane as white colleges. Some of the later opposition to McKenzie can be traced to the enforcement of higher standards.

Despite the unfortunate consequences for some students, McKenzie's plan brought new recognition to the school. For the first time Columbia University began to accept Fisk graduates into its graduate department without additional work. The University of Chicago accepted Fisk as a standard college, and the Carnegie Foundation's recognition of Fisk as an associate gave it widespread standing as a standard institution. In a 1924 editorial the *New York Times* contended that proper material support combined with the recognition accorded Fisk by the "highest educational authorities in the country" would place the school in "a position to give a scholarly training comparable with the best in American colleges."[8]

One of the characteristic features of Fisk had been its service to both black and white members of the community, but in recent years it had apparently lost touch. McKenzie hoped to rectify this error. Unfortunately he gave most of his attention to whites. Fisk had always attempted to support and be a part of the black neighborhood, but McKenzie entered into the activities of the white group more fully than any previous Fisk official. He was a member of the Kiwanis Club and the Chamber of Commerce, and was director of the Community Chest. He was usually involved in any campaign to raise money for charity or city improvement. In this way, he believed, friends could be won for Fisk, and white friendship for the school was stronger than during any preceding administration. Nashville business leaders spoke highly of Fisk and usually gave important visitors a tour of the campus. Some alumni, however, correctly believed that white good will was gained at too great a price—at a serious loss of principle.

Fisk continued to offer Nashvillians its musical talent for entertaining conventions and guests, church programs, building drives, and money-raising campaigns. More important though was the work done for the local black community. George E. Haynes's arrival had accelerated interest in social work and race relations, and this was the foundation upon which McKenzie built. His plan was "to build a satisfactory community around Fisk University—a community starting from a program which includes the physical essentials of decent existence." This would, he thought, arrest the suspicion and antagonism of local blacks. McKenzie had found that despite their great pride in Fisk, there was a feeling that the school was not truly neighborly. He wanted to offer extension work and a night school in the city.[9]

Under the leadership of Haynes and McKenzie many new friends were enlisted in the cause of social betterment of Nashville. Whites were especially impressed with the operation of Bethlehem House, a settlement house where social service students trained. City officials were persuaded to provide a playground for black children to be supervised by Fisk personnel. Soon, Haynes said, blacks and whites were working in close cooperation on several projects to improve conditions. The influence of the work pervaded the courts, industries, and the county and city charities, Haynes added.

In March 1916, a fire in East Nashville left over 2,500 people destitute. The Negro Board of Trade and the white Commercial Club raised money to reestablish families in homes with minimum furnishings. Over 320 black and 301 white families were assisted. The aid to blacks was made possible by the endeavors of Haynes and the Fisk senior class in cooperation with other local black colleges. Haynes's staff was so efficient that it was soon invited as a body to occupy an office adjoining the staff of the Commercial Club. The two groups worked together cordially until the homeless families had been resettled. According to Haynes, the incident laid the foundation for greater racial cooperation in Nashville in meeting problems of public welfare. Soon after the fire a conference of both races met to organize a public welfare league.

Fisk not only treated injury and disease, but tried to prevent them. During the winter of 1919 Ambrose Caliver was relieved of part of his duties as instructor of manual training to organize the Tennessee Colored Anti-Tuberculosis Society. Caliver served as director of the society for two years and as chairman of the executive committee for two more. Unfortunately, McKenzie's plans for the community did little to alter the view that Fisk personnel were unsympathetic to blacks. McKenzie was just not the man to calm these fears. He was aloof from both students and the black community. His determination to impose standards often seemed insensitive. And his personal associations were primarily with whites rather than blacks.[10]

The outbreak of World War I temporarily disrupted life at Fisk. It was a difficult time. Money and sometimes food and fuel were scarce. McKenzie always demonstrated a keen interest in peace plans, but there were no charges against Fisk of pacifism and feet-dragging in the war effort as there were during the Second World War. In 1917 the prudential committee voted to require all young men on campus to take at least one hour per week of military training. Soon after war was declared, two members of the faculty, Dexter N. Lutz, instructor of botany, and Dr. Leo E. Walker, teacher of chemistry and athletics, went into the service. They were joined by scores of Fisk students and graduates. At one time there were seventy-six stars (representing personnel and students) on the flag flying from Livingstone Hall.

When the war started there was no provision for training black officers. Fisk, Howard, Atlanta University, and the NAACP took up the question and were successful in getting a training camp established in the spring of 1917 at Fort Des Moines, Iowa. In October, 639 black officers, including several Fisk graduates, were commissioned. Eventually, approximately 200 Fiskites served in the war, at least 32 of them as officers. There was one major, James R. White '94, at least five captains, and twenty-six lieutenants. In addition, about twenty Fiskites were noncommissioned officers. Many of these men went overseas to fight "the battle to save democracy."

Fisk was not content just to send its alumni and students to war. In the summer of 1918 McKenzie agreed to utilize Fisk as a receiving camp for as many as 600 black troops. It would create difficulty, especially with student discipline, he said, but the school had no right to refuse to render the service. Dr. Haynes was called to Washington to head the newly created Division of Negro Economics in the Department of Labor. He was to advise the department on ways to improve working conditions for blacks and methods for securing their entire cooperation in the war production effort.[11] Isaac Fisher, black editor of the *Fisk University News*, called on blacks throughout the country to support the war, even though lynchings and brutality against blacks accompanied the crusade against the Germans.

The war slowed down the academic pace for a time, but it intensified Fisk's fight for racial justice. Soldiers returning from Europe, where they had risked their lives for their country, hoped and expected the situation for blacks to be improved in the United States. It took only a short time to recognize that the hopes were in vain. The Ku Klux Klan, which had been revived as early as 1915 in the South, spread to the rest of the country. Soon after the war it was a powerful organization that terrorized blacks, Jews, Orientals, and Roman Catholics. In some states high-ranking officials belonged to the Klan.

Lynchings continued during the war. More than 3,000 people accepted a newspaper invitation in Tennessee to watch a black man be burned alive. In 1918 forty blacks lost their lives in the East St. Louis riot. In the summer of 1919, designated by James Weldon Johnson as "The Red Summer," dozens of blacks were killed in twenty-five riots. In 1918 the *Fisk University News* called for good sense on part of both races to avoid what seemed to be rumblings of racial strife. Isaac Fisher said any organization unauthorized by the police power of the states and formed for the purpose of keeping the black man in his "place" was dangerous as well as unnecessary. He warned that men who had fought in the war would not be overawed by threats. Blacks had grown dissatisfied and restless with their lot. Indeed, he continued, a great many had "grown positively bitter in brooding over their own place in the system." Fisher, McKenzie, and the *News* received considerable attention. George Foster Peabody was so impressed with a Fisher article that he bought several subscriptions for himself and others, including Secretary of War Newton D. Baker.[12]

McKenzie and Fisher demanded racial justice, but they were not sufficiently militant to satisfy many blacks. Claude McKay's poem, which ended, "Like men we'll face the murderous, cowardly pack, pressed to the wall, dying but fighting back," would have distressed them. They believed answering force with force or even the threat of violence would only make conditions worse. McKenzie reflected both their views when he said: "In a large sense Fisk is the only college standing definitely before the public, both white and colored, for the spirit of conciliation and co-operation, and daring to breast the criticism of the critical Negro, the critical Southern white and the critical Northern white, and looking to the day when wisdom as well as success will justify this course."

Fisher spoke before Southern white groups, worked with the Southern Inter-racial Commission, and was appointed to the Commission on Churches and Race Relations by the Federal Council of the Churches of Christ in America. In a candid moment Fisher told a white admirer, "I have tried very hard to purge my heart of bitterness and unfairness and intolerance when I have written on race relations in this country; and the attitude you commend has not been taken without cost to me. I have been openly pilloried because I do not see 'red' all the time, and think in terms of goodwill sometimes."

McKenzie formed a voluntary organization with no dues and no duties to help solve the race problem. It was called the Triangle of Peace, a phrase he coined in 1918 to illustrate what he regarded as the three essential factors in the race problem. The symbol was a triangle with blacks, Southern whites, and Northern whites forming the three sides. Only with communication and cooperation between the three could any solution be reached; all who agreed were urged to register as members. McKenzie's plan was not unlike that of Booker T. Washington—his friend Fisher was a Tuskegee graduate and had worked for Washington—whose "life mission was to find a pragmatic compromise that would resolve the antagonisms, suspicions and aspirations" of the Southern white, the Northern white, and the black man, the three classes directly concerned. McKenzie cooperated closely with Chancellor James H. Kirkland of Vanderbilt, who publicly opposed lynchings, and Professor Edwin Mims of Vanderbilt, a Southerner and eloquent speaker who was primarily responsible for the law and order movement in Tennessee that practically took it out of the list of lynching states.

Although opposed to agitation, McKenzie vigorously protested the erection of a sign "This drinking fountain for whites only" in a Nashville park. City officials were asked to open the park to Fisk students. McKenzie also remonstrated against Jim Crow seating arrangements in Nashville auditoriums. As a member of the State Council of Social Agencies, he tried to secure proper facilities for mentally incompetent and delinquent black youths. Special arrangements were made for young white people in that category, he charged, but not for blacks. The state was asked to create a vocational school for wayward black girls. Fisher and McKenzie exerted considerable influence on a small segment of the Southern white population. In 1922 a prominent Southern white investment banker and trustee of the University of Tennessee, Bolton Smith, publicly declared his support of the Dyer Anti-lynching Bill. He had been persuaded to that view, Smith said, by a Fisher editorial in the *Fisk University News*.

Both McKenzie and Fisher were sincere and courageous in their stand. They believed their ideas were the only key to the solution of the race problem. Thousands of blacks and well-meaning whites agreed, but a powerful element of Fisk alumni were alienated by what appeared to be an unnecessary catering to Southern white opinion. Many Fiskites, Fisher said, were "bitterly opposed" to McKenzie's "attempt to win the South." McKenzie's plan frankly had no place for black assertiveness. While he decried violence, injustice, and segregation, gaining white trust was the major thrust of his program. He suppressed "radical" ideas and encouraged students to be unobtrusive. Only conservative blacks such as James C. Napier, member of the Fisk board of trustees, were entertained by the president.[13] McKenzie's view on race relations and his ideas on standards were reasons for increasing opposition that would eventually force his resignation.

Another consequence of the war, one to which McKenzie responded more effectively than he did to deteriorating race relations, was the demand for more educated blacks. During and after the war, blacks moved from rural to urban areas, from South to North. Within a decade the black population in Chicago doubled and other cities experienced similar increases. These communities demanded services—spiritual, commercial, material, and industrial—and they were looking primarily to persons of their own race for satisfaction. More and more blacks had resigned themselves to segregation; hence there was a need for more professional people and leaders.[14]

Expanded education required additional money, and philanthropic foundations were becoming increasingly inclined to give funds to black schools of college grade. The need for money at Fisk was obvious. The cottage in which music was taught was in bad repair. In one room loose paper flapped in the breeze. Water came through the walls. In the winter, heating was so ineffective that teachers heated bricks to keep warm. Alice May Grass, instructor of organ and piano, customarily kept one brick for her lap and one for her feet. When pupils came in for lessons, they too were supplied with hot bricks. McKenzie complained that toilet facilities were intolerable and bathing facilities completely lacking. "Fisk University cannot enforce its textbook teaching on home sanitation," the president wrote, "while violating the rules of sanitation on its campus, nor can it teach law enforcement while disregarding municipal ordinances affecting fire regulations." In 1915 the average salary was slightly less than $780 per year. The head of Fisk's highly regarded music department drew $622 annually.[15]

Money was badly needed for more than salaries. Over 300 women had to be turned away in 1919 because of lack of dormitory space. Comparison of income between white and black colleges showed the privations of the latter. During the 1920s, income from Yale, Harvard, and Columbia endowments, figured at 4 percent, was approximately one and one half million times greater than the total combined income of all private institutions for blacks in America.[16] Fisk's endowment was inadequate and the small amount gained from tuition covered only a minor part of total expenses.

McKenzie proved an effective and tireless fund raiser. Important persons like Secretary of War Newton D. Baker were persuaded to write letters urging support for Fisk. Funds most frequently came in small amounts, one to five dollars at a time, but in 1918 McKenzie secured from the Rosenwald Fund a promise of $2,500 a year for five years. He was also successful in getting money from Southern whites. In the school year 1918-1919, one Southerner gave $10,000 and the Nashville Commercial Club awarded a like amount. By 1920 the average annual salary had been raised to $1,000, buildings had been repaired, and the heating system improved. The annual budget had more than doubled since 1915—from $52,692.39 to $117,641.54.[17]

In the effort to raise money the Jubilee Singers were called into action once again. There had been groups styled after the Jubilee Singers in existence almost continuously, though they were not always from Fisk. In 1879 George L. White had organized a company of singers to travel over the United States. When he gave up the work in 1882, F. J. Loudin, a former member of the troupe, assumed management. Under Loudin, the singers made successful tours in the United States, England, Australia, China, and Japan. They were not affiliated with the university but many of them were Fiskites and their tours advertised the school. They received favorable notice and comment from, among others, President James A. Garfield, Harriet Beecher Stowe, and President Chester A. Arthur.[18] During 1889–1890, the American Missionary Association employed seven Fisk students as singers under the direction of Charles W. Shelton. The group was used to assist in raising money for the construction of Bennett Hall and for public relations for Southern schools.[19]

In 1899 a troupe of Fisk alumni and students was sent out in the school's behalf. Concerts were successful, but little money went to Fisk after expenses were deducted. Even so, then-President Merrill said, it was almost necessary to keep the singers in the field in self-defense. The phenomenal career of the original Jubilees had induced other institutions and private companies to capitalize on Fisk's reputation. Some of these troupes, Merrill added, had so frequently been musically and morally bankrupt that Fisk had "become a stench in the nostrils" of many Northerners. Lack of success resulted in the disbanding of this group of singers in 1903.[20]

It was decided in 1916 to experiment with a Jubilee Quartet directed by Professor John W. Work. It would be less expensive than a larger group and, it was hoped, would be of equal advertising value. The high point for the quartet was singing for President Woodrow Wilson at his request. It was a busy moment at the White House. Newton D. Baker had just left the president to take the oath of office as secretary of war. Congressmen were waiting impatiently to discuss legislation or to curry favor with Wilson. Messengers were scurrying back and forth with communications from the State and War departments relating to the latest events on the Mexican border. "Suddenly in the midst of it all," the *Washington Times* reported, "there burst forth the sounds of music from the cabinet room. Instantly the hubbub in the corridors and anterooms ceased. Swelling ever louder like the tones of an organ the strains swept through the Executive Offices." The Fisk University Jubilee Quartet was singing for the president. As Wilson shook hands with the singers, his eyes, according to the newspaper, were "a wee bit dimmed." After singing for the president the quartet went to the rooms of Joseph P. Tumulty, Wilson's private secretary. There they sang again to "the delight of a large audience," which included some distinguished members of Congress.[21]

Between 1916 and 1925 there were sometimes two groups of singers in the field, a student choir and the quartet. James A. Myers succeeded Professor Work as director of the quartet, which sang in Europe with great success. A concert in the Salle Gaveau, Paris, was completely sold out and a command performance at Windsor Castle for the king and queen of England was well received. When the National Music Supervisors Conference was held at Nashville in 1922 its president, F. A. Beach, said that no one thing was more influential in bringing the conference to Nashville than the Fisk Jubilee Singers. The Harvard Glee Club, the St. Olaf Choir, and the Jubilee Singers were classified by Beach as the three leading groups of a cappella singers in the United States. Of the three groups, Beach said, none could touch "the tone color" attained by the Jubilee Singers. "From the standpoint of folk singing," Beach added, the Fisk choir was "indisputably the finest in America."[22] The Jubilee Singers earned considerable publicity but little money for the school.

After meeting with favorable response in raising small sums for Fisk, the board of trustees on recommendation of President McKenzie, decided in 1919 to undertake a drive to secure two million dollars for endowment, new buildings, equipment, and reduction of the existing debt. Jerome Kidder was employed as executive secretary of the campaign. Kidder, McKenzie, the Jubilee Singers, and faculty worked on this campaign for the next five years. Appeal meetings were held throughout the country. One at the Hotel Astor in New York was attended by Governor Albert H. Roberts of Tennessee and a delegation of representatives of the Nashville Chamber of Commerce, who came to bear witness to the good Fisk had done their city. The *Southern Workman*'s editor believed the occasion was without precedent. "It marked," the editor wrote, "the awakened interest of public opinion in the South in regard to Negro education." McKenzie was again extremely successful in getting white support.

The first big break in the money drive came in March 1921, when the General Education Board offered $500,000 toward a $1,000,000 endowment, provided Fisk could match the sum. The General Education Board had already given Fisk some minor assistance; up to 1914 it had granted $140,000 to black colleges with half of it going to Fisk. Indeed, McKenzie may have conceived his idea of an endowment drive after reading General Education Board minutes. In 1914 a special committee of the board asked whether organized philanthropy "could not wisely take hold of the most promising Negro College—Fisk University—and develop it until it is fairly adequate to its task." The Carnegie Corporation quickly agreed to give $250,000, which left only $250,000 to be collected to meet the General Education Board's pledge. The response of white Nashvillians was heartening. In 1924 the *Nashville Banner,* not noted for friendliness to blacks, suggested that whites help in the campaign. "We believe that every consideration demands that Nashville meet its challenge in full," the newspaper said. "It owes it to the splendid institution, Fisk University, the most noted and notable college for Negroes in the world.... Fisk in its music and in untold other ways has advertised Nashville and contributed to Nashville an amount of art and service which could not begin to be measured by $50,000."[23] With such urging, citizens of Nashville raised the money. This was the first time any such sum had been contributed by a Southern city for any type of black education.

McKenzie was less successful in getting money from alumni. Dr. Ferdinand A. Stewart '85 gave the president a check for $1,000 in 1923, but the majority of the graduates were less generous. A Washington, D.C., alumnus informed McKenzie that he would support Fisk with money even though he disagreed with his racial policy. Other alumni, he continued, felt as he did, but they were showing their displeasure by refusing to give financial support. He said he could collect more money from the alumni if "I could convince them that the new Fisk has not formed an unwholesome alliance with Southern prejudice." McKenzie claimed it was possible to attempt to win Southerners of strongly opposed views without abandoning one's own convictions and principles.[24]

Despite lack of alumni enthusiasm, McKenzie was able to announce on 19 July 1924 that a million dollar endowment, the first ever raised by a black college, was fully subscribed. It was underwritten by the General Education Board, the Carnegie Corporation, John F. Slater Fund, J. C. Penney Foundation, and numerous individuals, prominent and otherwise. Completion of the endowment was a conspicuous recognition of more than a half-century of service in preparing black youth for leadership among their people. It was also recognition of the position of leadership which Fisk had achieved in meeting the growing need for black higher education in the United States. "Because Fisk has done its work remarkably well," the *Southern Workman* stated, "many groups of people, white and colored, North and South, have invested their money and their enthusiasm in its forward looking course." Hampton Institute sent its congratulations "for this public acknowledgement of the worth of an institution which has long been a pioneer in the field of collegiate education for Negroes."[25]

Unfortunately the million dollar fund was unavailable for immediate use. There was a stipulation: To secure payment all indebtedness— about $150,000—had to be cleared from the books. At the same time the endowment was being raised, expenses had increased. Between 1920 and 1924 some instructional salaries had been augmented by 92 percent. All salaries had been enlarged by as much as 37 percent. Expenditures expanded from $117,641.54 in 1920 to $164,439.27 in 1923. In 1922 a new and more costly plan to aid self-supporting students was implemented. All prerequisite courses requiring two quarters to complete were scheduled two times per year—fall and winter, and spring and summer. Students could work six months and then attend school for a like time. More persons were enabled to receive higher education, but it was expensive.[26] A new campaign was necessary to cancel the debts, but disturbances during the winter of 1924 that resulted in the resignation of McKenzie prevented any elaborate money drive. It remained for a new president to clear the school of indebtedness, thereby securing the conditionally subscribed $1,000,000 endowment.

7

The Student Revolt

STUDENT UNREST DURING THE WINTER OF 1924–1925, CULMINATING IN A strike in February 1925, forced the resignation of McKenzie and important changes in the school. The trouble can be traced to no single cause, but one source was the rigid regulation of students. Discipline in black schools was usually more strict than in the average American college, in part because black colleges for years had a number of lower grades. The kind of organization and methods best fitted to direct younger pupils were not necessarily appropriate for college students. Strikes and demonstrations in Northern white colleges, interfering little with the affairs of the school and accomplishing less, had been common. Though such occasions had come to be regarded as periodic and unavoidable occurrences among white students, this was not true in black schools. A college education was looked upon by blacks as a difficult and sacred attainment. Black students, economically circumscribed, had little time for demonstrations. They were concerned with acquiring an education which was received in a frequently poor college often long on religion and discipline and miserably short on facilities. Students who were fortunate enough to get to college were often so impoverished that leisure time had to be spent at odd jobs to feed and clothe themselves.

With the growth of a black middle class and the economic betterment of a small group by the First World War, more students went to college and fewer had to work. Newspapers, moving pictures, the radio, and Northern students going to Southern schools spread new ideas. The above changes, with the concept of democracy generated by the war, the aggressiveness of returning black soldiers, the Niagara movement, the founding of the NAACP, and the *élan vital* stimulated by the "Black Renaissance" or the "New Negro Movement," combined to send a new type of student to the black college. They were no longer the timorous students who refused to fight back.[1]

Neither the unreasonable regulations nor the spirit of unrest were peculiar to the McKenzie administration. In 1908 it was reported to the board of trustees that there had been some "serious cases of discipline" and a feeling of disquietude. Rules had been strict since the school was founded. Card playing, betting and gambling, and tobacco were prohibited. Dancing was considered a trap of the devil. When Miss K. M.

Marvin worked in the library during the first decade of the twentieth century, she refused to permit students to come in who even smelled of tobacco smoke. Occasionally she threatened to stand on the front steps and sniff each student who entered. In 1909 the prudential committee ordered all women to wear uniform suits to Sunday dinner; no finery was permitted. Those disregarding the rule were fined twenty-five cents for the first offense, suspended one day for the second, and suspended from the university for the third. The same committee deprived eleven young women of all extracurricular activities and social privileges for two months for attending "what was virtually a public dance." Some members of the committee wanted to send them home for a month.[2]

All students were required to attend the Sunday morning service and Sunday school at the university and to attend daily chapel devotion. Young men could not escort girls to religious exercises and young women were not allowed to be out after dark. Women of "proper age," though, were permitted to receive one caller each week between 4:30 and 5:30 P.M. In order to prevent members of the opposite sex from growing too fond of each other and "going steady" the faculty imposed a "two to one rule." If a young man dated a young lady twice, he had to call on another girl before escorting the former again. The same faculty voted that no ragtime music could be played on university pianos.[3]

Although discipline was strict before McKenzie became president, it became harsher during his administration. More rigid enforcement of rules coming at a time when students were becoming increasingly rebellious made an explosion almost inevitable. "I am increasingly convinced," McKenzie wrote, "that fidelity to school and college youth requires unfailing and constant supervision, constant insistence on regularity, reliability and fidelity." Discipline, he thought, was both a means and an end in itself in education. Much more must be demanded and expected than had been previously demanded in American institutions, McKenzie said. It was necessary, he believed, to "look for an efficiency" correspondent to that of military training camps. When in 1918 Fisk agreed to receive black troops on campus, the president said it would put the entire school to a degree upon a military basis to the "very great advantage" of the faculty. It would especially necessitate a rigid social control in the relationship of the sexes. "It will give us an opportunity," McKenzie stated, "to put ourselves where we ought to be without seeming to make any break with the past."[4] He believed in such a system for both white and black schools.

All the old rules were retained and new ones were passed. Possession of extension cords, electrical sockets, electric irons, and other appliances in the dorms was punished by confiscation of the article and suspension of the student. Weapons, fireworks, gasoline, benzine, "flame-producing stove, candle, article or device" were prohibited. Most of these rules reputedly were for safety, but to many of the students some of them seemed arbitrary and petty.

McKenzie was especially careful in controlling social relationships. Expulsion could result from a male and female walking together, not touching, even at high noon. After meals women remained in the dining room until the men were dismissed and in their dormitories. Women's presence on the campus or first floor of the dining hall ten minutes before or after meals was forbidden. Irregular attendance at meals, eating food secured off campus, and eating in dormitory rooms were punishable offenses. Packages to students from someone other than family could be examined by Fisk officials.

Dress regulations for women filled three pages of the catalog by 1920. All women were required to have two uniforms, a white one to be worn until November 1 and after April 1 and a blue one for the remaining period. The skirt could be gathered, but could have no more than three tucks or ruffles. No lace or embroidery trimming was allowed. White and navy blue crepe de chine waists, untrimmed, were authorized for school wear and shopping. Chiffon, georgette, organdy, or other thin waists and evening clothes of any kind were proscribed. For cold weather each woman was ordered to have a heavy coat "of plain wool material, dark in color, preferably blue; not plaid or of conspicuous color or trimmed in conspicuous color." Cotton hose and "strong shoes with sensible heels" were strongly recommended. Hats were purchased from the university. The uniforms were required for church, Sunday school, Sunday dinner, balls, socials, entertainments, shopping, visits to doctors or homes in the city, and all public occasions in town. Such regulations were usually endorsed by the faculty, though Augustus F. Shaw, professor of physics, threatened to resign in 1918 because of McKenzie's policy of "maximum separation." He recognized the danger of too great a freedom, he said, but believed there was greater danger in the separation policy than in the natural intermingling of the sexes.

Disciplinary cases were common on any campus and Fisk was no exception. Between 1917 and 1923 the prudential committee expelled six men for fornication, at least a dozen for gambling, one for possession of a deadly weapon, and one for threatening a fellow student with a pistol. Those expelled for gambling had been reported by students. Several who confessed to gambling were allowed to remain in school in view of their youth and having been influenced by older students. Two men found guilty of theft were permitted to stay on campus after promising to pay for the stolen articles. A more unusual breach of conduct in the eyes of McKenzie was chicken killing. It was reported that some students were catching chickens that wandered onto campus, killing them, and cooking them in their rooms at "parties." Those students, said the president, were guilty on three counts. First, he doubted the legality of the killings. Furthermore, it was against the institution's policy to utilize heat for nonessential cooking purposes and to have "irregular parties without very special reason and permission."[5] The culprits were never found.

Punishment for theft, fornication, and possession of deadly weapons was not considered unreasonable by Fisk students. They had no quarrel with McKenzie about such cases, but they did protest harsh punishment for minor offenses. A young man was suspended indefinitely for walking with a girl on campus. Another student was reported to the pruden-tial committee for walking parallel to a girl even though he was several feet away. There was a strong suspicion that he was talking to her. The case was dropped for lack of irrefutable proof. One woman was expelled because she threw a note to a man from her window and because she received a box of candy "clandestinely," meaning that it was accepted from a young man without prior faculty approval. In 1925 McKenzie called a special meeting of the prudential committee after learning that an electric curling iron had been found in a girl's room. Students could not leave campus, even to go home for Christmas holiday, without writ-ten permission from parents.[6]

Worse than the rules, the students thought, was the atmosphere of distrust and suspicion created by the watchfulness of the faculty. Stu-dents charged the faculty with having a spy system designed to catch them in the smallest violation of rules, and evidence suggests that they were not exaggerating. Unhappily for students a large number of parents agreed with the administration. One mother wrote in 1916 asking that her daughter be given less freedom. Home rules, the mother said, were "somewhat strict," and her daughter was given too much liberty at Fisk. The daughter had told her mother that home seemed more like school as to rules and regulations than the college. Another mother asked offi-cials to forbid her daughter to visit the city on Christmas Day. A little social life was acceptable, she wrote, but going downtown on Christmas seemed excessive. Other parents requested that their daughters be re-fused permission to receive young men. Fisk officials and parents were undoubtedly concerned for the students' welfare, but there are indica-tions that some of the faculty believed black young adults were less trust-worthy than whites.[7]

Rules at Fisk were no more rigid than at many other black schools. At Talladega College discipline was administered with a view toward "moral development of the students as well as the peace and good of the institu-tion." When it became evident that students lacked a scrupulous regard for regulations, they could be removed without specific charge. Smoking was prohibited and women were forbidden to receive male callers at Tougaloo College. All incoming mail passed through the hands of the preceptress who was authorized to inspect it. Storer College reserved the right to inspect letters and packages and dispose of them in "any way desirable." Lane College had rules similar to the above plus stipulation of what students must wear, including undergarments. Regulations at Atlanta University resembled those at Fisk.

After visiting more than fifty black schools and colleges in 1932, Langston Hughes said that setting foot on dozens of the campuses was "like going back to mid-Victorian England, or Massachusetts in the days of witch-burning Puritans." He observed the amusing spectacle of twenty-four-year-old men sneaking around like small boys to steal a drag from a cigarette. Card playing was an abomination and dancing was prohibited to both faculty and students at some schools. One college permitted women to dance with each other but not with males. The dances were reportedly unpopular. Separation of the sexes, Hughes said, rivaled nunneries and monastaries in their strictness. Such protection even extended to married women attending summer sessions. The wife of a prominent educator attended summer school at Hampton. When her husband called long distance she had to get special permission to go to the telephone. Permission could be secured only after officials made absolutely certain the man was her husband. These conditions existed in nearly all Southern black colleges; McKenzie was doing nothing not done by black educators. Where teachers failed to respond to new demands and were unable to see the new conditions as an opportunity for developing in youth a greater sense of responsibility and the power of self-control, unpleasant clashes were unavoidable.[8] Only wise and tactful leadership could prevent disturbances, and though McKenzie was in many ways an able man, he was not always wise and tactful with students. New demands brought increased suppression.

Strict discipline was only one cause of the student revolt. Compulsory chapel, a policy widely practiced in both black and white schools, was opposed by a few students. Students also demanded the right to have a publication of their own. The *Herald* had been combined with the *Fisk University News* in 1917. McKenzie claimed the *Herald* had been suspended to economize, but DuBois and others charged that the *Herald* had been suppressed to prevent student criticism. After consolidation of the two publications, students were to have at least twelve pages in the *News* on condition the staff could get 200 subscriptions among the students. Seemingly as important to students was the prohibition of fraternities and sororities. Fisk officials' opposition to fraternities was of long standing. When the question came up in 1915 the board of trustees voted that "fraternities and other secret or oath-bound societies" should be banned at Fisk. They did not accord with the type of democracy the school was trying to teach. Debating, literary, and academic societies were fine, officials thought, but exclusive social organizations were undesirable.[9]

Students further complained of the lack of an athletic association and student government. The faculty countered that if students were not so lethargic they could have both, though there is little doubt that student government would have been closely supervised by the faculty. It is true there was considerable opposition at Fisk to intercollegiate athletics, which were abandoned during World War I but reinstituted in 1919. Though a vigorous advocate of physical exercise, McKenzie had doubts about the value of intercollegiate activity. Fisk was committed to a policy of no training table, no professional players, no players of wavering scholarship, and no athletic coach. Unless something were done about professionalism, gambling, and trading of players, McKenzie feared black colleges would go through "the whole disgraceful career of white athletics."

McKenzie promised to support intercollegiate athletics if they could be retained without nullifying the value derived from intramural sports. This would, he said, involve many limitations upon intercollegiate sports as practiced almost universally in American colleges. He considered college athletics as genuinely amateur games, played for the pleasure of exercise and uninfluenced by spectators and gate receipts. He discouraged intercollegiate athletics, not for the purpose of annoying students, but because he was distressed at the many charges of professionalism and gambling in black colleges. Fisk continued to deemphasize athletics to the disappointment of many alumni.[10]

A more serious charge against McKenzie was that he was dictatorial and intolerant of dissent. Fisk administrations before McKenzie had been relatively democratic. Even under the strong-willed President Cravath, decisions ordinarily were made by the general faculty and faculty committees. McKenzie after the first few years ruled with an iron hand, and after attacks began around 1920 he demanded absolute loyalty. The morals of the faculty were guarded as closely as those of the pupils. Sooner or later he came into conflict with a majority of his teachers. Mrs. Arch Trawick, a white Nashville trustee and an enthusiastic McKenzie supporter, said she sometimes disagreed with the president but his "almost stubborn spirit and martyr's will were too strong for her." McKenzie was certain he was right and continued his policies despite attacks by friend and foe. His strong will and an apparently suspicious nature made compromise difficult for him. A member of the faculty accused McKenzie in a personal letter of sometimes being "somewhat unjust, supersensitive, I was going to say even overimaginative and perhaps unwarrantedly suspicious." The president once told an instructor that the important job he had to do required the "suppression of criticism of all sorts." In 1918 a few male students refused to attend study hall until McKenzie began to treat them like men. The president's response was to denounce them as Bolshevists. In 1921 students approached a trustee about McKenzie. The trustee investigated and reported repression, insult, and discrimination to the board and to McKenzie, but no attention was given his report.[11]

All of these factors contributed to student unrest, but to place the rebellion in its proper perspective it should be remembered that the 1920s witnessed a revolution in morals and manners throughout the United States. The postwar period—the Roaring Twenties—was a time of disillusionment and cynicism, of flappers and hip flasks, of bathtub gin and speakeasies, of revolt against old codes. According to the prewar code, young women were to look forward in innocence to a romantic love match. No male was to kiss them until the "right man" happened along. Majority opinion held it morally wrong for a girl to smoke, and rouge was an "insidious vintage." Long dresses were the custom. Suddenly women were smoking, cosmetics were used, and skirts began a spectacular ascent which continued until, in the words of one observer, the result was fearful to behold. "Petting" parties became a widely popular indoor sport. The dances, referred to by the *Hobart College Herald* as a "syncopated embrace," scandalized numerous parents and college administrators. The *Cincinnati Catholic Telegram* condemned new dances as absolutely indecent, the motions of which could not be described with propriety in a family newspaper. "The low-cut gowns, the rolled hose and short skirts," a Florida college president exclaimed, were "born of the Devil and his agents, and are carrying the present and future generations to chaos and destruction."[12] Problems of youth were the topic of discussion from coast to coast. It was only natural that Fisk students, aware of the revolution, would rebel against wearing uniforms, prohibitions against smoking, almost total separation of the sexes, and regulations more appropriate for 1866 than 1925. On the other hand, it was to be expected that some Fisk faculty would react to the new generation in the same troubled way as a majority of adults throughout the country.

Still, the students might not have revolted without the active support of some powerful alumni, and McKenzie's racial policy seemed to have been the most disturbing element to them. McKenzie's ideas and the opposition to them were discussed in chapter 6. It was charged that McKenzie wanted to build a great university, but to build it with white men, working for blacks and guiding them in strictly limited paths. DuBois said McKenzie knew the way to raise an endowment was "to win for his methods and opinions the imprimatur of white Tennessee." He had raised money, stated DuBois, but by yielding to the white Southern demand that Fisk teach and practice submission. DuBois's charges were not without basis. McKenzie at times seemed more concerned with local white opinion than with the desires of students and alumni. For example, Fisk students had been sent to sing to Jim Crow audiences. A Fisk alumnus wrote McKenzie that it was his methods, not his "high and constructive programs," that were being criticized. Fund raising for black colleges did present unusual problems because they were still dependent primarily on white gifts. Schools headed by blacks suffered the same fate. The old adage about "whose bread I eat his song I sing" applied to them too.[13]

There is little doubt that the president's belief in conciliation as the proper path to racial peace and his desire to win wealthy white friends influenced his actions. Raymond Wolters in a study of black campus unrest in the 1920s contends that most of McKenzie's policies leading to the Fisk revolt were motivated by his desire to get funds from educational associations which sympathized with the white South. The president had to convince philanthropists that Fisk "had not departed too far from the Tuskegee ideal, that its students were not radical egalitarians but young men and women who had learned to make peace with the reality of the caste system." Therefore, the student government association was dissolved, the *Herald* suspended, and dissent suppressed. McKenzie's views were endorsed by most of his faculty. One black professor at Fisk claimed the school was "slowly but surely" solving the race problem in Nashville and Tennessee. The Fisk belief that absolute honesty between the two peoples in all matters, he said, and "a growing spirit of tolerance on the part of each for the other" were "essential to a beginning of any sort of understanding." The fruit of McKenzie's labor was about ready for harvest, the professor thought, and numerous others agreed. McKenzie's methods, even if they would have attained racial peace, would not have gained civil rights and no doubt were wrong, but his views were not peculiar to whites.

The new postwar aggressiveness in the field of civil rights was by no means accepted by all blacks. Years after the Fisk difficulty, Langston Hughes charged black colleges with "doing their best to produce spineless Uncle Toms, uninformed, and full of mental and moral evasions." Tuskegee censored books on race problems to prevent "radical" volumes from falling into the hands of students. Tuskegee's president announced himself in favor of lower wages for blacks under the National Recovery Administration during the depression. After the young coach of Hampton was beaten to death by a mob in Birmingham a student protest on campus was discouraged by a black official. Hampton, he said, did not like the word "protest." It was not the school's way. The black president of Virginia State College summoned white town policemen when his students organized a protest against campus conditions.[14]

Students charged that McKenzie fired black teachers to replace them with whites, but the charges cannot be substantiated. In fact, the number of blacks on the faculty tripled under McKenzie. While the number of faculty remained almost constant, the number of black teachers increased from five in 1913 to fifteen in 1918. There were still fourteen blacks teaching at Fisk when the strike occurred. One black who was not asked to return was most unpopular with the local black community. The renewal of another man's contract was refused because there was evidence that his character was not above reproach. When he returned several years later, he was denounced by alumni and students for the same reason. It is true that McKenzie feuded with John W. Work, who left Fisk to become president of Roger Williams College. Work was not fired and the primary opposition to him came from the Department of Music, but McKenzie did not encourage him to stay. Students were correct when they claimed that department heads tended to be white.[15]

McKenzie's racial policy, rigid discipline, and limited freedom for students provided fuel for revolt and W. E. B. DuBois supplied the spark. The alumni had been restive for some time, but the opposition to McKenzie was not public. DuBois was kept aware of what was happening on campus by alumni and students, including his daughter Yolanda who was a senior at Fisk, but he hesitated to attack because the university "was in the throes of gathering a desperately needed endowment and it seemed unfair and unwise to raise a disturbing voice at so critical a time." But he could remain quiet no longer. In March 1924, DuBois referred to the "fight" at Fisk University in the *New York Amsterdam News*. It was, he said, "a fateful step in the development of the American Negro." It was not a question of discipline, DuBois contended, since discipline was not humiliation and insult; it did not call for taking black girls down back alleys to sing for white men; it did not call for refusal to entertain respectful student complaints. And, above all, discipline included freedom. DuBois was a national leader, editor of *Crisis,* and much admired by Fisk students. His announcement of a "fateful" fight no doubt gave encouragement to the student rebels. His view was endorsed by the New York Fisk Club. DuBois was scheduled to make the alumni address at Fisk in June 1924, and there was much anxiety on campus about what he would say. The apprehension proved justified. He announced that he had come to Fisk "to criticize and to say openly and before your face what so many of your graduates are saying secretly and behind your back." He attacked McKenzie in no uncertain terms, calling for an alumni boycott until Fisk had been reorganized in personnel and point of view. The visit to Fisk further convinced DuBois of the correctness of his views. The university had collected much money but in the process had lost its soul, he said. In the September issue of the *Crisis* DuBois wrote sadly that Fisk was to him "a place of sorrow, of infinite regret; a place where the dreams of great souls lay dusty and forgotten." Among the many friends of Fisk who believed that the university was off the correct path "none was more influential in sounding the alarm and organizing the opposition than its most distinguished alumnus, W. E. B. DuBois."[16]

The day after DuBois's speech, President McKenzie telegraphed the

New York trustees requesting an expression of confidence. Paul D. Cravath, chairman of the board, asked for a transcript of the speech, but there was none. He was unable to secure a copy from DuBois, who said he spoke from notes rather than a prepared text. Without seeing the speech, the board on June 14 prepared a letter expressing confidence in the McKenzie administration. McKenzie was complimented on his "so nearly successful" effort to raise the first million dollar endowment for higher education of blacks. No one could have secured the money, the board stated, unless the foundation upon which any such structure of credit must be built was firm and permanent. Since McKenzie had presided at Fisk there had been significant progress along all lines. He was commended for securing the endorsement of Harvard University, the University of Chicago, Northwestern University, and Columbia. These results were, the board proclaimed, in great measure traceable to McKenzie's "indomitable courage and perseverance in the face of seemingly insurmountable obstacles." Furthermore, the Carnegie Foundation had admitted members of Fisk faculty on equal terms to the benefits of its pension scheme.

The board praised McKenzie for the "unique achievement" of a $50,000 subscription from Nashville citizens. This was, said the board, a mark not only of progress by Fisk, but of a growing confidence in and enthusiasm for such work by Southern whites. Since some members of the board thought much of the opposition to McKenzie could be traced to increasingly rigid standards, especial mention was made of the favorable response of educators to that phase of McKenzie's work. If there had ever been any doubt where the board stood in the quarrel it was removed by the last paragraph of the letter. "The Board of Trustees not only earnestly and vigorously support the policies you have been pursuing at Fisk," the letter said, "but will support you in building up a faculty who are in sympathy with those policies. That you should have a united and loyal faculty in full sympathy with the standards you are seeking to maintain seems essential for success." The letter was signed by all trustees except Dr. Thomas Jesse Jones who was in Africa, and Dr. William N. DeBerry, an alumnus who felt he could not endorse the last paragraph.[17]

The board did decide to investigate. A committee composed of William H. Baldwin and L. Hollingsworth Wood conferred with McKenzie, Fisk officials, students, alumni, two black members of the board— Dr. Robert R. Moton and James C. Napier—DuBois, and the New York Fisk Club. Wood and Baldwin reported that DuBois was unable to produce purported proof of his many charges when specifically requested to do so. Other charges, they said, had been "completely controverted" by Mrs. Arch Trawick, a Nashville trustee, and, as the committee did not mention, McKenzie's close friend. They pointed out that DuBois had permitted his daughter to spend four years at Fisk (she was graduated in June). Most of the accusations, the committee felt, were "either bunk or deliberate distortion." Nevertheless, they recognized that there was "considerable feeling of unrest and dissatisfaction with conditions" at the university which no conscientious board of trustees would permit to remain unexamined. The committee recommended a thorough investigation at its November meeting.[18]

In the meantime DuBois had continued his attack against Fisk in the *American Mercury* and *Crisis*. After making his initial speech criticizing McKenzie, DuBois had asked students, staff, and faculty to help him prove his charges. He received a barrage of letters which characterized McKenzie as "an overbearing patriarch who suppressed critics, rewarded sycophants, and destroyed the confidence of black youth." He charged that the vision of Fisk students was being deliberately curtailed by discouragement of ambition and by propaganda. In order to win white sympathy, they were being humiliated and insulted. Black teachers were being dismissed and replaced with white instructors of mediocre ability. Student activities, he continued, were discouraged, and discipline was unduly severe. "Finally and above all," DuBois added, "at Fisk University today the president and most of the white teachers have no confidence in their students, no respect or hope for the Negro race and are treating them with suspicion and governing them by fear." Those were his conclusions based on interviews, visits, and letters, DuBois said, and if they proved true he suggested that Fisk needed a new president, a reconstituted faculty, and a reformed board of trustees. His accusations contained enough truth to make them difficult to refute.[19] Discipline was severe, students were treated with suspicion, and they were humiliated though perhaps not to attract sympathy.

On October 22 a group of students handed the board of trustees a statement of grievances against McKenzie. Students were allowed little initiative, the statement read, and they were urged not only to obey all rules, but to agree with university policies. They were not permitted expression of opinion. Discipline was unjust and unreasonable and students expelled from school experienced difficulty in securing their records from the university to enable them to enroll elsewhere. Furthermore, complained the students, discipline was supported by a widespread spy system. The statement condemned the teaching force: "Immature white undergraduates" were repeatedly brought in as teachers and Southern white persons were gradually being placed in positions of authority, students said. Moreover, McKenzie was deceptive, tyrannical, and was "making every effort" to increase the power and influence of the white South. Finally, neither the president, faculty, nor the trustees seemed to show any regard for the opinions of the alumni, parents, or the black world.

At the regular meeting of the trustees in November after "riotous beating upon tin pans," McKenzie invited the senior class and a committee of students to appear and present additional grievances. George W. Streator, secretary of the student committee, filed a statement containing eleven points. Students asked for: an opportunity to go before the faculty and be heard, a student council, fraternities and sororities, a recognized athletic association, modification of dress rules, increased privileges for upperclassmen, student employment in respectable positions on campus, a student publication, sympathetic chaperonage, fewer compulsory religious exercises, and examinations so arranged as to permit students time to go away for holidays. The committee orally reiterated existence of a spirit of distrust and oppression, the low quality of the faculty, and the race problem. The senior class added a few points to the committee's statement. It asked permission for senior women to chaperone underclassmen, prohibition of examination of personal packages, authorization for young men to escort girls to moving pictures on campus, and revision of laws affecting the laundry so it could be used daily. These quite reasonable requests were referred to President McKenzie, Mrs. Trawick, Napier, and Wood for settlement. At least three of these four people were unsympathetic with the students. Napier, the only black member of the committee, suggested the endorsement of McKenzie's administration. The letter sent to the president in June was adopted as official action of the board and placed in the minutes.[20]

The student petitions resulted in little change. The trustees did finally vote to grant an athletic association, a student council, modification of dress rules, and an alumni committee, but the modifications were slight. Though women were permitted to purchase their own hats they had to be of a conservative style and simply trimmed in black with no color. Cotton hose were no longer required for daily wear on campus. Little progress was made in forming a student council and athletic association. McKenzie, rather than calling the alumni committee together, sent them quotations commending his administration. Dissatisfied students continued mild agitation and New York alumni persisted in their effort to oust McKenzie. In early January 1925, alumni from all over the country met in conference with the New York Fisk Club. They returned to their respective communities, according to Dr. M. V. Boutte, a New Yorker, to form clubs to agitate for McKenzie's dismissal. The protest was unrelated to any racial issue, Boutte said—McKenzie's supporters and many others believed the agitation was meant to depose McKenzie in order to secure a black president—rather, it was provoked by McKenzie's policies which had "stifled the liberties and initiative of his Negro charges." The alumni in New York had taken over the former student publication, the *Fisk Herald,* and its editorial policy was against McKenzie.[21]

The board of trustees' position during this period was vague. Although it gave every indication of backing McKenzie wholeheartedly, members later claimed they had decided in November 1924 to ask for his resignation as soon as the "proper" time presented itself. McKenzie himself claimed to believe the board agreed with him.[22] After meeting with the board in January the president announced to the press that its policy would be to completely ignore the charges made against him. In a chapel talk to the students on February 4—a talk designated by students as the immediate cause of a disturbance which led to police intervention—McKenzie said most policies would be unchanged. He talked generally of discipline problems in other universities, pointing out that students usually believed discipline was too harsh. He reported that at a faculty meeting he had been directed to declare no modifications had been made in regulations affecting conduct, especially the prohibition against young men and women fraternizing on campus. The faculty was aware rules had been broken, McKenzie said, and they appealed for compliance. His speech was applauded.[23]

The applause must have been courtesy, for that night a number of students rose in wrath. Three other times there had been disturbances on campus after 10:00 P.M.—beating on pans and shouting—twice after printed statements by DuBois. On the evening of February 4 two student leaders warned Miss Clara Boynton, matron of the dining hall, that there would be a demonstration and that it would be useless for McKenzie or faculty representatives to come to the hall as they had during the other three demonstrations. They would continue, students said, until McKenzie's hair turned white. The disturbance began in Livingstone Hall. Forty-two panes of glass were broken, the chapel was turned upside down, and reputedly shots were fired. Throughout the demonstrations students kept up a steady chant of "DuBois! DuBois!" and "Before I'd be a slave." McKenzie and members of the prudential committee decided to call in the police. About thirty white policemen arrived on campus to quell the disorder caused by around a hundred students. McKenzie gave the police the names of seven students who were to be arrested for inciting a riot. Other students were taken to the president's office where they were forced to denounce the protest or withdraw from the university.

At the trial of the seven arrested men it was proven that McKenzie had no evidence of their involvement in the disturbance. Indeed, two of them had been away from campus that night. Still they were found guilty of disorderly conduct and given suspended fines of fifty dollars. When they threatened to sue McKenzie for malicious persecution he entered into an agreement with them. He would get their names stricken from the police records and permit other schools to accept them if they would refrain from further criticism of Fisk and its president. Four of the students were suspended. The April issue of *Crisis* ran pictures of six student leaders over the heading "Martyrs at Fisk."[24] McKenzie's calling the white police at a time when students were aroused by several months of white violence and police brutality in Nashville damned him in the black community. At least one white member of the board of trustees believed that his "reliance on the police betrayed an aristocratic personality, and more significantly, a lack of sympathy for the students."[25]

The demonstration was only the beginning of the student revolt. In support of those arrested and in protest against McKenzie's autocratic methods, approximately three-fourths of the student body went on strike, refusing to attend classes. Student leader George Streator boasted that "we don't need to do anything except tell the students: 'Boycott this or boycott that,' and believe me they do it to a finish." The strike was backed by the NAACP, *Crisis,* and much of the black press. In the *Crisis,* DuBois said he was "uplifted" by the revolt at Fisk. "At last we have real radicalism of the young," he said, "radicalism that costs, that is not mere words and foam." Hitherto much of what was called black radicalism was mere internal jealousy, striking at brothers and feeling brave, he stated. "But here is the real radical, the man who hits power in high places, white power, power backed by unlimited wealth; hits it and hits it openly and between the eyes; talks face to face and not down 'at the big gate.' God speed the breed!" The *Nation* thought the strike important because it demonstrated that the new generation, black or white, would not tolerate petty dictation. It indicated that young blacks had come of age, possessed a new self-respect, and were asking for their school the same type of social revolution that had taken place in many white colleges.[26]

The controversy continued to rage for several weeks. Students gathered evidence of the dictatorialness of McKenzie while the president collected letters supporting his policies. Older members of the faculty generally upheld McKenzie, believing the alternatives were McKenzie or lawlessness. Mary E. Spence, white professor of Greek, disagreed. The good of the university and of blacks necessitated a change, she said. White students, she thought, would have long ago revolted against the Fisk discipline. A majority of Nashville blacks opposed McKenzie while white Nashville rallied to his support. This gave some credence to press reports that the issue of race was involved in the disturbance. The *New York Times* claimed the demonstrations had been caused in part by the desire for a black president. DuBois said race was not involved, but then proceeded to talk about Southern white control of the school. In the mind of some Nashville whites and many Fisk students, McKenzie came to represent white supremacy. They praised him for calling the police to restrain students. In late February the president attended luncheon meetings of two white clubs. At each there was a standing ovation, shouting, and cheering the instant he appeared. Whites stopped him on the street to compliment him on the way he handled the student revolt. The president himself referred to the attack on Fisk and his character by "bolshevistic, if not anarchistic" elements of society. McKenzie and supporters were bitter toward DuBois, blaming his fierce attacks for the "riot" and strike. DuBois disclaimed responsibility, though years later he said he joined the fight until "Fisk deposed its dictatorial president." The students were offended by the charge that DuBois initiated the revolt. They had enlisted him only "after much persuasion," they claimed.[27]

The students themselves denied that they were motivated by race. They did not necessarily agree with McKenzie's policy, but they were seeking primarily a change in social regulations and greater student rights. An alumni investigating committee found no racial issue and neither did the board of trustees. And certainly the division was not completely along racial lines. A few local whites agreed with the students and some blacks, including a few members of the faculty, concurred with McKenzie. R. Augustus Lawson, a Fisk graduate, was on campus in February, and after trying to ascertain the facts, he decided McKenzie "should be upheld in his strong desire and effective effort to make Fisk all she should be in every good way." His own children would remain at Fisk, Lawson claimed, because he wanted for them "the Christian protection which Fisk had always furnished those who were honest and true."

At the request of interested parents, the principal of an Alabama Normal School went to Fisk to investigate. "After prolonged consideration," he wrote McKenzie, "I am convinced that the students of Fisk left you no other alternative but to summon the arm of the law to protect the lives and property entrusted to your care." Dozens of parents and some students wrote commending McKenzie for his stand. One father who had a daughter at Fisk wrote to thank McKenzie for calling the police to stop the "riot" before it reached the girls' dormitory. "While at Fisk last Tuesday," he continued, "and seeing the boys loitering on the steps of Jubilee Hall, some in the hall, smoking with hats on, we wondered what could these boys who forgot to act as gentlemen in a crisis like this do with a student council if they had one." DuBois claimed that some parents and alumni "turned upon their own children like wild beasts, ready to beat them into submission, insisting that even if the school authorities were wrong, it was the business of black boys and girls to submit."[28] Some of the parents' letters to McKenzie seemed to substantiate DuBois's view. Parents' reactions in some instances indicated that they viewed the student revolt as a part of the revolution in morals and manners in the United States, which was distasteful to them. Many of them still preferred the religious-oriented college with rigid rules. Furthermore their response revealed the dichotomy in black thought in the 1920s. Some of them approved not only of McKenzie's regulation of students but also of his racial policy.

An alumni investigating committee probably came closer to the truth of the circumstances surrounding the revolt than any other group involved. In June 1924, an alumni group had been appointed to aid in developing a program for improving the university. After the strike began the committee arrived on campus to examine the situation. It held hearings, listening to the president, students, alumni, interested whites and blacks from Nashville, and Fisk clubs throughout the country. The committee first of all found a great divergence of opinion among sincere and well-meaning people, but it was evident there had been unrest at Fisk for some time. All parties, the committee said, united in deprecating the use of "boisterous and unruly" methods in presenting grievances and were agreed that law and order must be maintained, the only difference of opinion being as to methods used. The "best" white opinion in Nashville, the committee found, believed that McKenzie had handled the situation wisely. Former Governor Roberts, who had represented the arrested students in court, claimed that McKenzie had made serious errors in dealing with the disturbance but had been wisely advised after the initial mistakes had been made so that legal problems had been well cared for.

Some witnesses said McKenzie had lost the confidence of Nashville blacks and the alumni with the result that many students would not go to Fisk. On the other hand the committee received letters indicating continued confidence and willingness to send students. Some who approved McKenzie's actions admitted it would be difficult to restore confidence. The committee played down the race issue. The strain on McKenzie had been great, and he had been forced to act from a position of great difficulty and delicacy from which errors could easily be made, the committee decided. Whether or not McKenzie's actions had been at all times wise, the committee added—and it was convinced he had made serious mistakes—he had always acted sincerely and in conformity with devotion to educational ideals as he saw them. After the hearings the committee made recommendations in accord with student opinion. In view of the trend of world thought toward a larger liberty, the committee said, the policies of Fisk should be brought to conform to a more generous appreciation of that tendency in modern life. It further suggested some method of alumni representation on the board of trustees and that greater efforts be made to enlist the support and interest of Fisk alumni.[29]

After the strike Fisk encountered more and more difficulty in securing funds. Most alumni refused to give money to the school and philanthropists were reluctant to award gifts to a school with so little stability. Facing an untenable situation, McKenzie on 16 April 1925 tendered his resignation to become effective at the end of the scholastic year. The student strike did not cause McKenzie's retirement—the board had al-

ready decided to ask for his resignation as soon as it could do so without
appearing to give in to what it considered student lawlessness—but it
probably hastened his departure. The board accepted his resignation
and granted him a year's salary.[30]

McKenzie is usually remembered by Fiskites, if at all, with distaste. He
made mistakes, some of them enormous ones, but he sincerely believed
he was acting in the best interests of Fisk and he did make important
contributions to the school. Dr. Thomas Jesse Jones, educational director of the Phelps-Stokes Fund and member of the Fisk board of trustees,
wrote in 1924: "May I say, with all emphasis, that in my opinion, Dr.
McKenzie is working out a phase of Negro education that is more important at the present time than that committed to any other man, white or
black, connected with the welfare of the Negro race." President Bruce R.
Payne of George Peabody College expressed sorrow at McKenzie's resignation and added: "What will become of Fisk! You have done so much
for it in the way of raising standards . . . and in the way of raising funds
for it,—in fact so much more than any other human being ever did,—that
I am distressed greatly to learn that you are leaving." A Fisk alumnus
wrote McKenzie that "I want you to understand that I have the highest
possible admiration for what you have accomplished and the beautiful
spirit in which you have worked. I have no doubt that in years to come
your administration at Fisk will stand out as the most significant epoch
in its history up to the present time."[31]

McKenzie had modernized Fisk in plant and curriculum. He had won
the confidence of educational foundations, thereby gaining for the university a considerable increase in its support and endowment. He had
raised standards and teachers' salaries. But his methods in so doing had
alienated a large proportion of the people he was serving. There was a
question of how long a black university, dominated by a white president
and white trustees and supported by white wealth, could carry on in
defiance of the wishes of its black constituency. Despite his accom-
plishments there is little doubt that McKenzie's retirement was in the
best interests of Fisk University. The time had passed when a paternalistic and dictatorial white president could successfully head the school.

8

A New Era

THE RETIREMENT OF MCKENZIE BY NO MEANS SOLVED THE PROBLEMS OF
Fisk. Many of the alumni, delighted at his departure, had little confidence in the board of trustees.[1] They adopted a wait-and-see attitude. At the same time, McKenzie had some "true and substantial friends" at Fisk, especially among the teachers. There was a question of what their reaction would be to his exit and whether they should be retained since they approved his policies. Furthermore, though a majority of students and alumni were pleased at McKenzie's resignation, a few of them were distressed at the change.

An alumna wrote McKenzie that Fisk was losing him "at a time when SHE most needs you." Her own son was involved in the student strike but he received no sympathy from his mother. White Nashville temporarily had lost faith in Fisk. Several local whites, especially those who believed blacks should stay in their "place," refused to pay pledges promised for the endowment. Friendship with local whites was perhaps not absolutely essential, but it would certainly be useful.[2] The board of trustees would have to walk carefully between two powerful forces in order to place the school back on its feet.

Desirous of selecting the proper man for the position, the board moved slowly in electing a new president. In the meantime university affairs were placed in the hands of an interim administrative committee composed of L. Hollingsworth Wood, chairman, representing the board of trustees; Professor Augustus F. Shaw, executive chairman and dean of the school; Professor Herbert A. Miller, on leave from Ohio State University; Miss L. Elizabeth Collinge, dean of women; Thomas M. Brumfield, assistant professor of Greek and Latin; and Mrs. Minnie Lou Crosthwaite, registrar. Shaw had opposed many of McKenzie's policies and Brumfield and Mrs. Crosthwaite were both Fisk graduates. To soothe further those who charged that all important positions were in the hands of whites, Ambrose Caliver was made assistant dean of the school. Upon the interim committee fell the burden of putting together the pieces left from the demonstration, strike, and resignation. A first problem was the disposition of requests of expelled students for reentry into Fisk. These students considered McKenzie's resignation as vindication of their actions and they wished to return to school, but several trustees opposed their readmission.

Especially disliked was George Streator, the leader of rebellious students. Mrs. Arch Trawick threatened to resign from the board and "release a condemning statement to the press" if he were readmitted. Paul D. Cravath, chairman of the board, was also opposed to Streator's readmission. When informed that the prudential committee was considering Streator's application, he personally intervened. Streator was, Cravath said, bound to be a disturbing factor on campus. His temperament was such that he could not avoid organizing mischief. Cravath opposed taking him back even after a long period of suspension. Cravath wrote still another letter to Professor Shaw, saying no self-respecting college would reinstate "leaders in a movement who pursued a course of such rowdyism and lawlessness" as Streator and friends. The prudential committee disagreed. In view of alumni anxiety for the return of those expelled, the committee decided to readmit them in the winter quarter of 1926. Cravath was by far the most powerful man on the board of trustees; it took courage to defy him. L. Hollingsworth Wood congratulated Professor Shaw and the prudential committee for having so much "backbone."[3]

The interim administration also tried to employ more black teachers. On at least one occasion a white woman was dismissed to make a place for a black faculty member. However, the proportion of blacks on the faculty changed little in the first years after McKenzie's departure.

The board of trustees made only a minor attempt to meet students' demands. At its May 1925 meeting, the board suspended the *Fisk News*, a faculty publication, and reestablished the *Fisk Herald* with a $500 subsidy. *News* editor Isaac Fisher, unpopular with the alumni because of his closeness to McKenzie, was invited to remain on the faculty. Instead, Fisher, who wanted to continue his study of race relations abroad, accepted the first Guggenheim Fellowship ever awarded to a black. The board further approved the principle of a black dean of women for Fisk if it should prove feasible. Most of the student complaints had to wait for the new president for settlement.[4]

The selection of the new president, Thomas Elsa Jones, a friend of L. Hollingsworth Wood and fellow Quaker, was announced on 18 February 1926. Born on 22 March 1888 in Fairmount, Indiana, Jones received his A.B. from Earlham College in 1912 and taught in public schools in Indiana for several years. Continuing his education, he won a B.D. from Hartford Theological Seminary in 1915 and an M.A. from the same school in 1917. After graduation Jones went to Friends Mission in Tokyo, Japan, where he remained until 1924 except for one year, 1917–1918, when he acted as director of the YMCA in Vladivostok, Siberia. While in Tokyo, Jones served as professor of economics at Keio

University. At the time of his election to the Fisk presidency, he was completing his Ph.D. at Columbia.

President Jones had no experience in race relations and little as an administrator in an educational institution, but he was young, vigorous, and bright. It was hoped that he would bring new ideas and infuse Fisk with new vigor. Upon arrival in Nashville in September 1926, he announced to the press that he was present as an educator and not as a man who expected to solve the race problem. "I am here to build a college that is second to none in the United States and my whole being is in the task," Jones added. He was brash, a poor businessman, and a worse lawyer, but he learned quickly and led Fisk into one of its most productive periods. James Weldon Johnson said no one could hear President Jones speak about Fisk "without feeling the galvanic force of his tremendous energy and enthusiasm. . . ." Jones was soon convinced that he was "right in the center of one of the most important developments not only in America but in the world."[5]

President Jones immediately began to try to pacify students and alumni. He began to bring in able black scholars and promoted Ambrose Caliver to dean of the university in the summer of 1927. To Caliver thus went the honor of being the first black dean in Fisk history.[6] More important, in June 1926 the board of trustees approved alumni representation on the board. For years some of the alumni had been agitating for the right to select a trustee. There had been Fisk graduates on the board, but they were not chosen by the alumni. According to the trustees' plan, the first year the alumni should nominate five persons from whom the board would choose three, one to serve for one year, one for two years, and one for three. Thereafter each year the alumni would present three names from whom one would be selected. There would always be at least three alumni on the board. Nominations could be made by the general alumni association, Fisk clubs, or local alumni associations having ten or more voters. Only graduates of the college, music, and normal departments were eligible. Each alumnus voted for three persons from a list circulated among them. The first three alumni trustees were Dr. Henry Hugh Proctor, Dr. Ferdinand Augustus Stewart, and Mrs. Minnie Lou Crosthwaite. Three blacks—Dr. William N. DeBerry, a Fiskite; James C. Napier, a Nashville businessman; and Robert R. Moton of Tuskegee Institute—were already on the board.[7]

To further improve the communications between the university and alumni the *Fisk News* was established as an alumni organ in 1927 and a full-time secretary and a recorder were employed by the university. Andrew J. Allison '13 was the first alumni secretary.[8] Within a year after the arrival of President Jones most of the alumni had rallied to the university's support. In January 1925, DuBois had listed Fisk as a liability to blacks, but in the March 1927 issue of *Crisis* he said Fisk was "moving

JUBILEE HALL (*Courtesy of the Fisk University Library's Special Collections*)

forward under its new progressive president," and he called on Fiskites
to give "till it hurts" in the new campaign for money. "The sincerity of
our demand for rights and reform can only be proven by our willingness
to help bear the burden of its cost," he warned. The alumni gave generously, as did students. The senior class of 1925–1926 presented the
board of trustees with insurance policies on all their lives totaling over
$18,000. In late 1927 Professor Mary E. Spence said the alumni for the
first time in years were once again united in their support of Fisk. She
believed President Jones was the only one who could have brought it
about. She and other alumni, Miss Spence said, had confidence in his
judgment.[9]

Perhaps DuBois and Miss Spence were too optimistic. Alumni were
supporting the school financially, but there were some who with good
cause still had misgivings about the board of trustees. Some white Southern board members seemed to have little respect for their black colleagues, and the black members responded to the lack of confidence
with mistrust. No doubt all board members were concerned with the best
interests of Fisk, but there were differences of opinion about the blacks'
place in American life. Even white Northern members gave alumni representatives cause for suspicion.

The board's most important member was Paul D. Cravath, son of the
founder and first president. Cravath, a lawyer, was an influential man in
New York City. In addition to his duties as trustee of Fisk, he was at one
time a director of the Juilliard School of Music, trustee of the David
Mannes Music School, and director of the New York Symphony Society
and the Metropolitan Opera. He had been a member of the board since
1895. Not only did he use his influence to collect money for Fisk, but he
gave large sums annually from his personal fortune. If any white trustee
was a friend of blacks it was Cravath. But in 1928 he told the *Nashville
Banner* that segregation was a natural process not a legal one. "It came
about of free will and is epitomized in the old formula, 'Birds of a
feather flock together,'" Cravath said. At the annual trustees meeting in
New York that same year Cravath invited all white members of the board
to lunch with him at the Broad Street Club. "Of course, you realize why it
is necessary that I must limit such a luncheon to the white members," he
told President Jones. "I think," he added, "embarrassment can be saved
by treating the luncheon as personal rather than as a luncheon of the
board." No wonder some blacks were skeptical. President Jones spoke of
walking a precarious line between two great forces, both backed by millions of concerned people. "One needs to draw continually from Divine
sources if he is to keep his balance and steadily move forward," Jones
said.[10]

Some alumni "dissatisfaction and fear" was reported again in 1930.
Much of the concern, the president believed, was because the new Fisk

library was built by a white contractor and the contract for the proposed chemistry building had been let to a white firm. Dr. DeBerry was assigned to explain to alumni that there was no discrimination; the university had accepted the lowest bid. The trustees' meeting in November 1930 "cleared the atmosphere" regarding black and white cooperation more than anything that had happened in the last two years, Jones reported to L. Hollingsworth Wood. "I think white people saw that my loyalties are firmly tied up with the group which I represent as President of Fisk University," Jones added, "and I think the colored people saw that it is time to shut up a lot of these vague and groundless rumors of discrimination." From every quarter he had received nothing but words of loyal support and commendation, Jones averred, even from alumni groups from whom he least expected support. Alumni suspicion was further allayed in 1933 when the trustees, upon recommendation of the general alumni association, increased alumni representation on the board from three to five, beginning in the scholastic year 1935–1936. Nevertheless, there were naturally nagging doubts by some alumni as long as Fisk had a white president and a predominantly white board of trustees.[11]

In the meantime President Jones and the faculty were trying to appease student demands. As far as a majority of students were concerned, the primary complaint against McKenzie had been the harsh regulations. In 1926 a faculty committee composed of the president, matron of the dining hall, director of physical education, director of health, and the chaplain met to determine what must be done to bring a spirit of trust and good will on campus. The consequent changes in rules would provoke an unbelieving chuckle from present Fisk students, but at the time they seemed momentous. Students were permitted to walk together during the day and they were given thirty minutes after supper two nights a week "to have a social time in the Jubilee Parlors." Also during this half-hour juniors and seniors were permitted to walk to the Chocolate Shop on campus. On special occasions, it was decided, upperclasswomen could go to town under proper chaperonage. Another student complaint under McKenzie was the policy of lights out at 10:00 P.M. Under the new rules lights were to be out at the same time in the women's dormitories, but the men could keep lights on as late as they desired.[12]

After much consultation with faculty, alumni, and trustees it was decided to allow "a few well chaperoned and carefully managed dances on campus." Permission to dance on campus evoked a good bit of criticism. Dr. S. N. Vass, secretary of religious education of the National Baptist Convention, excepted Fisk when discussing the Christian virtues of black colleges because the students gave a ball for President Jones as a climax to inaugural ceremonies. Dress regulations were liberalized. A dress committee composed of faculty and a woman from each class now made the rules. "Elaborate trimming" and coats of "flashy" color were still discouraged; the committee suggested "the more conservative browns, blues, gray and blacks." Hats were to be plain but high heels could be worn on dress occasions. Chapel attendance continued to be compulsory on Monday, Wednesday, Friday, and Sunday. Any student missing more than one-fourth of the chapel exercises during one quarter was suspended for the following quarters; several students were suspended for inattendance. Chapel was compulsory, President Jones said, because the Fisk program included a definite interest in religion and chapel attendance was as essential as class attendance. Moreover, he said, the exercises included only ten minutes of devotion. The remaining time was used for discussion of matters of general social or public interest. When students protested the practice again in 1928 the faculty voted overwhelmingly to continue the traditional policy.[13]

The question of smoking was too serious to be decided by the faculty alone. "Inasmuch as a change so important as permitting smoking on the campus at Fisk might involve the future reputation of the School," wrote Jones, "I deem it wise to refer this question to the Trustees." Some of the alumni, including Dr. Henry Hugh Proctor, a leading spirit in the initial revolt, were opposed to all smoking, but the students won. A smoking room was set up in the Chocolate Shop where men could smoke until 7:00 P.M., but there was to be no smoking elsewhere on campus. For the really dedicated smokers it was an agonizing wait from seven in the evening until the Chocolate Shop opened the next day. Inevitably some men smoked in their rooms. Finally Jones proposed to provide a room in the men's dormitories for smoking and then strictly forbid puffing in private rooms. The students made a counterproposal. They would cease smoking in the buildings if they could indulge their habit on campus. The faculty refused. "Some of us feel the cigarette stubs, the young men smoking in the presence of the young women, and turning Fisk into a smoking camp is a little more than we can stand," Jones reported. Finally in 1935 the women were also permitted to smoke. It was discouraged but was not absolutely prohibited.[14]

The student request for fraternities and sororities was also granted. President Jones informed the board of trustees in 1926 that it would eventually be necessary to permit such organizations. Nearly 60 percent of the men already belonged to fraternities at Meharry, which took them away from campus and developed a spirit of division and lack of loyalty. Many of the women were members of sororities in the city. This interfered with the "family spirit" on campus which Jones was trying to build. Since the students insisted on joining such societies he thought it would be better to have them on campus. The board referred the question to the president and faculty, giving them power to decide. After a year's study by a faculty-student commission, the long-banned organizations were welcomed to campus.[15] By June 1928, Fisk had four fraternities and two sororities.[16]

Student government was accepted by the interim administration. Previously there had been a student council, but it had been permitted to die apparently because of student apathy as well as faculty opposition. The new student council had charge of student decorum on and off campus, though faculty advisors had ultimate authority. Faculty members looked upon student government as far from perfect. President Jones said in September 1928 that students did not seem to be "taking too well to their new privileges." The *Herald* staff was not collecting material and the committee appointed by the student council to publish the fall issue was not functioning. The faculty thought the student council elections of 1928 were fraudulent. They insisted upon a new election, but students complained it would be useless. Student government, they grumbled, was just a farce since the faculty opposed any student autonomy. A *Herald* editorial in 1930 suggested that student government seemed to be maturing and becoming more effective, but it was several years before it was considered satisfactory. As one Fisk advisor said, student government is always "tricky" and "when it has come into a college as the result of a determined effort to break away from what students considered too rigid discipline, it takes experience, understanding, infinite patience and a very firm hand at the right places until traditions are well established."[17]

Some students were dissatisfied with the extent of their new rights. New freedoms merely caused them to want more. In a long editorial in 1927 the *Herald* called for sex education and openness in all matters. "The youth of today is tired of sham, tired of mock modesty, tired of hypocrisy," it said. Staid faculty members cringed in uneasy silence. There had already been criticism of smoking, dancing, short dresses, and silk hose. Students were considered too flippant. They were acting too much like the young people they were.

Passages such as the following taken from the *Herald* in 1934 dismayed the faculty. "Fo' give me, fo' give me, but have you seen 'The man from Harlem?' Yeh, man, there's many a dizzy frail chewing on her finger nails 'cause they all crave that man from Harlem. (Hot Cha!)." Even some of the alumni shook their heads gravely and sadly. A black woman living near Fisk who testified on behalf of the students during the strike complained in 1931 that she had made a mistake. Since McKenzie left, she stated, students were noisy and coarse and conditions were growing worse. Living near Fisk, she said, was "like living next door to an insane asylum." Chairman of the Board Cravath lamented the "alarming falling off in discipline," especially in the relations between sexes. If this impression should become current, as it already had among alumni, Cravath stated, it would hurt attendance. President Jones agreed that one of his most important problems was strengthening discipline.[18] Student unrest had not yet ended, for the social revolution at Fisk was not yet complete.

9

The Good Years

THE FIRST YEARS OF THE JONES ADMINISTRATION WERE ONES OF UNPRECE-
dented growth at Fisk. Within a short time of his arrival students had
been partially appeased and the misgivings of a majority of the alumni
allayed. It was thought that white Nashvillians would be more difficult to
mollify, but soon they were praising President Jones. In telling its
readers about Fisk "making its greatest progress in its history" the
Nashville Tennessean said in 1929 that "anyone who has been privileged to
meet Dr. Jones cannot but have been impressed with his candor, his
earnestness, his fairness, his simplicity, his efficiency." A Nashville
lawyer spoke for many of his friends when he wrote that he had formed
a very high opinion of Jones and was personally much attached to him.
He thought "that again the right man has been put in the right place."
    Certainly Jones was an energetic executive. An associate warned a
board of trustees member never to expect things to be methodically
planned and executed according to any pattern, since the president had
so many ideas a report could scarcely stay put long enough to be typed.
His friend and great admirer on the board, L. Hollingsworth Wood,
constantly cautioned Jones to slow down and to allow no particular problem to upset his digestion. The president was unable to heed the advice.
Baking soda for hyperacidity was his constant companion and he was
once hospitalized with ulcers.[1]
    Much of Fisk's progress was made possible by Jones's success in com-
pleting the million dollar endowment, which had been conditionally
pledged during McKenzie's administration but could not be paid until a
debt of about $150,000 had been eradicated. During the turmoil of
1924–1925 the debt had increased to over $300,000. The response from
the black community and alumni was encouraging. In October 1926,
black businessmen in Nashville launched a campaign to raise $10,000 to
rejuvenate the Memorial Chapel; they had already raised about $2,000.
In December Paul D. Cravath offered a donation of $25,000 if the
alumni would give a similar amount. A group meeting at Fisk for Jones's
inauguration raised $35,000 in less than thirty minutes. On 1 July 1927,
Cravath announced that Fisk had cleared its indebtedness, thus qualify-
ing for the $1,000,000 endowment fund. The debt had been paid by
gifts from more than 6,000 alumni and supporters of Fisk, Cravath said,

ranging from a few pennies to $1,000. He could have added that he had advanced still another $25,000 on unpaid pledges.[2]

Although completion of the endowment was a major achievement, Fisk's financial problem was not solved. In 1931–1932 endowment income was only $67,302 and expenses had increased enormously. The budget rose from approximately $250,000 in 1927–1928 to more than $323,000 in 1930–1931. It was necessary to continue what L. Hollingsworth Wood referred to as the "Fisk begging program." Fisk depended on gifts and grants for about 54 percent of its budget in 1932.

Total income almost quadrupled between 1923 and 1937, with much of the additional income coming from foundations. In the late 1920s and early 1930s philanthropic organizations singled out Fisk, Atlanta University, Howard, Dillard, Johnson C. Smith, and Hampton for contributions.[3]

There were also numerous benefactions from prominent individuals. Cyrus H. McCormick, who gave Fisk $2,000 in 1928 to help repair buildings, was only one of many donors. President Jones persuaded John D. Rockefeller, Jr., to give the commencement address in 1928. For days Nashville buzzed with excitement and Rockefeller's presence gained favorable attention for Fisk throughout the country. After praising Jones "as a man of broad vision and imagination, fearless and indomitable, whose hand he counted it a privilege to uphold," Rockefeller said he consented to make the address to "pay a tribute of admiration to the men and women of the South" and "to evidence his interest and belief" in blacks. Men who had money should make good use of it, Rockefeller stated, and he suggested Fisk as a good cause. James Dallas Burrus, who left his fortune to Fisk in 1928, claimed he was influenced by Rockefeller's speech. In 1929 Dr. John W. McClellan, a St. Louis black man, left Fisk an estate valued at approximately $100,000, though lawsuits lasting over a decade siphoned off most of it. Unfortunately the depression slowed gifts to a trickle.[4]

As usual the Fisk University Jubilee Singers were doing their share in advertising the school and trying to secure money. In early 1926 they traveled throughout the United States and Canada. A Canadian newspaper said of them: "Five colored vocalists and a tuning fork, and such singing as only the very greatest artists can achieve in ensemble. These are the Fisk Jubilee Singers and their profoundly devoted and emotional art." In October the troupe, composed of Mr. and Mrs. James A. Myers, L. David Collins, Carl J. Barbour, and H. W. O'Bannon, sailed once again for Europe. Duplicating earlier triumphs, they were greeted enthusiastically. A concert at the Salle Gaveau in Paris filled "every seat and inch of standing room." In February 1927, the singers appeared at the Palazzo Real at the command of the Italian king and queen before "one of the most aristocratic audiences that ever gathered in Italy." They also sang for Mussolini, much to his delight. They were well received by classical musicians in Italy. At a private concert in their honor Luisa Tetrazzini, an operatic soprano, sang arias and de Parchmann played Chopin to express their satisfaction with the singers' program. Back in France in 1928 they sang for the "Tiger" Clemenceau.

Upon their return to the United States, the *Nashville Banner* expressed the admiration of Nashvillians for the Jubilee Singers. "The Fisk Singers were received abroad as well as usual," the *Banner* proclaimed, "which is to say that theaters and concert halls were packed and jammed everywhere they appeared and that they sang for many of the personages and royalties of the lands they visited. The present group of Jubilee singers, in other words, is carrying on worthily the excellent traditions of artistry that have come down to them in unbroken succession." Soon after their return the singers were presented by the Detroit Symphony Society and later in the year they were the first black artists to appear in the Hollywood Bowl. The depression, of course, made it difficult for the singers to earn a profit and the board of trustees discussed disbanding them. When the question arose it was the white Nashville members who were most opposed. No, it could not be done, they said, the Jubilee Singers were an institution.[5]

Soon after the completion of the $1,000,000 endowment the General Education Board granted $400,000 to construct and endow a library. One-half of the sum was to be used for construction and one-half to begin a permanent library endowment. At the time of construction the library was considered one of the "most interesting and useful" in the country. After seeing the blueprints, the University of North Carolina librarian said it would be the South's most beautiful and modern library. Experts from around the nation examined and approved the plans. A special feature of the building was the murals, by a well-known New York artist, Aaron Douglas, depicting the black man's history. A former art critic for *Crisis,* Douglas later went to Fisk where he remained until his retirement in 1966.[6] The library's dedication in the fall of 1930 was accompanied by the Negro Library Conference. Seventy-one librarians from every Southern state and about a dozen Northern states attended. The purpose of the conference, arranged by the director of the Fisk library, Louis S. Shores, was to develop a "professional mindedness" among black librarians and to offer the opportunity for consideration of their common problems both in informal discussion and in formal conferences. Some well-known figures in the library world were engaged as speakers.[7]

Continued growth of the library was assured by the Julius Rosenwald Fund, the Carnegie Corporation, and the Laura Spelman Fund. The Rosenwald Fund awarded $15,000 per year toward operating expenses for seven years and an additional $25,000 for books if it could be matched from other sources. The Carnegie Corporation granted

$25,000 for books and the interest on $25,000 for ten years. The Laura Spelman Fund gave $1,800 a year to purchase books in the social sciences.

Between 1926 and 1936 the number of volumes in the library increased from 16,001 to 47,304, still a small number, but larger than in most black college libraries. In 1932 Fisk spent more for books and periodicals than Atlanta University, Talladega, Morehouse, and Spelman combined. An added feature of the new library was the Fiskiana Collection, consisting of primary materials on black education and the history of Fisk. New emphasis was also placed on the black studies collection. In 1931 Arthur Shomburg, a widely known collector from New York, became curator of black literature at Fisk. Through the years, especially under the direction of Arna Bontemps, the library gathered a notable collection of black studies materials.[8]

While President Jones was improving the school's financial condition he was reorganizing the faculty and administration. Blacks had been on the faculty under McKenzie, and Mrs. Minnie Lou Crosthwaite had been registrar, but usually blacks occupied subordinate positions. The policy begun by the interim administration of placing blacks in positions of greater importance was continued by President Jones. When Ambrose Caliver went on leave in 1929, Alrutheus Ambush Taylor became acting dean. In 1930 Taylor became academic dean and remained at Fisk until his death. Taylor had quite a varied career before joining the Fisk staff. He received a B.A. from the University of Michigan and an M.A. and Ph.D. from Harvard. He had taught at Tuskegee Institute and West Virginia Collegiate Institute. While in West Virginia he had been twice appointed by the governor as the state's delegate to the Social Workers Conference. Associated for three years with Carter G. Woodson as investigator for the Association for the Study of Negro Life and History, Taylor had published several articles from his findings. In 1928 he was awarded the Laura Spelman Rockefeller Memorial Fellowship for further study at Harvard. He first went to Fisk in 1926, soon became dean of men, then acting dean, and finally dean of the university. Taylor became a powerful figure on campus, thereby lessening alumni fears of white domination.[9]

In 1929 Juliette Derricotte was employed as the first black dean of women at Fisk. As a personality of great charm and force and with her broad contacts in religious work, Miss Derricotte was a strong influence on the young women who came under her charge. Unfortunately Miss Derricotte's career at Fisk was tragically short. On 6 November 1931, she and three Fisk students were in a car accident near Dalton, Georgia. An ambulance was called but never arrived. Whites living nearby took them to the offices of three white physicians in Dalton. Since the Hamilton Memorial Hospital in town had no black ward, there was no attempt to place the injured in the hospital.

The physician treating Miss Derricotte moved her to a private residence where white physicians placed their black patients who needed constant care. In the meantime one of the students had called friends in Chattanooga who sent an ambulance and physician to Dalton. Miss Derricotte was taken to the Walden Hospital in Chattanooga, where she died the following evening. The ambulance returned for the most seriously injured student, Miss Nina Johnson, who died before reaching Chattanooga. White officials denied that the injured women had been refused entrance to the Hamilton Memorial Hospital, though the white woman who had picked up Miss Johnson went to the hospital, asked where blacks could get treatment, and was sent to a doctor's office. No black had ever been treated in the hospital and none of the physicians attempted to take the two women there though they were obviously in serious condition. Whether they would have lived had they been taken immediately to the hospital is a matter of conjecture. They may have been two more of the many victims of segregation in the South.[10]

In addition to the two deans, Fisk added several other blacks to the staff, a number of them as research professors. New research professors included: Paul Radin, a Ph.D. from Yale in anthropology; Alain Leroy Locke, a Rhodes Scholar and Harvard Ph.D. in philosophy; St. Elmo Brady, one of the five black Ph.D.'s in chemistry in the United States; Elmer S. Imes, Ph.D., University of Michigan in physics; and Charles S. Johnson, Ph.B., University of Chicago in sociology. Other able blacks added to the faculty included John R. Cottin, languages; Z. Alexander Looby, in economics and government and later a strong figure in the Tennessee fight for civil rights; and Lorenzo D. Turner in English literature. In general the black faculty members were probably superior to their white colleagues. President Jones wanted to maintain a biracial faculty, but at the time there appeared to be more able black than white scholars willing to teach in black schools. As a result, the proportion of blacks on the faculty increased to more than one-half by 1936 and to about two-thirds by 1945.

Within a few years Jones had collected a strong, research-oriented faculty at Fisk. By 1930 the president was on the whole pleased with his staff. "I think we are now definitely out of the era of soul-saving, thrill-chasing, educational well wishing and are very much like any one of the first-class colleges," he said. The school was sometimes called the "New Fisk." Jones did experience some difficulty in the relations between old and new faculty. There was a faculty "purge" in 1934 that Jones thought solved the problem. In the fall he said the campus seemed more "united in a family feeling" than he had ever seen it before. The new faculty members were "keen, alert, cultured, and spiritual." "Our purging of last spring," he wrote, "seems to have done a great deal of good." If there really was a purge as Jones claimed, it was minor, for only a few members of the faculty left.

JULIETTE DERRICOTTE (*Courtesy of the Fisk University Library's Special Collections*)

Not all of the old faculty were pleased with the new regime. Jones was not always gracious in discharging older members to make way for younger, more aggressive personnel. One man who had served Fisk for seventeen years was discharged—though Jones had earlier guaranteed the man his position—on the grounds that he had been late to class (who had not been late? he asked), a microscope had disappeared from the laboratory, and because Fisk "was moving up." The president refused when asked for a written statement of the cause of the discharge. An appeal to the board of trustees was futile.

The number of higher degrees among the faculty more than doubled between 1925 and 1930. In 1925 there had been two Ph.D.'s on campus; in 1930 there were ten. There were no M.A.'s plus continued study in 1925 and there were twelve in 1930.[11] The upgrading of the faculty was in part due to the raising of salaries. Jones tried to end "the split family arrangement" which had evolved on the Fisk campus. Salaries had been so low that frequently a husband was forced to leave his wife elsewhere so she also could work. Miss Dora A. Scribner, who had been at Fisk over thirty-five years, received only $1,845 a year as professor of English in 1928. Salaries remained low for some of the faculty, but five members received $5,000 a year, four had salaries of $4,000, and two were paid $3,500 per year by 1933. These salaries were comparable to those paid in other small colleges of the country.[12]

Coupled with the faculty improvement was an increased emphasis on graduate work and the abandonment of the high school in 1927. The question of granting a graduate degree was raised early in Fisk history. Before 1890 graduates of several years' standing who had furnished proof of having pursued professional studies or of having engaged in teaching or other intellectual pursuits and had sustained good moral character were granted a master's degree. On this basis twelve M.A.'s were granted in 1879, sixteen in 1885, three in 1887, and four in 1888. In 1889 Fisk first announced its intention of offering graduate work. Graduates who could present evidence that they had made "satisfactory progress in liberal studies" after graduation were eligible for a degree. The requirement was supposedly equivalent to one year of systematic study. Since the Fisk graduate would generally have to pursue his or her advanced work as a nonresident, each professor was permitted to arrange a course of work in his or her field for graduates of the classical department. The professor determined authors to be studied, set a time limit for preparation, and arranged an exam. The professor submitted his or her conclusions to the faculty and if it decided the work done was equal to a year's regular study the student was recommended for an M.A.

In 1908 graduates of any department of the college, not just the classical department, were offered the privilege of doing graduate work. Requirements were strengthened in 1913. Each candidate had to present a thesis and display an elementary knowledge of French and German. Also necessary was one full year of work in the same field followed as an undergraduate. Candidates graduated by schools other than Fisk had to spend at least one year in residence. Fisk students could do their work in absentia but were required to present themselves at the university for a final examination.[13] After 1918 a year of resident study was mandatory for all who desired an M.A.

Most of the higher degrees granted by black schools before the 1920s were more in the nature of honorary than earned degrees. Then around 1920 Howard University reorganized its program and began seriously to offer advanced work. In 1927 Fisk followed Howard's lead. In that year arrangements were completed to offer graduate work in the history, sociology, English, philosophy, and chemistry departments. Soon afterwards, new emphasis was placed on graduate work in education. Under the new plan a student pursued in residence for one full year a course of study approved by the graduate studies committee. At the end of a year, a comprehensive examination was taken and an original thesis on an approved subject presented. An outside representative from a "distinguished university," including Harvard, the University of Chicago, and the University of Wisconsin, participated in the final written and oral examinations. By 1930 it was predicted that Fisk, Howard, Atlanta, and Dillard, supplemented by white schools which enrolled blacks, would meet the requirements of blacks for graduate education.[14]

Only a small number of degrees were awarded the first few years Fisk began offering graduate work. The first Master of Science degree was awarded in 1928 to Frederick Augustine Browne. Browne, who had received his bachelor's degree at Howard, joined the Fisk faculty as an instructor in chemistry after completing his master's degree. In 1929–1930 there were only four graduate students in anthropology, chemistry, and English, but by 1931–1932 the number of graduate students had risen to twenty-four in biology, chemistry, education, English, physics, and sociology. By the next year education had become the largest department on campus. There were eleven students in education, eight in chemistry, seven in English, six in sociology, and one each in biology and physics. Graduate requirements at Fisk were similar to those in good white universities, and as long as the students were limited the school had adequate facilities and the properly trained professors for offering such work.[15]

Soon the Fisk graduate program began to grow rapidly, probably too quickly for a school of Fisk's size. During 1933–1934 there were 93 graduate students and the number increased to 208 in 1937–1938 and to 242 in 1940–1941. A majority of these students were school teachers and attended only in the summers. The regular enrollment did not go above

80, and most of these were in education and sociology. In December 1938, Dean Alrutheus Ambush Taylor announced that 570 students from eighty-seven different colleges, thirty-four states, and two foreign countries had done graduate work at Fisk. At the end of the year Fisk had awarded 117 master's degrees, 43 of them in education, 26 in English, 16 in sociology, 12 in chemistry, and less than 10 each in anthropology, biology, history, mathematics, and music. Not one student who received a degree had failed to receive approval of the outside examiner. Usually the visiting observers were pleasantly surprised. In 1939 Laurence Hadley, professor of mathematics at Purdue, sat in on the examination for two candidates for master's degrees in mathematics. His private judgment was that Miss Annetta Bernice Baugh showed thorough preparation and passed her comprehensive exams with distinction. Her thesis, "Algebra of Two by Two Matrices," was labeled a splendid piece of work. "I consider it to be among the best which I have seen written for the Master's degree," he said. Professor Hadley was pleased with James Enoch Parker's exams and his breadth of training and grasp of subject. Parker's thesis was "highly creditable." Both students had worked under Professor Clarence E. Van Horn. Other examiners made similar reports about other students.[16] Fisk's graduate program continued to prosper.

The improvements in faculty, salary, library, and other facilities which made graduate training possible also brought greater recognition to Fisk. Fisk had been recognized as a standard college for years. Although it had made no application for accredited relationship with departments of education in other states, a "large number" of Fisk graduates had been accepted "as full candidates" for advanced degrees by the best graduate schools in the nation. Then, in 1930 Fisk became the first black college to be accredited as class A by the Southern Association of Colleges and Secondary Schools. If this association had not been so reluctant to rate black schools Fisk probably would have received the A grading before 1930.

In 1931 the New York State Board of Regents approved the Fisk course leading to the B.A. degree. More impressive, the leading national educational accrediting association, the Association of American Universities, gave Fisk an A standing in 1933. According to the *New York Times,* this indicated that Fisk was doing work on a parity with the highest standards of the best American colleges. For several years Fisk was the only black college accredited by the Association of American Universities. The A rating by the AAU not only labeled Fisk as outstanding among black institutions but as a distinctive school in the South. Only about 16 percent of the white public institutions and around 14 percent of white private schools had been approved in the Southern states.[17]

Fisk was generally accepted as a leading black school. In 1926 the *New*

York Times referred to Fisk as the Negro's "foremost college." Later the *Times* said education at Fisk was not one "adjusted" to blacks, nor one provided "instead" of a good education at a white school. "It is an education of the highest type provided where the Negro is economically best able to avail himself of it, and where he can exert the most direct influence to raise the standards of other schools." Speaking to Fisk students on "Jubilee Day" in 1933, James Weldon Johnson said: "Fisk is today a great university. It is a leader among the schools that have made progress of the Negro in America possible. And we should understand that the progress that has been made would have been impossible without such schools as Fisk." Fisk had, he added, helped enable blacks to generate within their race a vital part of the motive power essential to progress. Edwin R. Embree, president of the Julius Rosenwald Fund, believed Fisk was doing the "finest quality of work in general education" for blacks. He considered Fisk the ideal small college-university regardless of color. By the 1930s Fisk could lay claim not only to being an outstanding college for blacks and a superior school for the South, but to being one of the better small private universities in the nation.[18]

The quality of Fisk students, according to some of the teachers, failed to improve as rapidly as the faculty and facilities. In 1928–1929 approximately 8 percent of the students were dropped for poor scholarship. Some veteran observers on campus believed that the fault lay not so much with student inability as with too much socializing. After the student revolt there were many more extracurricular activities. Students in their zeal to take advantage of the new freedom, some faculty believed, went too far. Still Fisk claimed a better grade of students than many black colleges. Its reputation guaranteed the school numerous outstanding pupils. Furthermore, the students were largely urban. Of the freshman class in 1929 about 54 perent came from cities of more than 100,000 population. Another 23 percent were from cities with populations of over 25,000. There was nothing particularly special about urban students except that better secondary schools were usually available in the larger towns. Since Fisk accepted only the upper two-thirds of the graduating high school class and a majority of the students came from the upper one-third, a "relatively sophisticated and intellectually able" group assembled on campus each year. Children of successful alumni went to the alma mater, which was in a way a selective process.[19]

Even though a majority of Fisk students were from urban areas their secondary schools were generally inferior to white schools. An investigating team from Columbia reported that standardized tests given freshmen showed that Fisk did not secure "an exceptionally able" group of students as compared with white colleges, even though it was high in comparison with other black schools. Still, Fisk freshmen in 1929, 1930, and 1931 made higher gross median scores on standardized tests given to 173 colleges under direction of the American Council on Education than did first-year students in such Southern white colleges as the universities of Georgia, South Carolina, and Alabama. Fisk students on an average scored about eights points higher than their counterparts at Alabama. The discrepancy was much greater between Fisk and some of the smaller white schools.[20] Standards at Fisk were continuously raised. In the 1930s a comprehensive final examination was added for all seniors. The purpose of the exam was to dignify scholarship in the student mind, to introduce students more effectively to the culture of the past, to assist them in securing a whole view of a subject and its relationship to allied fields, and to foster independent thought and effort. The exam was given for major and minor subjects. Preparation for the comprehensive exam consisted of passing regular courses and independent study and reading under guidance of the faculty. The passing grade on the final comprehensive was a "C".[21]

Although Fisk students were usually able there seemed to be a greater lethargy about affairs of the world than among former students. A few students like Lawrence Reddick and John Hope Franklin wrote some interesting and provocative articles for the *Fisk Herald* in the early 1930s, but a campus leader could legitimately lament that on one occasion twenty-five students could not be found to meet a similar number from Vanderbilt to attempt to improve racial understandings. The *Herald* complained that the vital issues of the day were neglected.

The attitude of a number of Fisk students about blacks was disappointing. In 1930 W. A. Robinson, principal of the Laboratory School, Atlanta University, gave an "attitude test" to 107 Fisk students. Many of them had attitudes distinctly unfavorable to their own racial group. They had absorbed a surprisingly large number of white stereotypes. Over 27 percent of the males examined and 7 percent of the women said blacks liked to show off more than other people; more than 22 percent of both sexes agreed that blacks never became insane from worry like other people because when they worried they went to sleep; a similar number of men thought blacks were the only people in the world who shouted and were noisy in church; 41.7 percent of the males and 61.6 percent of the females agreed that when facts were faced white people could hardly be blamed for not wanting blacks in their swimming pools; 60.9 percent of the women and 47.2 percent of the men believed Jim Crow streetcars seemed almost justified by the way black men came on cars smelly and dirty and insisted on sitting down by people; 80.6 percent of the men and 78.9 percent of the women concurred that blacks were worse about being late for meetings than other groups; almost 20 percent said it was "extremely difficult" for black Americans to overcome the handicap of "their savage African ancestry"; 29.6 percent of the women and 16.7 percent of the men were convinced that much of the South's poverty could be traced directly to the inborn laziness and unproductiveness of the majority of the black population; 70.4 percent of the women and 83.3 percent of the men believed that "Negroes with more sense than race pride" would go to white companies for insurance; and over 40 percent of the men stated that if a member of their family were seriously ill they could not be blamed for calling a white physician if they had a choice of either black or white.[22]

Though the attitudes of Fisk students were conditioned by many factors, including family background, economic conditions, and antiblack propaganda, Fisk University still had somehow failed its charges. No matter how large the endowment was, how many higher degrees were on the faculty, or how many books the faculty wrote, so long as that many students believed white propaganda, Fisk had failed. One of the most cruel aspects of segregation and racism was the consequent destruction of personality, absence of racial pride, and even lack of independent judgment among those attacked. In 1933 President Jones said Fisk had endeavored to find young men and women of promise and to lead them step by step to a realization of their abilities and opportunities, overcome their inhibitions and fears, increase their self-confidence, and develop those gifts which had already given blacks a unique place in music, art, and literature. The endeavors in 1930 were unsuccessful. No wonder Langston Hughes charged that many black colleges were producing "Uncle Toms, uninformed, and full of mental and moral evasions."[23] The removal of antiblack attitudes among their own students was as yet an unsolved problem of black colleges.

10

Depression and World War

THE DEPRESSION THAT SWEPT THE COUNTRY AFTER THE GREAT STOCK market crash of 1929 naturally affected education, especially Southern black schools. While a cut in expenditures impaired the educational program of most Southern white communities, any curtailment in numerous black colleges already operating on the brink of bankruptcy frequently resulted in depriving students of the "barest essentials" of education.[1] Although it suffered less than many other universities, Fisk too felt the consequences of a nationwide depression.

Fisk students experienced such a "very hard" summer in 1930 that some of them were unable to return in the fall. Enrollment dropped from 439 in 1930 to 317 in 1934. In December 1932, students owed the university over $7,000 in tuition for the first semester. Thirty pupils left school the same year for financial reasons. Of the 141 students who failed to return to Fisk between 1934 and 1936, approximately 40 gave financial difficulty as their reason and 31 others transferred to cheaper schools. Since Fisk was dependent on tuition for about 20 percent of its budget, the tuition fee was one of the highest in the country. Tuition in 1936 was $205.85 per semester. Laboratory, music, and gymnasium fees were not included. Two Columbia University investigators reported in 1936 that wealth was "much too high a selective factor" in determining the Fisk freshman class. Fisk students received some aid after the National Youth Administration was created by President Roosevelt in 1935 to give part-time jobs to needy young people. The NYA granted several thousand dollars to Fisk in the late 1930s, but it was insufficient.[2] Gifts for scholarships tended to lessen.

The decline in enrollment, tuition, and gifts necessitated a drastic reduction in operating expenses. Money expended for educational purposes shrank from $346,149.90 in 1930–1931 to $243,358.92 in 1933–1934. In 1931 all departmental budgets were lowered by 27.5 percent and the next year an additional 5 percent cut was made. Tradition and space yielded to the dictates of economics. In the fall of 1932 Bennett Hall, a dormitory for men, closed for the first time in Fisk history. In October 1932, the faculty voluntarily contributed 5 percent of their year's salary toward making up the anticipated loss of income from students. Those who were reluctant were subjected to considerable pressure. By mid-1933 most faculty had suffered a 15 percent reduction in pay. In order to live on their diminished salary many of them moved out of university housing for cheaper rent in the city, which in turn reduced Fisk income even more.[3] Even with the lower salaries many teachers used their personal funds to help students stay in school.

By 1933 the situation was becoming desperate for Fisk faculty and students. Beginning in February Nashville banks refused to honor Fisk salary checks, and then on March 6 President Roosevelt closed all banks. Grocery stores went on a cash-only basis. The school gave employees three dollars each to live on until banks opened. The situation was slightly eased when Nashville banks began to issue scrip on checking accounts. The scrip was acceptable only to the bank which made the issue, but it could be used to purchase necessary food. Although fear of deprivation was soon ended, Fisk faculty like millions of other Americans suffered for several more years.

By stringent curtailments in operating expenses and reduction in faculty salaries, Fisk balanced its budget in 1934. Money could be used only for absolute necessities. In early 1934 President Jones asked the treasurer if curtains could possibly be afforded for Jubilee Hall. Neighbors had complained about students disrobing before open windows. But in late 1935 young women in the hall were still hiding behind doors and in closets to avoid public exposure while dressing.[4]

It was during the depression that Fisk began seriously to consider a merger with Meharry Medical College, which was also in severe financial straits. There had long been considerable cooperation between the two schools. From time to time Meharry housed its books in the Fisk Library. Meharry professors examined and treated Fisk students and finally its campus had been moved just across the street from Fisk. Since many Fisk graduates had gone on to Meharry to become physicians there was a close relationship between the alumni of the two schools. To encourage greater cooperation Meharry and Fisk in the 1930s began to select four men who served on both boards of trustees. By 1940 the two colleges had joint libraries, student health services had been transferred to Meharry, and in 1942 the operation and maintenance of both campuses was placed in charge of H. H. Miller of Meharry who became general superintendent of building and grounds. Furthermore, there was an intercollege committee on discipline and recreation and joint use of the student union, Livingstone Hall, Jubilee Hall, dining rooms, tennis courts, a guest house, and other facilities. Some instructors taught at both schools. When a subcommittee from the two institutions met in 1943, there was no question about the efficacy of a merger, but there was disagreement as to how the unification should be accomplished. Fisk representatives wanted all Meharry property transferred to the Fisk board of trustees. Meharry wanted both schools to dissolve their charters and adopt a new one which would form the basis of a partnership. Inability to reach an agreement as to methods prevented the proposed merger from being achieved.[5]

Fisk officials who advocated a merger with Meharry were motivated by more than financial circumstances created by the depression. There were scores of black colleges competing for limited amounts of money from philanthropic foundations and for students. Other schools, including Atlanta University, Morehouse, and Spelman, which composed the Atlanta University Affiliation, had recognized the wisdom of unity. In 1936 when Fisk was concerned about a dwindling enrollment, seventeen Southern and border states and the District of Columbia graduated only about 13,000 blacks from high school annually. Approximately 900 blacks were graduated yearly in Tennessee. For the limited number of students who would go to college Fisk competed with 7 other institutions in the state and 110 in all the South. Even though Fisk and some of the other schools drew students from Northern communities, there was no need for more than a hundred colleges to service the small percentage of black high school graduates who would attend college. Moreover, Fisk did not occupy the privileged position of previous years. The school had not lost prestige—it was a much better school than in 1900 or 1910—but other colleges were improving. At one time Fisk was the only grade A accredited black school in the South. If it had competition it came from other private schools, but during the last two decades more state schools throughout the South had improved. They could charge less tuition because they were supported by public funds. Tuition at Fisk was almost twice as high as at other black colleges except Howard University. And undoubtedly expenses of education would rise. Fisk could exist without a merger with Meharry, but unification would relieve some of the financial difficulties for both schools and provide an attractive center for black higher education.[6]

Even without a Meharry partnership Fisk after the first few years of the depression continued to improve its financial standing. In January 1936, the General Education Board agreed that if Fisk would raise a minimum of $150,000 by 30 June 1937, it would thereafter match any contributions gained by the university up to $1,500,000. Mrs. Dwight W. Morrow made the first donation of $1,000 in memory of her late husband, who had been ambassador to Mexico. Fisk met the condition of the General Education Board and then in November 1937 the Julius Rosenwald Fund gave Fisk 5,000 shares of Sears, Roebuck, and Company stock valued at $335,000. Contributions to be matched by the General Education Board by this time totaled $850,000, of which $150,000 in pledges and cash had been given by Nashville citizens who once again recognized the value of Fisk to their community.[7]

By 1938 Fisk had an endowment of $2,447,412.94 and a physical plant valued at $1,589,302.97. A check of the annual budget revealed the school's tremendous financial growth. Expenditures at decade intervals were: 1909–1910, $61,487.14; 1919–1920, $117,641.54; 1929–1930, $221,000; 1939–1940, $405,998.37. Nevertheless, the school still relied on private gifts for over $100,000 annually for operating expenses, and one of its major sources vanished when Paul Cravath died in 1940. Cravath had made generous annual contributions and could always be depended upon when a few thousand dollars more were needed. He left $300,000 to Fisk to be paid upon the death of his wife. The money was to be used to erect a building in memory of his father, the first Fisk president. When Fisk received the money in 1953 the board of trustees decided to use it to endow professorships.[8]

Despite Fisk's success in augmenting its endowment it became increasingly obvious that the many black colleges could not continue to compete successfully for private gifts and foundation support to finance the swelling costs of education. In 1943 a group of college presidents were called together by Dr. F. D. Patterson, president of Tuskegee Institute, to discuss the possibility of establishing a cooperative fund-raising organization for accredited private black colleges. Benevolent associations had advocated some type of cooperation for years. In 1944 the United Negro College Fund was launched. Twenty-seven institutions including Fisk became members and five more joined the next year. The UNCF campaign to raise $1,500,000 was opened on 3 May 1944 by John D. Rockefeller, Jr. Each school sent representatives to specified areas to appeal for funds for the entire group. Only $765,000 was collected the first year, but in the next fifteen years approximately $20,000,000 was raised by the United Negro College Fund. Through the UNCF and private grants Fisk raised its endowment to $3,900,000 by 1946.[9]

The depression accelerated rather than retarded Fisk's aid to the community. The traditional policy of community service received new impetus under President Jones. In his view Fisk was a school that extended its services throughout life not only to its pupils. "As a liberal arts college of the highest type in a world of rapidly changing relationships," Jones said, "Fisk University bids its students discover truth, not alone in books, but also through moving, changing, ongoing human experiences in real community life." Services by faculty and students ranged from small to consequential. On Christmas Eve 1928, students, including the Jubilee Singers, went caroling to collect money for the purchase of a moving picture projector for the Bethlehem House for underprivileged. In the summer of 1930 Fisk faculty operated a program to train fifty black teachers of play and recreation for work in city parks. At the same time the library sent the "Book Tower," a list of new and useful books, to Fisk clubs throughout the country, especially in rural areas where such information was unavailable. The library also loaned needed books to alumni and offered a reference service.[10]

The university sponsored numerous training courses in Nashville. In

October 1927, a community training center was organized for religious workers. The school usually lasted twenty weeks with up to twelve course offerings. Ministers and laymen varying in number from 50 to 110 and of several denominations studied missions, problems of Christianity, and Sunday school organization in the annual institute. One year four of the students were presiding elders. The university expanded its usefulness when in the fall of 1937 the Fisk University Social Settlement was opened. The settlement, developed by Professor Charles S. Johnson, offered recreation and social activities, a People's College to provide practical education for adults, and a Children's Institute to furnish preschool education for underprivileged youngsters. The People's College offered courses in business, economics, history, civics, journalism, chorus work, current literature, dramatics, and advanced reading and arithmetic. Handicrafts and workshop classes were given and prenatal and baby clinics held. The settlement was staffed by five full-time and over thirty part-time workers. Part-time employees included a health officer, psychiatrist, psychologist, dentist, and a dietitian.

In 1946 an adult education program for "functionally illiterate" blacks in Nashville was inaugurated by Fisk and Tennessee A & I State College. The program was sponsored by the United States Office of Education, the American Association on Adult Education, and the National Conference on Adult Education. A functional illiterate was defined as a person aged twenty-five or over who had not completed the fifth grade. Dr. George N. Redd of the Fisk Department of Education said the program's purpose was "education for citizenship."[11]

Fisk did more than try to educate the local community. After a six-year fight, Nashville blacks were able to get a charter for a Boy Scout organization in late 1933. President Jones and Dr. St. Elmo Brady, professor of chemistry, led the agitation for such a charter. Jones also tried unsuccessfully in 1933 to alter the discrepancy in park space for whites and blacks. Although whites in Nashville, according to Jones, enjoyed 30, 170 acres of parks, the blacks were crowded onto 38.5 acres. John W. Work, Jr., founded the Agora, a club interested in all matters of civil concern to blacks. Several Fiskites, including Professor Thomas M. Brumfield and Dr. C. O. Hadley, have served as president of the organization.[12]

Of more far-reaching consequence were some of the studies about blacks made by the Fisk social science department. In 1928 Fisk and the Tennessee State Department of Public Health began a study of comparative death rates of Tennessee whites and blacks. After an examination of one million cases of morbidity and mortality among the two races, Dr. Elbridge Sibley published in 1930 *Differential Mortality in the State of Tennessee*, which tried to evaluate the influence of economics and educational factors on health conditions. The blacks' death rate was almost twice that of whites and the greatest difference occurred in late adolescence and early adulthood. Pneumonia, typhoid, pellagra, and tuberculosis were the greatest killers, with the latter claiming the largest number of victims.

Fisk, the state health department, and the Julius Rosenwald Fund began a study to discover the reason for the tuberculosis differential between the races. Fisk did not wait for results of the study to begin action. Recognizing education as one of the best means of effecting a change in health habits, Fisk, Meharry, and Tennessee A & I joined and formulated a plan to test the effectiveness of an educational program in correcting conditions responsible for the higher black mortality rate. A five-year health program was begun in three experimental schools. A later survey showed a large improvement in health habits of the children concerned. Fisk, also in cooperation with Meharry Medical College, engaged a professor to conduct courses at Fisk on prevention and control of disease for future teachers and professional people. Fisk employed an expert "to integrate" the findings of the social science department with the welfare programs of the state departments of social institutions and public health.[13] Such studies and programs could exert influence beyond the borders of Tennessee.

The Fisk social science department made several other useful surveys, including economic, social, and political problems of blacks. Studies of Southern sharecroppers helped form the basis of the federal government's resettlement program. These studies also resulted in better housing projects in several states. Authors and individual inquiries will be discussed in chapter 11.[14]

One outgrowth of the social science department's studies was a greater cooperation with local white colleges. With the growth of more rigid segregation in the 1920s interrelationships between Fisk and white universities had declined. Dr. Alva W. Taylor, professor of social ethics at the Vanderbilt School of Religion, almost lost his position in the early 1930s because he taught a class at Fisk and arranged for his Vanderbilt graduate students to join Fisk students in seminars on current questions. But in 1942 Fisk, Vanderbilt, Peabody, and Scarritt College jointly employed a professor and cooperated in sponsoring a Southern Rural Life Conference. A rural life program initiated by Fisk received the blessing and support of the other three schools. The object of Fisk's program was twofold. Since there was a dearth of effective leadership in rural communities, Fisk proposed to prepare qualified persons to assume leadership responsibilities. These leaders were to assist in the rehabilitation of both human and natural resources in the small black neighborhoods. Second, Fisk intended to use its resources and research findings to attack problems of social and educational reconstruction facing many of the communities.

To train rural leaders Fisk in 1943 set up a center at the Allen-White

School in Hardeman County, Tennessee. This center placed Fisk students in direct contact with the everyday life of a farming community. Each interested student spent six weeks in the center. While interning the student assumed responsibility, under supervision of the center director, for a community project. Some worked with community religious or social organizations and others planned and directed important school activities, took part in preparation, preservation, and production of food, cared for livestock, and built and maintained equipment for school and community use. The project was intended not only to train students, but to improve living conditions and to stimulate a spirit of self-help in the communities.[15]

An Urban Life Studies program was also instituted. It was an interdepartmental program emphasizing "racial adjustment" in education, in health and religion, and in economic and industrial problems. The urban program was operated in cooperation with the Julius Rosenwald Fund and the American Missionary Association.

Just as the Fisk faculty seemed to become more productive in response to the depression crisis, the students appeared to become more aggressive and increasingly concerned about national and world problems. Students were still dissatisfied with changes made after President McKenzie's resignation and they had not forgotten the influence exerted by the revolt and strike. In 1933 there was an attempt to call a student mass meeting to protest "wrongs," but it was prevented by the student council president. President Jones referred to the proposed meeting as a "tempest in a teapot," yet unrest was sufficiently widespread to cause concern. Mrs. Minnie L. Crosthwaite, member of the board of trustees, was asked to investigate. Her inquiries revealed considerable divergence of opinion. Students believed in some ways the pendulum had swung too far since the days of McKenzie and in others it had moved not at all. They complained of the inadequacy of student government, which leaned toward the fraternities and sororities of which government officials were members, they said. Interestingly enough, some students lamented the predominance of social over academic activities. They wanted greater recognition of scholastic attainment. The faculty must have been surprised at this charge against them.

Students wanted to know why three of the teachers whom they most admired resigned in one year, and they grumbled that faculty committees were tardy in answering their petitions. Furthermore, students charged that the *Fisk Herald* was so effectively censored that it was not really expressing students' ideas. A few students believed that Dean Alrutheus Ambush Taylor exerted too great an influence over President Jones, while others were fearful that Taylor would be replaced by a white dean. Other reasons for unrest were: dissatisfaction with the character of physical education for women, bathroom conditions in

Jubilee Hall, the closing of Bennett Hall, and—a not unusual complaint on college campuses—the need for closer faculty-student contact. Perhaps the latter accusation was the most valid of all since the primary problem seemed to be lack of adequate communication between students and the faculty and administration. In 1934 the *Baltimore Afro-American* claimed Fisk students were upset because of segregated facilities for the Fisk Choir while on tour and because of campus gossip about a black professor and a white woman. But unrest never closely approached the intensity of the previous revolt.[16]

Of more importance than the students' complaints about the administration was their revived concern with civil rights. A tragic lynching pointed up the need for their involvement. In late 1933 Cordie Cheek was seized just off the Fisk campus, taken to a spot between Glendale and Columbia, Tennessee, and murdered. Apparently a party-line telephone was used to inform citizens of Maury County of the time and place of the lynching. Law officers were accused of being deeply involved in the episode. Fisk officials formed a citizens committee, with Judge John R. Aust, a white Nashville trustee, as chairman, to try to bring the murderers to trial. Although the committee was unsuccessful the incident served to arouse Fisk students; the victim could well have been one of them. The Denmark Vesey Forum led Fisk students "as one body" in protest against the lynching. The *Crisis* accepted the protest as a sign that young blacks were breaking with tradition and exhibiting a new spirit.[17] When in late 1934 President Roosevelt visited the campus to hear the Fisk Choir sing one of his favorite spirituals—"Aint Gonna Study War No More"—he was handed a petition signed by 250 students protesting the Scottsboro case in Alabama, the lynching of Claude Neal at Marianna, Florida, and violence in general.[18]

The students' new spirit of protest provoked administrative actions which elicited charges of "Uncle Tomism" and "McKenzielike tyranny." The Fisk Singers under Mrs. James A. Myers were contracted to sing at a Jim Crow Nashville theater in early 1934, an agreement President Jones said was made by Mrs. Myers. When the program was advertised it created resentment on campus. Jones was in Washington but Dean Taylor called a faculty meeting and after due consideration canceled the engagement. On the next day, a group of students led by Ishmael Flory, a graduate student from California, arranged what was supposed to be a mass meeting. Only a few students came, but pictures were taken and Flory wrote a story for black newspapers. Flory claimed that Jones mysteriously left town after having arranged the affair, that a mass meeting of students had forced a cancellation, and that the same situation existed as when President McKenzie had been on campus. The indignant administration asked Flory to withdraw from school. A faculty committee reviewing the expulsion upheld it by a vote of 37 to 7.[19]

Naturally the incident created much interest. Flory claimed he had been expelled for daring to protest Jim Crowism. Even his advisor, Charles S. Johnson, had voted for his withdrawal, Flory complained. The *Crisis* in two separate articles denounced the Fisk administration for a "tyrannical display of authority" and for Uncle Tomism. The Denmark Vesey Forum circulated a petition demanding Flory's reinstatement. Norman Thomas, a recent Socialist candidate for president, telegraphed: "unthinkable for Fisk to support policy of Jim-Crowism." A telegram received from the Washington, D.C., chapter of the National Student League read: "we believe the expulsion of Ishmael P. Flory to be an act of Uncle Tom of the meanest variety. We protest the action of Fisk University. . . ." According to *Crisis* the whole student world, black and white, was shocked by Flory's dismissal. Jones, on the other hand, argued that such drastic action as expulsion was taken "not merely because of gross inaccuracies of statement and rather vicious misrepresentation" of the university in this one incident, but because of similar articles published on previous occasions. Jones thought Flory had violated "both his opportunity and trust" as a graduate student, therefore "we separated ourselves from him." Later the president seemed to show signs of panic when he told the board of trustees that excitement had been generated by the administration's discipline of "a young Communist" student. Many students supported President Jones on this issue. Both those who favored Jones and those who supported Flory appealed to the powerful New York Fisk Club, which had supported students in 1924–1925. The club appointed a committee to investigate.[20]

A faculty report to the board of trustees said that while some misunderstanding arose about "an alleged denial" of freedom of speech and a faculty Jim Crow attitude, students recognized the unfairness of charges and helped settle the matter. The attack against Jones occurred at about the same time the *Chicago Defender* denounced DuBois for making a speech in Chicago in which he contended segregation was not logical but intimated nothing was to be gained by fighting it. Flory was never reinstated and the incident was soon forgotten by most critics, but it was probably the beginning of criticism and distrust of Jones which reached a peak during World War II. Previous criticism had been limited primarily to the board of trustees. In 1933 Alumni Secretary Andrew J. Allison had told the Nashville Fisk Club that Jones was trying to undermine the general alumni association, cut off its budget, and operate the organization himself, but a personal conference between Jones and Allison ended the criticism.[21]

The Flory misunderstanding failed to dampen student spirit. Protests against lynching continued and membership in the NAACP rose. In 1937 Fisk students under leadership of the university minister, W. J. Faulkner, tried a new experiment in race relations. Thirteen students and Faulkner visited fourteen white Methodist churches in Nashville.

Fisk representatives spoke and then entertained questions from the congregation. All students who participated thought the experience had been rewarding. The program faltered quickly, but it was at least an attempt to improve race relations.

An editorial in 1937 proved that the *Fisk Herald* had not lost its zeal for a battle. The *Herald* denounced Germany for persecuting Jews and expressed pleasure that the victims could find refuge in the United States. But, the editorial added, "While America may offer haven to the Reichland's expelled Jews, she cannot sincerely condemn the Reichland for that which stains her own hands. *Clean out your own back yard neighbor.*" The much maligned board of trustees indirectly placed its stamp of approval upon the policy of protest when in 1938 it voted to award DuBois an honorary Doctor of Literature degree.[22]

Student discipline problems during the 1930s were not serious. In 1934 a gambling ring was discovered by Coach Henderson A. Johnson on the fourth floor of Livingstone Hall. In March 1935, President Jones said there were a few cases for discipline as was usual in the spring. There was some minor grumbling about regulations. Certain restaurants were off limits to all Fisk students, including those that sold alcoholic beverages, those with a dance floor "adjacent thereto under the same roof," any that furnished private tables and doors that could be locked as entrances to private dining rooms, any with a rear entrance, those with booths inadequately lighted, and those with "private passages to property with an unsavory reputation."[23]

The composition of the student body changed during the depression years. A larger number of Northern young people began attending Fisk. The increasing percentage of Northern students was in part because of their greater ability to pay Fisk's high tuition fee and in part because of Fisk's spreading reputation. Fisk's already enviable image was enhanced during the 1930s by the growing amount of scholarly activity at the school. The number of students from the north-central and north Atlantic states increased from only 15.9 percent in 1929 to more than 42 percent in 1943. There was a corresponding tightening of standards. In 1936 Fisk began to accept only the upper one-third of high school graduating classes. In that same year at least 40 percent of the students' parents had received collegiate training, which gave Fisk a somewhat unusual student body.[24]

During the depression crisis Fisk faltered momentarily. Enrollment declined and salaries were reduced, but within a few years Fisk was making renewed progress. The endowment was virtually doubled, community service was increased, and a constant flow of scholarship came from the school. After a low in 1934 enrollment began to rise slowly and standards were continually raised. Despite serious obstacles the depression decade was one of the most productive in Fisk history.

World War II probably had a more adverse effect on Fisk than the depression, largely because of administrative instability. In late 1940 President Jones sent his resignation to the board of trustees, to be effective as soon as possible after 1 January 1941. It was time for new leadership at Fisk, Jones said. A money campaign had floundered, thus necessitating retrenchment. Since there were no funds to employ additional personnel, the teaching and administrative duties of the faculty had to be increased. Jones thought a new president might infuse new life into the university. A more pressing reason for his resignation, though, was Jones's desire to become director of the Civilian Public Service, American Friends Service Committee. The objective of the Civilian Public Service was to organize conscientious objectors on a basis constructive to the nation. Being a conscientious objector himself, Jones believed he could not refuse the position. Rather than accepting his resignation, the board of trustees gave President Jones a leave of absence for 1941.[25] Throughout the war the president spent several months each year away from campus. The burden of administration fell primarily upon Dean Taylor.

Jones's decision to become head of the Civilian Public Service created problems with both the faculty and alumni. A group of teachers formed a "Teachers Association" or "Teachers Union" on campus to protect their interests. Though the organization had no recognition or authorization from the administration or board of trustees, its members were dissatisfied with the administration in Jones's absence and corresponded frequently with the board.[26] The "unfavorable conditions" on campus came to the attention of alumni. Realizing that it was a critical time in the history of the world and Fisk they formed in 1941 a "Special Alumni Committee on the Present and Future Status of Fisk." After investigation and consultation, the committee made a number of recommendations to the board. First, the alumni said, Fisk needed a president constantly at the helm. Jones had been an effective president, the committee added, and it regretted that he felt his pacifist views might be against the best interest of the institution. The alumni believed Jones could be loyal to his own convictions about war and still permit the institution to function as an integral part of the nation's defense. But they wanted a decision. If he could not do it, then a new president was needed. The absence of leadership had already manifested itself, the committee added, in pressure groups among the faculty. If a new president were elected the committee suggested that sympathetic consideration be given to a black man. They remembered "too keenly and regretfully, the unfounded assumption" of friends that the appointment of a black to the presidency of Fisk would be a mistake. It might be well for the board of trustees to know, wrote the committee, that no one factor was more disturbing to blacks than the policy so often pursued of deciding their destiny without regard to their opinions or wishes. At the same time the committee expressed a desire to maintain a "broad interracial outlook" at Fisk.

In a final paragraph the committee returned to the weighty matter of participation in the national defense program. All Americans had a vital stake in the emergencies of the hour and sustained patriotism and morale were important factors. The apparent lack of concern of the administration over this matter and the reluctance of the school in making possible student participation in the emergency was having a stultifying effect on them. Some initiative by the trustees to "get Fisk into the stream of things" was essential because there was no such initiative at the school. The alumni hoped the trustees would see the question of Fisk's cooperation in the national defense effort "in its true perspective and not from any moral conviction as to their duty in opposing preparedness." The board of trustees made a statement advocating preparedness while President Jones promised that he would attempt to return to campus more frequently than he had in the previous few months.[27]

Despite the president's views, Fisk supported preparedness and, later, the war effort. Months before Pearl Harbor, alumni statements in the *Fisk News* announced that blacks would do their part. There was no hysteria, but neither was there any question about the stand of a majority of Fiskites. When the war began, the faculty organized to do what it could. Professor St. Elmo Brady was in charge of civilian defense and blackouts. Almuni Secretary Allison supervised the sale of war bonds and stamps. W. J. Faulkner was placed in charge of service to soldiers. As a part of the Fisk war effort the Jubilee Singers entertained at army camps under the auspices of the USO. Numerous Fisk students dropped out of school and volunteered for the armed forces. President Jones may have been a Quaker conscientious objector, but Fisk was far from a pacifist institution.[28]

The number of Fiskites who served in the armed forces and died for their country during World War II is difficult to determine, but their record was commendable. At least sixty served as officers. Albert H. Dyson, Jr., became a lieutenant colonel in the army, and during his four years of service he won the Bronze Star, American Service Medal, Philippine Liberation Medal, and the Asiatic Service Medal. Paul S. Binford was promoted to major in the Ninth Cavalry Regiment. The following attained the rank of captain: William S. Banks, Jr., Lyman D. Brown, James A. McLendon, Robert M. Hendricks, Jr., Clarence W. Griggs, George Levi Knox, Wilbur Martin, and Irma Clayton Wertz. Banks, who was promoted to captain in October 1943, was the first black to gain that rank in the Ninty-Second Infantry Division. When Knox became captain in 1944 he was the third-highest ranking black officer in the Army Air Force. Captain Griggs, a chaplain, was killed in action on 12 April 1945, on Okinawa.

Captain Wertz was one of several Fisk women who became officers. After graduating from Fisk, she had studied at the Atlanta School of

Social Work, the Chicago Academy of Fine Arts, and the Bryant-Stratton Business College in Chicago. Before entering the service, Captain Wertz was assistant director of Parkway Community House in Chicago. She was in the first training class to graduate from the Women's Army Corps training center at Fort Des Moines, Iowa. Another fifty (probably more) Fiskites served as first and second lieutenants. Over two hundred others were known to have served in the lower ranks. Sergeant Lawrence M. Hayes, as director and arranger, was in charge of what was believed to be the largest black Marine band in the Pacific. Numerous Fisk alumni and students who were not in the military served abroad and at home in the Red Cross. No doubt the exploits of many other Fiskites who fought valiantly are unrecorded. The Fisk contribution was recognized when in April 1945, the S.S. *Fisk Victory* was launched at Richmond, California.[29]

Meanwhile, the Fisk campus was the scene of increased activity. While some institutions appeared to wither away under war conditions, Fisk experienced its biggest years ever. Total enrollment in the fall of 1944 was 653, the largest in Fisk history. Enrollment would have been greater had facilities accommodated more students.

Honors continued to come to the school. In 1945 it was granted a charter to establish a chapter of Alpha Kappa Delta, an honorary sociological fraternity. Fisk was the first black college to be awarded such a charter. Students too were receiving distinction. In 1945 over 100 black and white students from fifty colleges and universities from thirteen Southern states met in conference at the University of North Carolina. Their aim was to defend the ideals of human justice, freedom, and democratic action. Charles D. Proctor of Fisk was elected president of the conference.[30]

Although enrollment rose, honors were won, and the faculty continued to produce scholarly material, all was not well at Fisk. The alumni were concerned when President Jones refused to recommend Professor St. Elmo Brady for tenure. Jones contended that Brady was uncooperative and that he spread misunderstanding and discontent among the alumni. Brady thought the president was persecuting him. Some alumni believed Brady was not recommended for tenure because he was black, even though other blacks had been granted tenure. Jones and Brady temporarily settled their differences, but some alumni were still dissatisfied. Moreover, irritation arose again between alumni members and white Nashville members of the board of trustees. White trustees had on occasion boycotted the trustees' meetings in Nashville and some of them seemed to have little respect for blacks. Blacks, on the other hand, often did not trust the Southern white members on the board. This mutual distrust did not mean that all white Nashville trustees lacked faith in blacks. It was far from true and many of them, such as Bernard Fensterwald and Lee J. Loventhal, gave generously of their time and money to Fisk.[31]

Alumni discontent in 1945 led the general alumni association to propose "a fair, impartial and thorough inquiry into the state of the university." "Diffuse, undocumented and disturbing" rumors were circulated about life at Fisk, the alumni association said, and "feelings of unrest and discontent" were felt by faculty and students. Knowledge of such conditions had spread over the country, it added. The general alumni association recommended a survey by a commission of recognized experts, sponsored jointly by the board of trustees and itself. The board agreed, but before a survey could be completed Fisk was under a new administration. In 1945, after twenty years at Fisk, President Jones resigned, effective 1 July 1946, to become head of his alma mater, Earlham College in Indiana.[32]

Jones could be proud of his achievements at Fisk. During his administration the university measurably raised its standards, increased its facilities through the construction of the chemistry building and the library, and made substantial strides in raising an endowment. Student enrollment had doubled and more Northern youth began to travel south to study at Fisk. He had improved the library and had assembled an interracial faculty whose scholarly contributions were envied by much larger and wealthier schools. It was under Jones's administration that Fisk became the first black institution to acquire a class A rating by the Southern Association of Colleges and Secondary Schools and the first black college to be placed on the approved list of the Association of American Universities. Finally, President Jones played a role in making Nashville a national center by attracting scholars to the university from all parts of the country to participate in Fisk's conferences, festivals, and institutes.[33]

When President Jones left Fisk in June 1946, administrative responsibilities were placed in the hands of a committee of three men: Dean Alrutheus Taylor; Isiah T. Creswell, controller; and William Hume, chairman of the Nashville Board of Education. Meanwhile, the board of trustees began a systematic search for a man of stature for president. It was unnecessary to look far. In October 1946, the board announced the appointment of Fisk's first black president, Professor Charles S. Johnson.

There had been some agitation among Fiskites for a black executive, but in selecting Johnson the board was inspired by his capabilities not his race. Johnson was eminently qualified for the position. When he became president, the internationally recognized scholar had written seventeen books, chapters in fourteen others, seventy-two articles, numerous book reviews, and had served as editor of three magazines. Having recently returned from Japan as one of the educators summoned to make recommendations for the reeducation of the Japanese, Johnson was scheduled for a November trip to Paris as a United States delegate to the United Nations Educational, Scientific, and Cultural Organization. There was no question about his reputation as a scholar and educator.

Moreover, he had received substantial administrative experience as director of the Race Relations Institute and as chairman of Fisk's social science department.[34]

Johnson was a famous man of extraordinary talent, but Fisk was worthy of him. It compared favorably with white educational institutions of university grade. The *New York Herald Tribune* claimed in 1947 that Fisk was "one of America's major institutions of learning. Its high academic standards and elevated cultural tone, as well as its seniority, have long justified its familiar appellation, 'the Negro Harvard.'" The school had an endowment of around four million dollars and an enrollment of almost one thousand of the better black students in the country. Yet it had problems—a limited plant—and the unfavorable position which most private institutions occupied with respect to income as compared with tax-supported schools.[35] Maintenance of Fisk's standing in the educational world would challenge the genius of Johnson.

11

Fisk as a Center
of Scholarship and Culture

A 1932 UNITED STATES OFFICE OF EDUCATION STUDY DEPLORED THE LACK of research and publication in black colleges.[1] Too heavy teaching loads, too many supplementary duties, lack of funds, poor salaries, library deficiencies, and absence of encouragement and incentives were reasons for the black scholars' small yield. By 1930, there was little that could be considered as serious effort at research and experimentation in black schools other than Fisk and Howard. A 1937 study of black institutions showed that only Fisk had undertaken several investigations of more than local importance. Fisk had been of great service, said the report, in the fields of racial, social, economic, and business problems. It was a center of social and economic research. Edwin R. Embree, president of the Rosenwald Fund, thought in 1931 that Fisk was probably the finest black college in the land. Its scholarly ideals were being realized, he said, largely because it had the "pick of the country" for its faculty and student body.[2]

There had been a few publications in the early years at Fisk, but it was not until Jones's administration that scholarly work became outstanding. Under Jones came the trend toward research professorships, publication, and graduate studies. During the five years preceding 1933 more than a dozen volumes in sociology, anthropology, economics, health, literature, philosophy, and religion were published at Fisk. At this time less work was being done in the sciences, though Professor St. Elmo Brady was a recognized authority on alkaloids, and the physics department was attempting to describe the curve of molecular motion in certain diatomic gases. In 1935–1936 the Fisk faculty published two books, three songs, and sixteen articles. Four years later thirty-nine books, six songs, and eighty-six articles had been written by Fisk teachers in a little over five years. The school was doing research on a larger scale than any other black college. The output of scholarly work decreased little, if any, during the war. In 1945 over ten songs, four books, forty articles, fifty-two newspaper columns, and more than one hundred book reviews were written by Fisk teachers.[3]

It does not detract from important contributions made by several individuals on campus to say that some of the most influential research at Fisk was done by the social science department under Charles S. Johnson's leadership. Born in Bristol, Virginia, on 24 July 1893,

Johnson attended Wayland Academy, which was then part of Richmond's Virginia Union University. He completed the academy course and graduated from Virginia Union in 1916. While in school he worked to support himself, sang in a quartet, participated with the debate team, served as president of the student council, and acted as editor-in-chief of the college journal. Johnson did further work at the University of Chicago, where he received a Ph.B in 1917. While at Chicago he assumed responsibility as director of research and investigation for the Chicago Urban League. In 1918 he enlisted in the army, where as regimental sergeant major in the 803rd Pioneer Infantry Regiment he took part in the Meuse-Argonne offensive.

Johnson returned to Chicago a week before the tragic race riot of 1919 and later presented a plan to study causes of the riot. Acceptance of his plan resulted in Johnson's appointment as associate executive secretary of Chicago's Commission on Race Relations, a postriot creation of the Illinois governor. The commission's investigation was published as *The Negro in Chicago*. In 1921 Johnson became director of research for the National Urban League with headquarters in New York. As director he founded the periodical, *Opportunity: a Journal of Negro Life*, which he edited until 1928. Unlike *Crisis*, it emphasized black opportunities rather than grievances. Its objective was to stimulate pride in past racial achievements and to show there was hope for the future. Articles in *Opportunity* covered topics ranging from musicians, actors, artists, poets, city life, home, school, recreation, and health. Under Johnson's editorship the magazine attained a high degree of excellence.[4]

When in 1927 the Laura Spelman Rockefeller Memorial made possible the establishment of a department of social research at Fisk, Johnson seemed a logical choice to be its head. The department's purpose was to make original studies of folklore, music, and psychology and to train black research workers for education and social-service positions. With the greatest reluctance, the National Urban League released Johnson in the fall of 1928 when he joined Fisk University's faculty. Within a short time Johnson had created a first-class Department of Social Science that was bringing in large grants from foundations. The rest of his adult life was devoted to explaining blacks to whites and whites to blacks. Moreover, he sought to make Southerners and Northerners and city and country people understand one another. Johnson's scholarship was never tainted by emotionalism as he surveyed the glaring paradox of blacks in American democracy. He searched for a common ground of understanding between races that would cure the inconsistency. The universal recognition he won for his work indicated that at many points the paradox he assailed could be surmounted.[5]

Professor Howard Odum, noted sociologist from the University of North Carolina at Chapel Hill, once stated, "In a studied manner I say

CHARLES S. JOHNSON (*Courtesy of the Fisk University Library's Special Collections*)

that there is no more able sociologist in America today than Charles S. Johnson." On another occasion Odum said Johnson's research had been appraised as making a major contribution to the "whole field and method of social science in the United States." In 1945 when Professor Edgar T. Thompson of Duke University was lamenting the absence of new ideas among Southern sociologists he excepted Fisk and the University of North Carolina. In those two places, Thompson claimed, "a genuine spirit of scientific research in sociology" could be seen in action. Results produced by Fisk and North Carolina were "distinguished throughout the whole sociological fraternity," he added. Thompson thought the contrast between the character of the two universities' studies was striking—North Carolina was interested primarily in the South while Fisk studies ranged the world—but in both "one felt the presence of enthusiasm and life." Although Fisk sociologists studied Southern life they were more interested than most meridional sociologists in the "comparative use of nonsouthern experience in the analysis of Southern society." Fisk investigations were not confined to "southern horizons or to southern historical levels," stated Thompson, but "they seek to wrench analysis clear of the particularistic assumptions of a single culture and to put the phenomena of southern life in a wider context of relationship and meaning." Especially were Fisk sociologists concerned with making a contribution to the comparative study of race relations. Gunnar Myrdal, the Swedish sociologist who directed the research resulting in the monumental *American Dilemma,* was "full of enthusiasm" about Johnson and the Fisk Department of Social Science. In *Negro Status and Race Relations in the United States 1911–1946,* published by the Phelps-Stokes Fund, it was stated that "among Negroes none has made a more important contribution" toward "Negro progress" than Professor Johnson.[6]

Johnson's ability was recognized by awards and appointments. In 1930 he won the William E. Harmon Gold Medal for distinguished achievement among blacks in the field of science. In the same year he was appointed the American member of an international commission to study alleged enforced labor and slavery conditions in Liberia. Johnson served on President Hoover's Housing Commission and on the Committee on Farm Tenancy under President Roosevelt. In 1933 he founded and acted as codirector of the Institute of Race Relations at Swarthmore College. Johnson was elected the first black trustee of the Julius Rosenwald Fund in 1934. He received the most distinctive honor accorded a black man in scientific meetings when in 1937 the American Sociological Society elected him as vice-president. Johnson was honored in 1940 by being the first black invited to speak to a statewide meeting of Missouri social workers. Honors continued to be heaped upon him throughout his life.[7]

Although Johnson was the guiding genius of Fisk's social science department, he was by no means the only able member. Much of research was cooperative and several books credited to Johnson were partially done by other members of the department. Men such as E. Franklin Frazier, Bertram W. Doyle, Horace Mann Bond, and Paul K. Edwards were able scholars. When Professor Robert E. Park, eminent sociologist from the University of Chicago and a pioneer in the study of race relations, retired in 1935 he became a visiting professor at Fisk until his death in 1944. The present social science building at Fisk is named in honor of Park and Johnson.

The social science department's ability was demonstrated by their activity in professional meetings. At the American Sociological Society meeting in 1933 Johnson read two papers and Frazier and Harry Walker each read one. During the same meeting Johnson gave still another paper to the Conference on a Scientific Approach to Race Relations. The department published twenty-three books between 1928 and 1940 that were destined to have considerable impact. A sample of the titles follows: *The Negro in American Civilization, Shadow of the Plantation, The Collapse of Cotton Tenancy: Summary of Field Studies and Statistical Survey, 1933–1935,* and *A Preface to Racial Understanding* by Johnson; *The Negro Family in Chicago* and *The Free Negro Family* by E. Franklin Frazier; *The Education of the Negro in the American Social Order* by Horace Mann Bond; *The Southern Urban Negro as a Consumer* by Paul K. Edwards; *The Etiquette of Race Relations in the South* by Bertram W. Doyle; and a translated *History of Ancient Mexico* by Fanny R. Bandelier. Books such as *Shadow of the Plantation, The Free Negro Family,* and the volumes by Bond and Edwards gave the federal government a better understanding of black problems. Fisk reputedly exerted appreciable influence on New Deal legislation affecting the South. As an example of the power exercised by the department, some merchandizing companies began to employ black salesmen after Edwards's *The Southern Urban Negro as a Consumer* apprised them of the value of blacks in the marketplace. As an experiment, the Rumford Baking Powder Company engaged two Fisk graduates who quickly demonstrated the efficiency of black sales personnel.[8]

Under Johnson's leadership Fisk became a center for research and field investigation in the entire area of race relations. Fisk expanded its program in 1944 when the university and the American Missionary Association inaugurated the annual Institute of Race Relations. Since Fiskites faced unusual strains arising from the incomplete attainment of democratic ideals, the school had long sought to kindle well-informed, objective discussion and thought on human relations. In the view of Fisk officials, adjustment of social conflicts was the only hope of survival for a decent human civilization. The American Missionary Association was also concerned with race relations, and Fisk and Charles S. Johnson seemed to be reasonable choices for the location and the director for an institute.

The first annual institute drew 137 black and white community leaders for three weeks of study of current problems. An intensive course was given in race and culture and in problems and methods of realistically dealing with the racial situation. Institute participants discussed prejudice and discrimination of all kinds and concerning all races. It was designed for educators, social and religious workers, labor and civic group leaders, journalists, youth leaders, government employees, members and staff workers of interracial committees, and other interested persons.

Over the years a distinguished group from all fields of endeavor constituted the institute's leadership. Among those who participated in the institute at various times were: Brooks Hays, Arkansas congressman; Kenesaw Mountain Landis, lawyer, columnist, and first baseball commissioner; Thurgood Marshall, special counsel for the NAACP and later U.S. Supreme Court justice; Henry Steele Commager, noted historian of Columbia University; James P. Mitchell, U.S. secretary of labor; Countee Cullen, black author; Kenneth Little, from the London School of Economics; and numerous professors and community leaders. Within a few years over 1,000 community officials had attended the institute. A *Christian Science Monitor* reporter who attended in 1950 said the mood there would not comfort enemies of democracy. Social change in the face of complexities was not being pushed to the point of explosion, but the men and women deeply felt the shame of discrimination and second-class citizenship imposed upon them. Still, he stated, they were intensely loyal citizens. The reporter believed the Institute of Race Relations was making itself felt around the country. People were learning how to deal with the problem and how to negotiate changes. When Johnson retired as director of the institute he was succeeded by Dr. Herman H. Long, one of the South's chief authorities on racial tensions.[9]

Johnson and a few members of the social science department did not do all the research and publishing at Fisk. Fisk was a small school, but a large percentage of its faculty was productive. It would be useless to catalog all of the Fisk faculty publications, but a few of them can be mentioned. In addition to his administrative duties Dean Alrutheus A. Taylor wrote his third book about Reconstruction, *The Negro in Tennessee, 1865–1880. The Negro in South Carolina during Reconstruction* and *The Negro in the Reconstruction of Virginia* had been published before he joined the Fisk faculty. Most historians of the post–Civil War period had either ignored blacks or pictured them as ignorant, uncivilized, and corrupt. Taylor attempted to show the true role and life of blacks after the war. Professor Theodore S. Currier contributed a monograph, *Los Corsarios del Rio de la Plata.* Fisk also made a contribution to the knowledge of slavery when its scholars conducted interviews with a number of former slaves.

Preston Valien, who succeeded Johnson as chairman of the social science department, between 1941 and 1951 wrote these books: *A Research Brief on Negro Migration; Low Income Housing Areas of Nashville, Tennessee; Juvenile Delinquency in Nashville and Davidson County; A Background Study of Family Life in Tennessee with Special Reference to the Welfare of Children;* plus numerous articles. Lyman V. Cady, professor of religion, published *Liberal Theology, An Appraisal; Wang Yang-Mings Intuitive Philosophy;* and *Biblical Basis of Christian Ethics.* Beryl Parker, lecturer in education, wrote *New Education in the German Republic* and *Austrian Educational Institutes.*

In the late 1940s a group of new faculty members, including George N. Redd in the department of education, began publishing. Between 1946 and 1950 Redd and S. O. Roberts published nearly a score of articles, most of them concerning black education. More work also was done in the sciences, starting in the late 1940s by such people as Nelson Fuson, Elihu Fein, Harry T. Folger, Lee Lorch, N. W. Riser, and Marie-Louise Josien.

Not only did the Fisk faculty publish, but after World War II scholars from other schools began to travel to Fisk to do research, especially in the black history and Fiskiana Collections. Fisk has a large number of fine manuscript collections including the Mary E. Spence Papers, George E. Haynes Letters, Charles S. Johnson Papers, and the Charles Waddell Chesnutt Collection.

Fisk also had some fiction writers. The best known such writer in the 1930s was James Weldon Johnson, author, poet, educator, public servant, composer of popular songs, diplomat, lawyer, scholar, and crusader for black rights. Johnson was born in Jacksonville, Florida, on 17 June 1871. After attending the local public schools he went to Atlanta University where he was graduated in 1894. He later studied at Columbia, became principal of the Stanton Central Grammar School in Jacksonville, and read law. In 1901 Johnson stopped teaching school to work in New York City with his brother J. Rosamond, who had completed a course in the Boston Conservatory of Music. Together they produced light opera, the words written by James and the music by his brother. They also wrote special songs for such stars as May Irwin, Anna Held, Lillian Russell, Bert Williams, George Primrose, and Fay Templeton. Some of their songs were "I've Got Troubles of My Own," "Since You Went Away," "Louisiana Lize," "The Maiden with the Dreamy Eyes," "The Maid of Timbuctoo," "Oh! Didn't He Ramble," and "Congo Love Song." The latter, written for Fay Templeton, brought $13,000 in royalties.[10]

In 1906 President Theodore Roosevelt appointed James Weldon Johnson as United States consul at Puerto Cabello, Venezuela. He later served in the same capacity at Corinto, Nicaragua, where in the midst of various revolutions delicate and difficult tasks were entrusted to him. Once during a tense situation a detachment of the United States fleet was placed at his disposal. Johnson left government employ when Woodrow Wilson became president and refused to approve his promotion to a position in the Azores. In 1914 he joined the NAACP staff and worked with the organization for several years while continuing his own writing. His publication of *Fifty Years and Other Poems* in 1917 made him "something of an advance herald" of the Harlem Renaissance. "As a precursor, participant and historian of the Renaissance," John Hope Franklin said, no one man had as much influence as Johnson on the rise of the new literary movement among blacks.[11]

Johnson resigned as secretary of the NAACP in 1931 to accept the newly created Adam K. Spence Chair of Creative Literature and Writing at Fisk. Commenting upon his decision to go to Fisk, Johnson said, "I feel that on this favorable ground I shall be able to help effectively in developing additional racial strength and fitness and in shaping fresh forces against bigotry and racial wrong." Johnson and his wife, the gracious Grace Nail Johnson, were delightful additions to the Fisk campus. Johnson was as successful in teaching as in everything else he had undertaken. His duty was to guide students who were ambitious to be writers and gave evidence of talent. He had entire freedom to organize and carry on the work as he pleased. Frequently students met in the Johnson home for spirited discussions of literature and blacks' role in America. In his autobiography, *Along This Way*, Johnson said he was "almost amused" at the eagerness with which he met his classes. "The pleasure of talking to them about the things that I have learned and the things that I thought out for myself is supreme," he stated, "and there is no less pleasure in drawing from them the things that they have learned and the things they have thought out for themselves." A Vanderbilt scholar who visited one of his classes told Fisk President Jones he was "much moved" by Johnson's extraordinary ability and perception. Fisk was indeed fortunate in having a man of such caliber, he added. George Foster Peabody wrote to congratulate "Fisk and our whole country" for adding Johnson to the faculty.[12]

Johnson continued his writing at Fisk. Among his works were *Along This Way; God's Trombones; The Book of American Negro Spirituals; Black Manhattan; The Autobiography of an Ex-Colored Man; St. Peter Relates an Incident; Negro Americans, What Now?; English Libretto of the Grand Opera; Goyescas, Self-Determining Haiti;* and *Native African Races and Culture.* For his work he won the Harmon Award in Literature, the Spingarn Medal for outstanding achievement, and was the first recipient (for *Black Manhattan*) of the W. E. B. DuBois prize of $1,000 for black literature.

Johnson was also noted for his poetry. One critic said *God's Trombones*, a book of blacks' sermons in verse, was one of the finest things yet accomplished by a black poet. "The Creation" and "O Black and Unknown Bards" compared favorably with the best poetry produced in

America, the critic added. Professor Charles S. Johnson regarded James Weldon Johnson as "the first Negro to provide an objective and detached appraisal of the internal workings of the Negro mind, under the stress and frustration of his racial status in America." Johnson's most significant discoveries, he added, "were of those positive and creative values that lay unrecognized in this human reservoir, and of the need for Negroes themselves to exercise their own internal resources and power to complete their emancipation, in order that they might live and move with confidence in the society of American citizens." To this end James Weldon Johnson directed all his energies and his many skills.[13]

Johnson was a popular lecturer. Between 9 and 14 April 1933, he was a guest lecturer four times at Swarthmore, twice each at Bryn Mawr, Haverford, Temple, the University of Pennsylvania, and Princeton. In November and December he went on a lecture tour through Illinois, Indiana, and Wisconsin. Beginning in 1934, Johnson spent the fall quarter of every year as visiting lecturer of creative literature at New York University. At NYU he organized a new course through which he interpreted the black contribution to American culture.

Johnson's reputation did not gain him special consideration from Tennessee whites. Once, Poppy Cannon (later Mrs. Walter White) and another white woman visited the Johnsons. After a pleasant evening Johnson took them back to the hotel. Over his protest they rode with him in the front seat. He stopped in the shadows, outside the beam of light from the hotel entrance. When they put out their hands to shake his, he cut short their thanks and returned to the car. The women wondered what was wrong. The next morning they realized he was trying to protect them. An early call from the management rudely asked them to vacate the hotel. Someone had seen them ride home with a black man. This was just one example of the type of humiliation suffered by most black members of the Fisk faculty at one time or other.

On another occasion Johnson was attacked in a speech reported in a Knoxville newspaper. He was vice-president of an international club formed by students and faculty of Fisk, Scarritt, and Vanderbilt. The president was a white woman from Scarritt. Frederick W. Millspaugh, in a speech in February 1932, denounced what he called an international club composed of white women and black men. Johnson was, he charged, "known to be a member of a free love cult, and the American Civil Liberties Union, an organization akin to the Communistic group and decidedly Red." The club sometimes discussed sex, Millspaugh said, and added: "I can't conceive of the decency of discussion of those subjects between a young lady studying to be a missionary and a buck Negro from Fisk University. . . ." Fortunately Johnson had a philosophy which helped protect his sensibilities from ridiculous attacks. Johnson said he endeavored to live by the following pledge for the greater part of his life:

"I will not allow one prejudiced person or one million or one hundred million to blight my life. I will not let prejudice or any of its attendant humiliations and injustices bear me down to spiritual defeat. My inner life is mine, and I shall defend and maintain its integrity against all the powers of hell."[14]

Johnson's career was ended in 1938 when a train struck his car near Wiscasset, Maine. He was instantly killed and Mrs. Johnson was badly injured. Arthur D. Spingarn said of him after his death: "To few men is it given to live a fuller or more useful life. In each of the fields he entered he performed distinguished service and in some of them he rose to unique heights. Everything that he did during his entire life was not only a personal achievement, but directly and consciously enured to the benefit of the American Negro." It was fitting that in 1944 the United States launched a liberty ship, the S.S. *James Weldon Johnson.*[15]

Another Fisk writer of note was Arna Bontemps, who became director of the library soon after Johnson's death. Born in Alexandria, Louisiana, Bontemps was moved to California as a small boy. There he attended public and private schools and received his first college degree in 1923. Bontemps early achieved writing success. In 1926 he won *Opportunity*'s Alexander Pushkin Award for poetry with "Golgotha is a Mountain." The poem was later set to music by John W. Work. In 1927 Bontemps received the same award for "Nocturne at Bethesda." He soon moved to New York City and became one of the most productive members of the "Negro Renaissance." His first novel, *God Sends Sunday* (1931) emphasized the exotic and sensual aspects of black life. The novel was later dramatized by Bontemps and Countee Cullen as the "St. Louis Woman." The play opened 6 May 1946 at the Martin Beck Theatre in New York. Some blacks objected to the leading character, Della Green, because she was a prostitute, but the play was a hit in spite of some unfavorable notices. Characters in "St. Louis Woman" were played by Pearl Bailey, Ruby Hill, Rex Ingram, and Juanita Hall.[16]

Soon after *God Sends Sunday* came four more books: *You Can't Pet a Possum, Sad Faced Boy, Black Thunder,* and *Drums at Dusk,* the latter two historical novels. He became one of the most successful writers of children's books. In the meantime events were occurring which would eventually land Bontemps at Fisk. His first book was published during the depression and, in Bontemps's words, the "lively and talented" young men he had met in Harlem "were scurrying to whatever brier patches they could find." He found one in Alabama. He arrived in time to witness the Scottsboro trials, "a cause célèbre of the 1930s" in which nine young blacks were tried for raping two white women. After taking stock of the situation, he moved his family to Chicago. The Windy City proved little better. Twice his apartment was burglarized and nearly every week his family saw a robbery or something equally dismaying. He had fled

ARNA BONTEMPS AND STUDENTS. *Left to right, sitting:* Helen E. Harris, Bontemps, M. L. Hogan; *standing:* Ameer Ali, Robert C. Orr, Shirley Davis Fuller (*Courtesy of the Fisk University Library's Special Collections*)

"the jungle of Alabama's Scottsboro era to the jungle of Chicago's crime-ridden South Side, and one was as terrifying as the other." Unwilling to exchange life in Chicago "for the institutionalized assault on Negro personality" in Alabama, Bontemps suddenly began to find the Fisk campus attractive. "If a refuge for the harrassed Negro could be found anywhere in the 1930s," Bontemps wrote later, "it had to be in such a setting." The atmosphere at Fisk, a nationally known scholar told him, was "yeasty." It appealed to many black intellectuals.[17]

Bontemps became director of the library and continued his writing. For a time he turned to nonfiction. *They Seek a City*, written with Jack Conroy, was a study of black migration from the time of the underground railroad. *They Have Tomorrow* was a series of biographical sketches of talented young blacks. His *Story of the Negro*, a history of blacks in American culture, received the Jane Addams award in 1956, and his *100 Years of Negro Freedom* received good reviews. Bontemps also continued to write fiction and poetry. He wrote and edited over a score of books and his poetry has been collected in more than a dozen anthologies. Bontemps twice received a Julius Rosenwald Fund Fellowship for writing and also a John Simon Guggenheim Foundation Award.

A worthy colleague of Bontemps was poet Robert Earl Hayden, who went to Fisk in 1948 after teaching at the University of Michigan. In 1940 Hayden began to attract considerable attention with his *Heart Shape in the Dust*. His other works include *The Lion and the Archer, Figure of Time*, and *A Ballad of Remembrance*. The latter collection of Hayden's works was awarded the prize for anglophone poetry at the First World Festival of Negro Arts at Dakar, Senegal, in 1966.[18]

By the 1930s Fisk had gained a reputation not only as a source of scholarly works and literature, but also as a center of art and music. Although Fisk had collected a few paintings, little emphasis was placed on art at the university before the Jones administration. Fisk began to exhibit the works of well-known black artists, especially in connection with the Annual Festival of Music and Fine Arts, which was inaugurated in 1928. Eminent musicians and artists were brought to campus and art works were displayed. After viewing a collection of paintings and etchings in 1928 a *Nashville Banner* reporter labeled the display "remarkable." The second annual exhibit, the *Banner* proclaimed, clearly demonstrated that blacks were "a force to be reckoned with in the progress of art in this country. . . ." President Jones said some local whites, after inspecting the exhibits, "became rather frightened," as if they feared blacks "might out-do the white people in this field as they have in the field of singing."[19]

In 1931 Fisk acquired a notable collection of its own. Approximately 300 pencil sketches and water colors by Cyrus Leroy Baldridge were given to the university by Samuel Insull, the flamboyant Chicago businessman. The drawings were done by Baldridge during a year's exploration in West Africa. Not only did the drawings have considerable artistic merit, but they constituted an important record of a rapidly passing civilization. Charles S. Johnson said it was generally agreed that the Baldridge drawings were the best illustrations of African life available. The *New York Times* announced the gift to Fisk with the headline, "Fisk University Becoming a Cultural Centre" and the words that Fisk was in the process of "becoming a veritable art centre in the South." The paper also mentioned the library murals done by Aaron Douglas, which were referred to as depicting "the engrossing story of the Negro's climb upward from savagery and bondage. . . ."[20]

Fisk placed a new emphasis on art when in 1937 Douglas was persuaded to join the faculty. Douglas was born in Topeka, Kansas, in 1889 and received a degree from the University of Kansas in 1923. In 1925–1926 he studied under Winold Reiss in New York City. He received a Barnes Foundation Fellowship in 1928, Rosenwald Grant for study in Paris in 1931, and a Rosenwald Travel Grant to tour Haiti and the South in 1938. His works have been exhibited many times, including one-man shows at Coz-Delbos Gallery and A. C. A. Gallery, both in New York City. Douglas's murals, usually allegorical scenes showing black cultural background or historical life are in the old Fisk Library, 135th Street Branch of the New York Public Library, and at Bennett College.[21]

Fisk's growing reputation for the fine arts brought other collections to the school. In 1949 Georgia O'Keeffe, one of the most famous women artists in the United States and widow of pioneer artistic photographer Alfred Stieglitz, presented Fisk with the Alfred Stieglitz Collection of Modern Art. The collection of over 100 works contained originals by Cezanne, Picasso, Rivera, Renoir, Marin, Hartley, O'Keeffe, Severini, Signac, and Toulouse-Lautrec. In addition to the paintings, water colors, lithographs, etchings, and pieces of sculpture were nineteen photographs on chloride by Stieglitz himself, who was a genius in creative expression with the camera. The collection was formally opened to the public in the Carl Van Vechten Gallery in November 1949. It was considered the outstanding collection of its kind in the South and one of the most important collections in the country. "Incontestably an eye-popping show" the *Nashville Tennessean*'s art critic told his readers after visiting the gallery.[22] The number of art works at Fisk was further augmented in 1952 when Mrs. Irene McCoy Gaines, in memory of her uncle George W. Ellis, who for twelve years served as secretary of the American legation in Monrovia, Liberia, gave the university 252 pieces of African art. The gift was part of the George W. Ellis African Collection formerly in the Smithsonian Institute. Ellis had been an authority on West African culture and on African art. Also in 1952, Carl Van Vechten presented Fisk with the Florine Stettheimer Memorial Collection of Books on Fine Arts, a set of some 1,200 selected volumes.[23]

Fisk was more famous for its music than other art forms. Olga

Samaroff Stokowski of the Juilliard Foundation and former music critic of the *New York Evening Post* in 1929 said, "the work being done at Fisk is remarkable . . . the type which the Juilliard Foundation is eager to help." On another occasion she stated, "In many different ways I have been highly impressed with the musical work being done at Fisk University." After teaching former Fisk students, examining others for Juilliard Foundation scholarships, and having heard the Fisk Singers do choral work, she added, "I have gained the conviction that the musical department . . . is one of great significance and importance to the whole country." The *New York Herald Tribune*'s music critic, Virgil Thompson, claimed Fisk had one of the largest and best music departments in the South, a department which had long been a pioneer in musical studies.[24]

Fisk's reputation for music had been building almost since the school opened. While the Jubilee Singers were winning praise for their renditions of spirituals, other students in the Mozart Society, founded by music lover Adam K. Spence, were studying classical works. There was always much emphasis on music. Each year the anniversary of the Jubilee Singers' first tour was celebrated as Jubilee Day with a musical program. In 1885 the music department was created, guided at first by President Cravath and Mrs. Julia Chase Spence. In 1886 graded courses for the piano and cabinet organ were introduced. The next year Miss Jennie A. Robinson became director of music. She remained at Fisk for over thirty years. Music did more to endear Fisk to Nashville residents than any other one thing.[25]

After the turn of the twentieth century, when only a small amount of original scholarship had come out of black schools, Fisk had made contributions in music. By the 1890s interest in spirituals at Fisk had declined. John W. Work, a Fisk graduate who returned to teach Latin, began popularizing the songs and collecting new materials. Within a few years he had restored folk music at Fisk. The publication of *Folk Songs of the American Negro* in 1907 by John and Frederick Work and *The Folk Songs of the American Negro* by John in 1915 stimulated a new study of folk music in America.[26]

John W. Work, Jr., later won international recognition as a composer and collector. In 1940 he published *American Negro Songs and Spirituals*. He won first prize in a competition offered by the Fellowship of American Composers for "The Singers" in 1946. It was presented by the Detroit Symphony Orchestra. When Virgil Thompson heard Work's "Yenvalou" suite in 1947, he said it was one of the finest pieces of contemporary music in the whole American repertory and was the finest on a Haitian theme.[27]

In the meantime Fisk's music department continued to improve its reputation for performing European music. In 1927 a Vanderbilt professor heard the Mozart Society sing "King Olaf." He had never listened to a choral work performed with "greater and more uniform excellence," he wrote. The music critic for the *Nashville Banner* claimed that the Mozart Society sang the "Volga Boatman's Song" better than any of the Slavic choral groups he had heard.[28]

In 1928 the curriculum was strengthened and the music department became the School of Music and granted a Bachelor of Music degree. Five years later the purely musical course of the Bachelor of Music degree was replaced by a new course of study leading to a Bachelor of Arts and a Master of Arts with a major in music. Fisk produced numerous concert artists, and the annual Festival of Music and Fine Arts brought many noted performers to campus.

During the 1930s Fisk became famous for its choir. Weekly broadcasts of the Fisk School of Music over the Columbia network so impressed the country that the network production manager invited the university to broadcast on the "Hello Europe" hour on 15 February 1932. Approximately ninety stations in the United States and forty abroad were on the hookup. The station received complimentary letters from Poland and other countries. A choir tour in 1933 won praise from music critics of the *Boston Transcript, Musical Leader, New York Times* and the *Prompter*. The latter called the choir, "perhaps the most famous Negro singing group in the world...." T. Tertius Noble, a well-known choir master was guest conductor during the tour. Dr. Noble had accepted an invitation to conduct the Fisk choir singing one of his own compositions at commencement exercises in June 1932. Impressed with the choir's ability and response, Noble asked the privilege of conducting it on the tour. The choir was then under the general direction of Ray Francis Brown of the Fisk School of Music. At Carnegie Hall the choir won plaudits for a concert which included pieces from Bach, Palestrina, F. Melius Christianson, Gretchaninoff, Rachmaninoff, and Tchaikovsky. The choir continued to sing over national networks and made nationwide tours with great success.[29]

An able music faculty was gathered at Fisk. In 1939 Catherine Van Buren, a well-known soprano concert singer, joined the staff. Another member of the faculty was Lois Towles, who received her training at the University of Iowa and the Juilliard School of Music. According to the *Nashville Tennessean*, she made her debut before a Nashville audience in "a concert of surpassing brilliance." The pretentious program, the *Tennessean* claimed, was one few women pianists would care to attempt. The reviewer thought Miss Towles would "one day bring to the piano what Marian Anderson... brought to the voice." John F. Ohl, professor of music and author of *Masterpieces of Music Before 1750: Fifty Musical Examples from Gregorian Chant to J. S. Bach, with Historical and Analytical Notes*, was known for his choir directing.[30]

Fisk's reputation as a music center was further enhanced by the

George Gershwin Memorial Collection of Music and Music Literature, founded by Carl Van Vechten. Van Vechten was a New York music critic, author, photographer, and collector. Arna Bontemps was a friend of Van Vechten and persuaded him to give Fisk his music collection. Van Vechten's gift contained books on music, published music, manuscripts, letters, photographs, phonograph records, and scrapbooks. Soon after its founding, others added gifts to the collection. Among those who made presentations was W. C. Handy, who gave some of his own works. Bontemps had edited Handy's *Father of the Blues.* The library collected original letters of Franz Listz, Beethoven, Charles Gounod, Giacomo Meyerbeer, Adelina Patti, Felipe Pedrell, Richard Wagner, and Carl Maria Weber and dozens of original manuscripts. Soon after the collection was opened, Bontemps said, scholars were on campus to utilize it.[31]

12

The Extracurriculum

THE EARLY AMERICAN COLLEGE, FREDERICK RUDOLPH SAID, FREQUENTLY neglected "intellect in the interest of piety." Worldly joys were often neglected in the interest of preparing for eternity. But the American college students rebelled. College became a battleground where piety and intellect fought for superiority, "an arena in which undergraduates erected monuments" not only to "the soul of man but to man as a social and physical being." The struggle continued until some college officials no doubt wondered how students could see the curriculum through the extracurriculum and a few students believed the greatest benefits of college resulted from organizations, institutions, and student activities.[1]

Fisk students fought the same battles as other college students. Extracurricular activities at first were limited primarily to religious work. A student was more likely to attend or even hold a prayer meeting than to engage in an athletic contest; he or she was more apt to go to a revival than to a ball.

Organizations to stimulate the intellect came first on the Fisk campus. As mentioned in chapter 2, the Union Literary Society was organized on 31 January 1868. The society, primarily a debate club, discussed issues of contemporary interest. Although women were permitted to participate in the Union Literary Society, in 1882 they formed their own organization, the Young Ladies Lyceum, which provided practice in speaking, debate, and parliamentary usage. The previous year Beta Kappa Beta had been organized for both sexes. It too was mainly a discussion group.[2]

Some of the extracurricular organizations had a strong religious orientation. In 1889 Professor H. H. Wright called together some of the "best young men" on campus, persuaded them to take the White Cross pledge, and the White Cross League was formed. The society's pledge was: to treat all women with respect and try to protect them from wrong and degradation; to endeavor to stop all indecent language and coarse jests; to maintain that the law of purity was equally binding upon men as women; to attempt to spread these principles among companions and younger brothers; and to use every possible means to fulfill the command, "Keep thyself pure." The *American Missionary* proudly reported in 1890 that one member of the White Cross League had persuaded three or four nonstudent couples who had been living together unlawfully to be married and that other members stated the pledge had acted as a restraining influence on them personally. Meetings were primarily religious. The order of events in an 1894 program was as follows: reports, annual address, prayer, hymn, and benediction. On occasion there were guest speakers. One talked on "Significance of the Sexual Instinct."[3]

Before President McKenzie's resignation in 1925, Fisk clubs remained primarily academic or debating organizations. The Extempo Club in 1916 sponsored talks and debates on personal appearance, table manners, oration, work, purity of speech, temperance, reform, social efficiency, possibilities of the Republican party, possibility of the United States entering the war, and the manner by which Germany secured her food and munitions of war. The Decagynian Club studied famous people, and the Tanner Art Club discussed notable art works. The D. L. V. Club and the Dunbar Club were interested in literature. In 1916 the D. L. V. Club investigated the making of a short story. Both organizations encouraged academic excellence.[4] The Mozart Society appreciated classical music and was usually busy preparing a program for special events. Publication of the *Fisk Herald,* strongly supported by all the clubs, was considered one of the most important nonacademic activities. All of the above societies were formed before or around the end of the nineteenth century.

Fisk debators were especially active. In 1907 they debated: "Resolved, that President Roosevelt was justified in dismissing three companies of the Twenty-fifth Infantry." The three companies were black troops given dishonorable discharges without sufficient inquiry after they were charged with shooting up a town. The judge's decision favored the negative. Debates with other black schools were common, but on rare occasions contests were arranged with white colleges. A debate scheduled with Northwestern University was almost postponed because Northwestern officials insisted the chairman be white. Fisk complied with the request. In 1930 Fisk's debate team, composed of Lawrence Reddick, L. D. Jefferson, and Edwin B. Keemer, defeated Northwestern. They took the affirmative on "Resolved, that the several states should be allowed to adopt the Ontario system of liquor control."[5]

An extracurricular activity that eventually became part of the curriculum was drama. The Dunbar and D. L. V. clubs' interest in drama received impetus with the formation of the Stagecrafters in 1926, probably in response to a student complaint during the strike of 1925 regarding the lack of drama on campus. The Stagecrafters met with considerable success. They frequently produced plays by black authors, though they by no means restricted themselves to black material. In 1940 a $2,500 General Education Board grant facilitated the Stagecrafters' work, and they were well on their way to becoming one of the outstanding black dramatic organizations. Arna Bontemps claimed Fisk had one of the top black little theaters. A summer theater was organized with workshop courses in stage lighting, play production, and play directing. Finally in 1955 the university's educational policy committee approved a major in drama and speech. The Stagecrafters provided many hours of entertainment for Nashvillians, black and white. When Fisk presented Anton Chekhov's "The Cherry Orchard," the *Nashville Banner* reported that a classic play of powerful proportions received classic treatment "at the amazingly skilled hands" of the youthful Stagecrafters.[6]

There were sufficient organizations for stimulating the intellect, and with the introduction of fraternities and sororities in 1926 social aspirations were satisfied. With the arrival of purely social clubs, the literary societies tended to decline, not from lack of interest or because fraternities and sororities adopted their purpose, but because the social organizations demanded a higher level of loyalty and introduced new political complications into student elections.[7] For a time at least, responsibility to fraternity or sorority superceded liability to clubs, and nonclass activity leaned more toward the social. Extracurricular enterprises at Fisk by 1930 closely resembled those in a majority of other colleges. Despite the temporary loss of popularity, the number of academic societies—such as the Science Club, Biology Seminar, History Club, and Mathematics Club—increased.

Like white college students before them, the Fiskites were not content with only clubs that served the intellect and a system of fraternities and sororities that catered to social needs. They also created organizations to provide physical activity. Students, including W. E. B. DuBois, had for years requested a gymnasium before one was finally built in 1888. No attempt was made to produce athletes; all training was directed toward the "development of such sound, vigorous, evenly balanced, strong, and graceful bodies that they shall be efficient and enduring instruments for the use of well-trained minds in the hard work and stern conflicts of life."[8]

Dissatisfied with the boredom of routine physical exercises, the Fisk men organized what was reportedly the first Southern black football team. Football was relatively new in American colleges. The first recorded intercollegiate game was between Princeton and Rutgers in 1869. The two schools played three games with twenty-five men on each team. The game bore little resemblance to football as it came to be known later. It was then the English variant rugby, but when the Intercollegiate Football Association accepted new rules in 1881, there was little left of rugby in American football. By the 1890s football was a widely popular college sport. The first team at Fisk was organized in 1893 or 1894 by Charles Snyder, who had played on a Hartford, Connecticut, high school team. Snyder taught the game to Fisk men and served as captain of the first team.

DEBATE TEAM, 1910. *Left to right:* Joseph E. Ellison, Robert N. Arthurton, James E. Stamps, Clarence H. Payne (*Courtesy of the Fisk University Library's Special Collections*)

The early team was named after President Erastus Milo Cravath, "the Sons of Milo." Later the name became "Fisk Bulldogs." At first there was no football coach—the players coached themselves and decided who would participate. Absence of a coach did not retard their game. On Thanksgiving Day 1895, "a most enthusiastic game of football" was played between Fisk and the Nashville Giants. The Giants were "shamefully defeated." Between 1899 and 1904 Fisk lost only one game. In 1903 a disputed match with Meharry was decided in favor of Fisk when the presidents of the two schools called in a spectator, nationally famous Walter Camp, to arbitrate. Warren G. Waterman, a graduate from football-mad Yale who went to Fisk in 1899 as instructor in civil government and natural science, served as the first coach. Fisk football, minus protective equipment, was not without hazards. During the Merrill administration, John Hughes was buried under a pile of tacklers, was carried off the field, and later died with complications from broken ribs.[9]

While white schools were being charged with professionalism—one year the University of Oregon played in three successive games with three different schools and each time played against the same man—Fisk was playing a strictly amateur game. In 1907 the team was coached by John W. Work, professor of history and Latin and leader of the Jubilee Singers. The football team went on a two-week tour, played four games, and sang over a dozen concerts. Sometimes the game was played and the concert given on the same day. By 1915 Fisk was a little more serious about intercollegiate athletics. The team won 4 and tied 2 with a score of 0 to 0. Fisk scored 145 points throughout the season, while its opponents tallied only 3. By this time some students were complaining that athletics were for a chosen few to the neglect of many others who needed physical training. "So long as large numbers of our young people of both sexes, are narrow-chested, thin-limbed, their muscles growing soft as their fat grows hard . . . there will be a need of athletics," a student wrote, and not for football players alone.[10]

Intercollegiate sports were abandoned during World War I but were renewed in 1919 with sensational results. In a game with Talladega, "Jack Rabbit" Poole, often called the 135-pound wizard, took a punt and skirted the right end for a victorious 60-yard touchdown. On Thanksgiving Day Fisk defeated Morehouse College 39 to 0, which, Fiskites claimed, made their school "the undisputed champion of the South." Fisk continued its winning ways, but in the meantime President McKenzie was becoming disillusioned with the sport. In 1921 when the Wilberforce team visited Fisk, a nasty rumor of their misbehavior on the train was circulated. President J. L. Peacock of Shaw University told McKenzie that Howard University paid players' expenses at school and even hired them from other universities. Indeed, Peacock said, he had in his possession a letter one of Shaw's players had received. Furthermore, he said, gambling at the Howard-Lincoln annual game was notorious. If gambling and professionalism continued to exist, McKenzie thought, intercollegiate sports should be discontinued. Despite pressure from alumni—and football in white and black colleges always held great appeal for alumni—Fisk continued the policy of absolutely no special treatment for football players and no athletic scholarships.[11] McKenzie had no intention of becoming involved in the scandals experienced by white schools.

After McKenzie resigned, football received new emphasis to please students and alumni. Henderson A. Johnson, a 1924 Fisk graduate, was employed as director of intercollegiate athletics. Johnson, a competent student, had made an amazing athletic record at Fisk. A four-year letterman—freshmen could play at Fisk—he served as halfback and captain of the team for three years. The New York Age wrote that as a "triple-threat man and outstanding in every department of the game, he has been hailed as one of the greatest backs of all time." "Tubby" Johnson, as he was fondly known, was considered one of the smartest college coaches. Though little money was spent on football—less than $6,000 in 1929—Johnson built a highly regarded team. National black newspapers were filled with stories of Fisk football in the late 1920s and early 1930s. In 1929 the team had an 8 and 1 record and in 1930 a 9 and 1 record. Joseph Wiggins, back, and Booker Pierce, tackle, were selected to the All Southern team in 1930. Wiggins, who weighed only 162, was one of the best backs in the country. "He can do anything on a football field. He can kick, run, pass and tackle in a sensational manner," the Chicago Bee proclaimed. Fisk won the Southern Football Championship in 1910, 1912, 1913, 1915, 1919, 1922, 1928, and 1929.[12]

While most alumni were cheering vigorously over Fisk's improved football fortunes, there was minor grumbling about the use of professional players. George Streator, of student strike fame, charged Fisk with professionalism, of "casting aside her standards for a trifling football team." The administration, Streator said, knew Fisk was using professionals. Two of Fisk's best players in 1929 had been on the Atlanta University football team the preceding year. After Atlanta discontinued the sport they had gone to Fisk. This could hardly be considered unethical in view of the absence of regulations for football in black colleges. After all, "Hoss" Lane starred at North Carolina A & T for eight years and "Beef" Martin played at Johnson C. Smith for seven seasons. Black intercollegiate athletics were encountering the same problems experienced by white colleges a few years earlier. In the early days of football in white schools it was not unknown for the coach of a college one year to be a star player at another university the next. After investigation President Jones fired the assistant coach because he had played the men from Atlanta and because he had reputedly promised some of the players he would furnish part of their tuition and expenses.[13]

After the "scandal" of 1930, football declined rapidly at Fisk. In 1931 the team's record was only 1 and 8. In 1932 it had a winning season, but

this was apparently only a temporary aberration. The next year it had
the misfortune to go scoreless in five of the first seven games. The best
the team could do in 1934 was a 0–0 tie in one game and losses in the
rest. According to the *Fisk Herald,* the once famous Bulldog eleven had
now become a "scrappy Fox Terrier." The backs of the 1934 team
weighed only 132, 138, 138, and 133, but, said the *Herald,* "when the four
'ponies' get together, watch for some fast stepping." Two of the guards,
"Little Arthur" Jackson and Gerald "Jew" Ross were known as "the
midget guards of the South."[14] President Jones encouraged the abandonment of intercollegiate athletics and a movement toward intramural
games. Perhaps, he said, games between colleges could be played on a
tournament basis, the best team from each school playing champions
from other universities. In his attempt to stimulate intramural games in
1934, President Jones himself played on a faculty football team against a
student team. For his trouble he suffered several broken ribs, which
confined him to his bed for a few weeks. Broken ribs did not alter
President Jones's attitude toward intramural athletics, but after the dis-
astrous season of 1934 and resulting alumni dissatisfaction he tried to
repair Fisk's waning football fortunes. He even allotted $135 to Coach
Johnson in 1937 as travel expense for visiting prospective athletes who
were good students. Of course such a paltry sum was virtually useless
when other schools were spending thousands of dollars on recruiting.
Fisk won only one game, 2 to 0, in 1935 and none in 1937. President
Jones could truthfully say in 1941 that intercollegiate football was the
weakest sport at Fisk.[15]

Football was suspended after 1941 and, except for a homecoming
game in 1943, it was not resumed until 1946. In the first postwar game
Fisk defeated Miles College, Birmingham, Alabama, 12 to 0. The athletic
program was expanded in 1948. A full eight-game schedule was arranged in football, facilities were expanded, the tennis court was reno-
vated, and new equipment was purchased for intramural athletics. Fisk
football contests were not limited to black schools. The homecoming
opponent in 1954 was Taylor University, a white school in Upland,
Indiana.[16] Although Fisk had some good seasons after 1948 and produced some fine players, football was not permitted to become a big
business as in many schools. For example, Fisk clung to the policy of no
athletic scholarships.

Basketball was organized at Fisk in 1903 but remained intramural
until 1926. The team rather consistently had winning seasons though
there were a few bad years. The *Herald* in 1935 reported Fisk's participation in a tournament as follows: "The Fisk varsity journeyed to Tuskegee, entered the tournament . . . attended a few social functions and
returned home. Unfortunately they did not emerge . . . as victors, but
Fisk was represented and no one actually expected them to be victorious."[17] Fisk baseball and track teams also performed creditably.

13

Alumni

ONE MARK OF A GREAT UNIVERSITY IS THE DEGREE TO WHICH ITS STUDENTS are equipped to cope with the demands of life. Judging by their successes, Fisk students were usually well prepared. The alumni distinguished themselves in almost every field of endeavor. From 1875, when the first class graduated, to 1963 Fisk awarded 4,778 undergraduate and 683 graduate degrees. Of this number 317 continued in school and won the M.D., 128 the D.D.S., 88 the Ph.D., 23 the Ed.D., and 524 master's degrees. Approximately one-fifth of Fisk's undergraduates have received advanced degrees.[1]

Fisk students entered a wide range of occupations with heavy concentrations in medicine, business, social service, homemaking, and teaching. A larger number entered the field of education than any other profession. In 1900, of the 371 living graduates whose occupations were known, 119 were college professors, principals, and teachers in public schools. Hundreds of others who had attended Fisk were teaching without degrees. In 1915 approximately 50 percent of Fisk graduates were teachers. It was estimated that around 75,000 children in the South were being taught by Fiskites. By 1930 the number teaching had declined to about 40 percent of Fisk's graduates.[2]

Several of those affiliated with public schools were in supervisory positions. In 1900 at least forty-six Fisk graduates were principals. W. E. Mollison, a former student, served as superintendent of schools of Issaquena County, Mississippi, in the early 1880s. He was also a lawyer and editor of a county newspaper, the *Spectator*. J. N. Calloway '87 taught at Tuskegee and then in 1902 went to Togoland, German West Africa, at the request of the German government to introduce the cultivation of cotton. Others served the cause of education in other ways. C. O. Rogers '24, principal of Jackson High School, Corsicana, Texas, became president of the Texas State Colored Teachers Association. Mrs. Ida Hauser Duncan '27 served two terms as president of the North Carolina Teachers Association. Others with different occupations played a role in education. In 1964 Dr. J. Andrew Simmons '25 was elected to the Bedford Hills, New York, Central Board of Education by an almost two to one majority, and in 1965 Clifton G. Dyson M.A. '34, a businessman, was appointed to the Florida State Board of Regents.[3]

Numerous Fisk graduates earned higher degrees and became college teachers. The first Fiskite to win the Ph.D. was A. O. Coffin '85, who received a degree in biology from Illinois Wesleyan University in Bloomington, Illinois, in 1889. A former slave, Coffin averaged 97 percent on all his course work at Illinois Wesleyan, a mark that had never been excelled at the university. One of his professors said that of the men who had taken the degree in the previous fifteen years, Coffin easily stood among the top half-dozen. By 1943 fewer than 400 blacks in the United States had received Ph.D.'s. Of that number at least sixteen had earned their first degree at Fisk. Others taught in college without the doctorate. A government survey in 1932 indicated that only Howard University among black schools had supplied more teachers than Fisk.[4]

Although most Fiskites who taught in institutions of higher learning were associated with black colleges, they were by no means restricted to schools for their race. In 1964 Fisk graduates were teaching in approximately fifty black colleges. They were also teaching in at least sixteen predominantly white schools, including Dartmouth College, the University of Massachusetts, University of Michigan, Hunter College, Brooklyn College, University of California at Los Angeles, and New York University. William L. Cash, Jr., served as professor of psychology and chairman of the department of Counseling and Guidance at the University of North Dakota. John Hope Franklin, a Harvard Ph.D., became chairman of the history department at Brooklyn College in 1956. It was thought that no other New York college had ever before appointed a black chairman of an academic department. Franklin, author of several books, including *From Slavery to Freedom* and *Reconstruction After the Civil War*,[5] had been a Guggenheim Fellow and Pitt Professor at Cambridge. In 1964 he became professor of history at the University of Chicago. Three years later he became chairman of the history department. Professor Franklin is past president of the Southern Historical Association and of the Organization of American Historians and is presently John Matthews Manly Distinguished Service Professor of History at the University of Chicago.

Numerous other Fiskites worked with white organizations. From 1939 to 1948 Lawrence D. Reddick B.A. '32, a Chicago Ph.D. in history, was curator of the Schomburg Collection of Negro Literature and History in the New York Public Library. He resigned to become chief librarian of Atlanta University.[6] Fisk women have not lagged far behind the men in pursuing graduate degrees; at least thirty of them have won doctorates. Edna M. Colson '15, Eliza Atkins Gleason '30, and Mildred Bryant Jones, Normal '97, all of whom received the Ph.D. in 1940, were the first Fisk women to earn doctorates. Elsie Lewis '32, who received her Ph.D. from the University of Chicago, later became chairman of the Howard University history department.

Several Fiskites have served as college presidents. John H. Burrus, who became president of Alcorn Agricultural and Mechanical College in Mississippi in 1882, was only the first of a number of distinguished Fisk graduates to head institutions of higher learning. Burrus was followed at Alcorn by Thomas J. Calloway '89. Calloway's ability was recognized when the United States government selected him as one of the twelve commissioners of education to collect and arrange statistics for the World's Exposition in Paris in 1900. C. H. Duncan '85 became president of Swayne College in Montgomery, Alabama, his first year out of school. Ernest H. Anderson '80 was president of Prairie View Normal and Industrial College in Texas for several years. John M. Gandy '98, head of Virginia State College, was honored in 1930 by his appointment to the National Advisory Committee of Educational Specialists. Gandy had earlier served as president of the National Association of Teachers in Colored Schools.[7]

Author and minister William Lloyd Imes '10 assumed the presidency of Knoxville College in Knoxville, Tennessee, in 1943. One of the better-known black college presidents was Charles H. Wesley '11, who at different times guided both Wilberforce University and Central State College in Wilberforce, Ohio. He went to Wilberforce in 1943 after serving as dean of the graduate school at Howard University. Author of more than a dozen volumes about black Americans, Dr. Wesley became director of research for the Association for the Study of Negro Life and History upon his retirement from Central State College. Wesley, who received his Ph.D. from Harvard, also studied at the Guilde Internationale in Paris and the Howard University Law School.[8] Honorary degrees from eight universities have been bestowed upon him. In 1967 James R. Lawson '35 became president of his alma mater.[9]

Several Fisk graduates engaged in religious work. The early university faculty was almost as concerned with training educated ministers as it was in producing teachers. An educated black ministry was badly needed, the faculty thought, and the black preacher occupied a position of considerable leadership in the community. Some Fisk students gained a national reputation in religious service which gave them influence beyond the walls of their church. One of the best-known black ministers was Henry Hugh Proctor. Born in Fayetteville, Tennessee, in 1868, Proctor entered Fisk after a few years in public schools. Upon graduation in 1891 he attended the Yale University Divinity School. A Yale professor said Proctor was "one of the very best students in his class, perhaps the most effective preacher in his class, and on the whole, I think, the best orator in the Seminary."[10] At the graduation ceremony Proctor was selected by the faculty as one of the class speakers. Immediately after graduation he accepted the pastorate of the First Congregational Church of Atlanta, whose membership grew under his leadership from 100 to 1,000.

Increasing membership was only a small part of Proctor's contribution. He ministered to the physical as well as the spiritual needs of his flock and in so doing he established what has been called the first institutional church for blacks. A gymnasium, music school, day nursery, kindergarten, employment bureau, a home for girls, and a Bible school were organized by the church. The church also maintained a slum mission. A white critic who denounced the "social complacency and non-aggressiveness" of "the select city churches" claimed Proctor's was a brilliant exception. Proctor's attempt to meet the social needs of his charges was rewarded. In the 1920s, two-thirds of the church's 1,000 members owned their homes and not one was illiterate. The purpose of the church, said Proctor, was "to serve man in his threefold nature, body, mind, and spirit." Visitors from all over the country went to Atlanta to examine Proctor's institutional church. Among the guests were President William Howard Taft and former President Theodore Roosevelt.[11]

His successful ministry gained Proctor city-wide influence. After the terrible Atlanta race riot of September 1906, Proctor received a surprising call from a white Atlanta lawyer, Charles T. Hopkins. They talked, devised a plan, and both called in friends. The group, which expanded to include about forty black and white men, worked together to restore peace. Proctor and his committee organized the "Coloured Co-operative Civil League," which continued to meet with whites from time to time. Proctor later dated the beginning of the movement for interracial cooperation in the South from that first mixed meeting after the riot. On one occasion a white "Georgia cracker" came to the Proctor home. Mrs. Proctor was frightened, but much to her surprise and delight the man took her husband by the hand, said he approved his work, and had come to pray with him.

During World War I Proctor volunteered as a chaplain, but age prevented his enlistment. After the armistice he received a telegram from General John J. Pershing's headquarters to come to France to help sustain the morale of those who were forced to remain in Europe. Proctor, Helen Hagan, a pianist, and J. E. Blanton, a singer, traveled throughout France staging programs for black soldiers. Proctor later moved to New York, where he was elected moderator of the Congregational Association of the city, the first black to be so honored.[12]

William N. DeBerry enjoyed a career similar to Proctor's. After graduating from Fisk in 1896 and Oberlin he entered upon a thirty-year pastorate at the St. John Congregational Church in Springfield, Massachusetts. Stressing the "social idea" in his ministry, DeBerry established a home for working girls, a school of domestic training, a handicraft club for young people, a free employment agency, and a welfare league for women. His influence was sufficient in Springfield to ban the showing of the racist picture "The Birth of a Nation." DeBerry received the first Harmon Medal for distinguished service in religion. A few months later, in May 1928, the William Pycheon Medal of the Springfield Publicity Club was presented to DeBerry for "distinguished service" to the city. In 1935 he was appointed to the Springfield Board of Public Welfare and later to the Governor's Commission on Religious and Racial Understanding.[13] Both DeBerry and Proctor served on the Fisk board of trustees.

Numerous other Fiskites did yeoman's service in religious work, some of whom went to Africa as missionaries. Mrs. Althea Brown Edmiston '01, a missionary to central Africa, compiled a dictionary and grammar for the great Bukuba Tribe, which had no written language. Buford Gordon '17 was elected to the bishopric of the African Methodist Episcopal Zion Church in 1944. He was the first Fisk graduate to become a bishop. William Lloyd Imes, previously mentioned as president of Knoxville College, was pastor for several years of the St. James Presbyterian Church in New York City, the largest black Presbyterian congregation in the United States. For years George W. Moore '81 was a missionary and superintendent of Southern church work for the American Missionary Association.[14]

Even more numerous than ministers were physicians. In one year alone six Fiskites graduated from Meharry Medical College. In 1927 it was estimated that in recent years at least 11 percent of Fisk graduates became physicians, pharmacists, and dentists, and some of them achieved more than local fame. Allen A. Wesley '84, Chicago Medical College '87, had a successful practice in Chicago and later served as surgeon-in-chief of the Provident Hospital in that city. During the Spanish-American War he entered the Eighth Illinois Volunteers as a major. While in Cuba he successfully handled over 2,000 cases of malaria. His regiment enjoyed a remarkable health record.[15]

After graduating from Fisk in 1885, Ferdinand A. Stewart entered Harvard Medical School. He graduated from Harvard with first honors in his class of more than one hundred and was the only black man admitted as a fellow in the Massachusetts Medical Society. Upon his return to Nashville he engaged in private practice and served as professor of pathology at Meharry. He was elected president of the Negro National Medical Association in 1900. Despite his numerous activities in the medical profession, Dr. Stewart gave freely of his time and money to Fisk University.[16]

A Fisk '92 and Meharry graduate, D. W. Sherrod, settled in Macon, Mississippi, where he developed a lucrative practice, including a majority of white patients. His statewide reputation brought him wealth and prestige. In 1928 he purchased a city block in the business district of Meridian, Mississippi, valued at $100,000. A life-long Republican, Sherrod was a state committeeman to every national Republican convention between 1912 and 1928.[17]

Dr. Charles V. Roman also enjoyed a national reputation. In 1928 the *Pittsburgh Courier* claimed that since the death of Booker T. Washington no black man in the South had "stood out more prominently" than Roman, an ear, eye, nose, and throat specialist. He was invited by President Herbert Hoover to attend the Conference on Child Welfare and Labor held in Washington in 1930. Roman studied at the Chicago Medical School, the Royal London Ophthalmic Hospital, and the Central London Hospital in London, England. He taught physiology and hygiene and was the examining physician at Fisk.[18]

George Sheppard Moore, son of Ella Sheppard Moore of Jubilee Singer fame, attended Northwestern University Medical School after completing his work at Fisk in 1906. For thirteen years he practiced in Nashville and lectured at Meharry on medical psychiatry. Later he joined the United States Veterans' Facility Hospital, Tuskegee, eventually becoming clinical director. While at Tuskegee, Moore performed delicate cerebrospinal surgery. His skill at such surgery led the United States government to send him to various states to do similar operations. Ernest R. Alexander '14, who was the only black in his class at the University of Vermont Medical School, achieved the unique distinction of taking all honors offered by the university in medicine. Working in Bellvue Hospital and Harlem Hospital in New York City, Alexander became a well-known dermatologist. He taught postgraduate courses at Columbia University College of Physicians and Surgeons.[19] Many other Fiskites performed valuable service as physicians.[20]

Fisk also sent a sizable number of students into law. In addition to his work as an educator, farmer, and businessman, John H. Burrus practiced law. William R. Morris '84 was admitted to the bar in 1887 by the Illinois Supreme Court. Later he moved to Minneapolis, where he was the first black to appear before the courts of Hennepin County. A. M. Thomas, Jr., '81 won praise from the Yale law faculty. These men were practicing law successfully at a time when there were very few black lawyers in the country.[21]

At least two Fiskites became president of the Cook County Bar Association in Chicago. James B. Cashin '16 served as president from 1934 to 1936. In 1945 Zedrick T. Braden '21 was elected president. Mrs. Sophia Boaz Pitts '11 worked for the federal government as a lawyer.[22]

Several Fisk lawyers advanced to positions as judges. James A. Cobb, former student, was appointed judge of the District of Columbia Municipal Court. Otis M. Smith '45 was made associate justice of the Michigan Supreme Court. Wade H. McCree '41, who had been criticized by the *Fisk Herald* for shaving his head while a freshman, was sworn in as judge of the Third Judicial Court in Wayne County, Michigan. Later President John F. Kennedy named him to the United States District Court. In 1977 McCree was nominated for United States Solicitor General. Governor

Orville Freeman appointed L. Howard Bennett '35 to the Minneapolis Municipal Court, while Charles W. White '21 became judge of the common pleas court in Cleveland, Ohio. The first black justice of the New York City Court of Special Sessions was former student Myles A. Paige, appointed in 1936.[23]

Several other attorneys achieved prominence.[24] One of the five members of the United States delegation to the United Nations General Assembly in 1954 was Charles Mahoney '08. Mahoney was president and general counsel of the Great Lakes Mutual Life Insurance Company. In 1966 President Lyndon B. Johnson appointed Constance Baker Motley, a former student at Fisk, to a federal district court judgeship. Previously Mrs. Motley had been second-ranking attorney in the legal defense fund of the National Association for the Advancement of Colored People. She left the fund in 1964 to become New York's first black woman state senator. A year later she was named to the $35,000-a-year post of borough president of Manhattan. She was Manhattan's first woman borough president, and the first black woman federal judge.[25]

Many other Fiskites were rewarded with high appointive government offices. L. Howard Bennett, mentioned previously, was made principal assistant to the deputy assistant secretary of defense for civil rights. Mrs. Dorothy Inborden Miller '19 was appointed director of home economics, Division X-XIII, Washington, D.C., in 1933. Governor of New York Herbert Lehman appointed the dermatologist Ernest R. Alexander to the State Advisory Council on Employment. In 1963 Roy K. Davenport '31 took an oath as deputy undersecretary of the army for personnel management. Randall L. Tyus '32 served as Small Business Administration employment policy officer in Washington, D.C., and a special assistant for program analysis in the Health Information Research Utilization Branch, Washington, D.C., was Joseph H. Douglass '37.[26]

Most of the people just mentioned were appointed to office, but some Fisk graduates fought their way into office through the rough and tumble of American politics. Samuel A. McAlwee, an 1883 graduate, won election to the Tennessee legislature while still a student. He took his seat in the lower house in January 1883 and was twice reelected. The Tennessee legislature designated McAlwee to superintend the black exhibits at the 1885 New Orleans Exposition. He was also president of the West Tennessee Colored Fair Association and the Memphis Fair Association. As a delegate to the Republican National Convention in 1884, McAlwee helped nominate James G. Blaine for president. As a legislator he worked for more humane treatment of the insane and secured the passage of a bill to establish an asylum in the western part of the state. McAlwee, an eloquent champion of civil rights and a constant enemy of mobs and lynching, fought a losing battle. Even before his election,

Tennessee had passed "Jim Crow" laws and the rest of the South was following suit, and lynching was on the rise. McAlwee later moved to Chicago where he became a highly paid lawyer.[27]

Miss Cora M. Brown '35, an attorney, was a Michigan state senator for two terms. She was later defeated in a primary campaign for the United States House of Representatives. A Democrat, Senator Brown supported Adlai Stevenson for president in 1952, but in 1956 she backed President Eisenhower. Postmaster General Arthur Summerfield appointed her as special associate general counsel of the post office in 1957. Other Fiskites served on the local level. Benjamin A. M. Green '09, a banker, was elected mayor in the all-black town of Mound Bayou, Mississippi. John Edward Porter '80 was twice elected county clerk of Graham County, Kansas, and Harold M. Love M.A. '49 was elected Nashville city councilman in 1962.[28]

Two Fisk students have served in Congress. After graduating with honors from Fisk in 1909, William L. Dawson attended Northwestern University Law School. Illinois elected him to the United States House of Representatives in 1943. He successfully sought reelection every two years until ill health prevented his running in 1970. He died soon after the November election. In addition to his duties as a representative Dawson served as vice-chairman of the Democratic National Committee. In 1945 Dawson was joined in the House by Adam Clayton Powell of New York. When they were both reelected in 1954 and Charles C. Diggs, Jr., of Detroit was sent to the House it was the first time in the twentieth century that three black men were in Congress at one time. Diggs was a former Fisk student. He had dropped out of Fisk during World War II to join the army as a private. When the war was over he enrolled at Wayne State University. After serving in the Michigan state senate, Diggs was elected to Congress as a Democrat.[29]

Another Fisk politician, James W. Ford '18 was viewed with mixed emotions by his former mentors and friends. At Fisk, James "Rabbit" Ford was known as a fleet-footed athlete and a good student. He joined the army during World War I to help "make the world safe for democracy." Like many other young Americans he became disillusioned and in 1926 he joined the Communist party. He ran for vice-president on the Communist ticket in 1932, 1936, and 1940. Some Fisk officials who had looked with favor upon Ford, the student, looked with apprehension upon Ford, the Communist. Nevertheless, he was permitted to speak at the university in 1940. In answer to criticism from local whites and some alumni, Andrew J. Allison, alumni secretary, said it was an example of independence and freedom of speech, which Fisk had always advocated. "Again and again," added Allison, "it has been emphasized that here on Fisk campus is one of the finest examples of true democracy at work in the United States." Anyway, the speech was nonpolitical. Another Fisk student, Merrill Work '24 ran for the New York assembly from the Brooklyn district on the Communist ticket.[30]

At least three Fiskites were in politics outside the United States. Gabriel Dennis, secretary of state of Liberia, represented his country at the United Nations Conference on International Organization at San Francisco. Gabriel Jummelle M.A. '45 served as finance minister, labor minister, and public health minister of Haiti, and Franck Legendre M.A. '45 was a senator in the same country.[31]

Only a very few Fiskites became farmers, though several of them taught agriculture. The Burrus brothers effectively taught improved farming methods at Alcorn A & M, and they owned a farm. Many members of Tuskegee's staff came from Fisk and it was a Fiskite who was selected by the German government to introduce cotton in Africa. Gaston T. Cook '22 became secretary of the Florida Farmers Cooperative Marketing Association in 1931. The organization had twenty-two local societies.[32] Most Fisk graduates who were interested in agriculture farmed only as a hobby or were concerned with teaching better farming methods.

Several Fisk students went into business, particularly, it seems, into insurance. Many of them became high-ranking officials in respectable companies. Dr. Lewis B. Moore '89 became national field executive in the Lincoln Reserve Life Insurance Company with headquarters in Birmingham, Alabama. By 1931 William H. Fearonce '14, Thomas B. Wilson '23, Cutee A. Renfro '29, Henry W. Sewing '16, Cleveland A. Terrell '21, and Luther W. Moor '98 were all managers of life insurance companies. Lemuel L. Foster '11 became manager in the late 1920s of the Victory Life Insurance Company, New York City, the largest ordinary life insurance branch office owned and operated by blacks. Dr. P. P. Creuzot '11 was elected president of the Unity Insurance Company of New Orleans. Attorney Charles H. Mahoney '08 was president and general counsel of the Great Lakes Mutual Insurance Company of Michigan and at the same time was a Detroit bank director. A. Maceo Walker '30 was president of the Universal Life Insurance Company with headquarters in Memphis, Tennessee, and was president of a bank in the same city. In 1955 Walker was elected head of the National Insurance Association in Cleveland—the youngest president in the history of the organization. Henry W. Sewing '16 in 1947 established his own company, which sold fire and life insurance and real estate. In addition, Sewing became president of the Douglas State Bank in Kansas City, Kansas, and manager of the ordinary department of the Kansas City district of the Atlanta Life Insurance Company. G. E. DeLorme '28 was manager of the Atlanta branch of the latter company.[33]

Others were self-employed businessmen. The Hemphill Press in

Nashville, Tennessee, was owned and operated by Gray W. Hemphill '99 and his two sons, Stanley '25 and Sumner '36, all Fisk graduates. Another family firm was run by William S. Cannon '20 in Atlanta, Georgia, who dealt in cosmetics. D. J. Scott '04 was a partner of Scott Brothers, merchants in Savannah. As early as 1910 the company did a business of $12,500. Other graduates were photographers, real estate brokers, and morticians.[34]

A group of students in Chicago formed a manufacturing organization, the Chemical Products Company, headed by Charles A. King '17. Julian Harris '17 was in charge of manufacturing operations. Both men were commercial chemists. Every director of the corporation was a Fisk graduate except one, and his mother was a Fiskite. The company produced toilet articles, ink eradicator, artificial rubber stoppers that would not oxidize, and household products marketed under the trademarks of "Yvonne" and "Chem-Pro-Co." The *Chicago Banker, Merchant and Manufacturer* welcomed the company to Chicago, pointing out that each associate already had an enviable reputation in the city.[35]

The Haarlem Research Laboratories, Incorporated, manufacturing chemists, was directed by A. Maurice Moore, Jr., '24. The laboratories under his supervision produced not only for the United States, but for other countries. Many other Fiskites became well-known scientists. In 1945 Miss Carolyn Parker '38, a physicist, was one of two women affiliated with the Air Technical Service Common Headquarters, Wright Field, Ohio. Robert A. Ellis '48 worked with Project Matterhorn, Forrestal Research Center in Princeton, New Jersey, while Louis P. Clark, Jr., '33 was a weapon systems specialist and consultant for the General Electric Company. Others in chemistry, physics, and mathematics too numerous to mention were and are associated with large research companies throughout the United States.[36]

Fisk produced at least one reputable architect, Calvin McKissack, a partner in the McKissack and McKissack Company of Nashville. During World War II the government awarded him a contract to construct the Tuskegee Aviation School. With a payroll of some 1,600 persons per week, one-fourth of them white, the job was completed to the satisfaction of army engineers before the contract date. No racial friction occurred among the mixed working men. After the war, McKissack and McKissack received the bid to construct Scribner Hall for Fisk. McKissack in 1958 signed a three million dollar contract as supervising architect for constructing several buildings at the University of Haiti. He served on the Fisk board of trustees.[37]

It is not surprising that Fisk, with its emphasis on music, produced several notable teachers and performers. Fisk music teachers were scattered throughout the South. In May 1935, all Birmingham, Alabama, the *Chicago Defender* said, "was agog over hearing the 3,000 high school

trained singers under the direction of Prof. Harold McCoo, graduate of
Fisk. . . . Over 10,000 persons were thrilled by the execution of the high
school singers whom he has only had under his training for six months."
Some of the songs rendered were John W. Work's compositions and
some were written by McCoo. The John W. Works, father and son, were
fine teachers as well as composers and collectors. Harold J. Brown '23
was a composer and choral conductor. In 1927, 1928, 1930, and 1931 he
won the Wanamaker Musical Composition contest and in 1929 the Harmon Award. Roy Tibbs '07, director of Howard University glee club, was
commended by the *Washington Tribune* for "doing as much or more than
any other one person in Washington to raise the standard of music
among Negroes." He was so proficient in music that no one, the *Tribune*
added, questioned the ability of any group or individual under his direction. One of two black members of the Organists Guild, Tibbs was a
popular performer.[38]

Several concert pianists studied at Fisk, including R. Augustus Lawson
'96. Within two years of his graduation, Lawson was among the important minor concert players. A protege of Mrs. Charles Dudley Warner,
wife of the American author and editor, Lawson studied at the Musical
Conservatory in Hartford, Connecticut. He settled in Hartford, where
he reputedly possessed the largest private music studio in the country.
The only black member of the Connecticut Association of Music
Teachers, Lawson won fame both as a teacher and a performer.[39]

Perhaps the most widely acclaimed singer to come out of Fisk, at least
until recent years, was Roland Hayes.[40] His rise to fame is almost as
romantic as that of the Jubilee Singers. Hayes rose from the depths of
obscurity and poverty. As a young boy in Chattanooga, Tennessee,
Hayes worked in an iron mill and did odd jobs. After hearing him sing in
the church choir, music teacher Arthur Calhoun persuaded Hayes to
take a few lessons. William Stone, a white employee of the *Chattanooga
Times,* heard him perform locally and with a black assistant helped Hayes
raise some money. Armed with a few dollars, Hayes was on his way to
Oberlin College when he heard of Fisk University. After listening to him
sing, Miss Jennie Robinson of the Fisk music department decided to give
the poverty-stricken boy with the beautiful tenor voice a month's trial to
see how studious he was. For four years he stayed at Fisk, waiting on
tables and doing other odd jobs to pay his way. At the end of four years
he was employed by the Fisk Singers to perform in a Boston concert. He
decided to remain in Boston, where he was given lessons by Arthur
Hubbard, a local music instructor. After giving his first concert in Boston Symphony Hall on 5 November 1917, Hayes slowly won recognition.

Traveling to London, he was invited to sing at Buckingham Palace and
to give a concert in Wigmore Hall. Suddenly Hayes was acclaimed as a

great artist. A subsequent trip to Germany won praise from critics for his German diction and his deep understanding of their lyrics. As had happened with many American artists, recognition abroad opened new doors at home. When the Boston symphony orchestra engaged him and Bostonians paid to listen, it meant that Hayes was received into the American "aristocracy of art." The *New York Sun* music critic, W. J. Henderson, said of Hayes in 1926: "This man who was born on a level little above that of a slave, now carries himself before the public with the authority of a cultivated gentleman, sings in four languages with fluency and correct accent, is master of the great song literatures of Germany, Italy, France, England and the United States, and is welcomed with the most cordial applause wherever he appears." Hayes was successful, Henderson proclaimed, "not merely because of the beauty of his voice or the fervor of his Negro emotion but chiefly by reason of the high quality of the art which governs them."

Hayes credited Fisk with considerable responsibility for his success and in 1930 performed at the university without fee to raise needed funds. Two years later Fisk awarded the first honorary degree in its history when it presented Hayes with a doctorate of music. Fisk departed from its time-honored practice of conferring no honorary degrees, the board of trustees said, because of Hayes's eminence not only in music but in the field of human relations.

In 1948 at the age of sixty Hayes was still filling the concert halls. A performance in Carnegie Hall was followed by a great ovation. His voice was sometimes hoarse, the *New York Times* wrote, but he had the quality that kept people coming back year after year. It was an intense appreciation and perception of beauty coupled with deep human compassion.[41] Hayes's renderings of the black spirituals were frequently no less than marvelous, an art which Fiskites claimed he learned while studying at their university.

Fisk also had some popular performers. In the 1930s James M. Lunceford '25 and band were wowing New York. The *Pittsburgh Courier* said he was "the toast of the Cotton Club" in New York City. Critics predicted that he was following in the footsteps of Duke Ellington and Cab Calloway. In 1934 he was heard regularly over the National Broadcasting System. A few years later, Lunceford's band successfully toured Norway, Sweden, Holland, Denmark, Belgium, England, and France. Soon after its return, the band was playing in New York's Apollo Theater and touring the country. Lunceford was considered one of the "most talented and distinctive orchestra leaders in the business." "His rhythm is hot," the *Kansas City Call* proclaimed, "his melodies are sweet and his orchestra as a whole is one of the most popular in the nation."[42] The *Call* had a basis for comparison. Between 1925 and 1940 Kansas City was a hotbed of jazz. Lunceford's orchestra boasted a reputation of being "the best-educated, best-disciplined, and best-dressed sepia band in the nation." All members were college men, six of them Fiskites.

Even Louis Armstrong and Lionel Hampton had indirect connections with Fisk. In 1920 a young lady born in Memphis and on vacation from Fisk was demonstrating sheet music at a Chicago music store for three dollars a week when a trumpeter, Sugar Johnny, and his New Orleans band, advertised for a piano player. Lillian Hardin tried out for her first jazz-playing job. When Miss Hardin asked the band for music, they politely told her they had none and never used any. When she asked what key the first number would be in they told her: when you hear two knocks, start playing. It was a case of sink or swim, and swim she did. She never returned to the music store or Fisk. Four years later she married another young musician, Louis Armstrong. After they separated, Miss Hardin formed her own orchestra. In 1965 she was still playing professionally.[43] Gladys Riddle Hampton, a Fisk student, managed her husband Lionel's band. She was also president and treasurer of their publishing company, Swing and Tempo.[44]

At a time when black newspapers were few and usually short-lived, several Fiskites were successful editors. As early as 1883 Edwin F. Horn, a former student, was conducting a newspaper in Indianapolis, Indiana. The city editor of the *Chicago Conservator* in the late 1880s was Lewis W. Cummins '85. By 1890 at least five other papers, usually small ones, were edited by Fisk graduates. They were: the *Nashville Tribune*, edited by Samuel A. McAlwee, the politician, and W. A. Crostwaite; the *Galveston Test*, edited by H. C. Gray; the *Dallas Tribune*, with R. S. Holloway as associate editor; and the *Tennessee Star*, edited by George T. Robison '85.[45]

Julius N. Avendorph, who went to Chicago from Fisk and secured a position in the office of the president of the Pullman Company, became society editor of the *Chicago Defender*. According to the *Defender*, Avendorph was qualified for his position because he was one of the best-known men in Chicago's black social circles. He had formed several social clubs and founded the annual Paul Laurence Dunbar Memorial. In the late 1920s A. Maceo Smith, who was in the real estate business in Texarkana, Arkansas, began a weekly newspaper.[46]

There were several Texas editors. J. Alston Atkins '19, an attorney, edited the *Houston Informer and Texas Freeman*. In 1931 he was selected as the speaker for the annual meeting of the Texas Commission on Interracial Cooperation. The *San Antonio Register* was edited by Jasper Duncan '16. Later Duncan became chain editor of the Scott Newspaper Syndicate in Atlanta, Georgia.[47]

Several Fisk women have been involved in the newspaper business and at least one became editor. Mrs. Mayme Osby Brown was managing editor of the *East Tennessee News* for nearly five years before she accepted a similar position in 1934 with the *New Orleans Louisiana,* a weekly sheet. The managing editor in the 1930s of the *Negro Liberator,* an organ of the New York League of Struggle for Negro Rights, was Merrill Work, mentioned previously as a politician.[48]

William Lloyd Imes '10, pastor and college president, was selected as religious editor of the *New York Amsterdam News,* while W. S. Ellington '19, a Baptist minister, edited the *Abdemelach and Debbora* magazine. Carter H. Wesley published the *Houston Informer* and fourteen branch newspapers. He was called one of the foremost publishers in black journalism. J. F. McClellan edited the *Nashville Independent* for a short time.[49]

Fisk also produced some novelists and poets. From the time James Weldon Johnson was added to the faculty the university had one or more writers on campus. Arna Bontemps remained at Fisk and was joined from year to year by numerous visiting creative writers. Their presence created an atmosphere encouraging to students with creative potential. Poets from Fisk have been rare. Herman J. D. Carter '31 published a book of poems, *The Scottsboro Blues,* in the early 1930s. Several of his poems have been included in anthologies, and numerous of his short stories have been published. At a later time the playwrights William E. Demby '47 and Benjamin Tanner Johnson '49, both of whom spent time in Rome, Italy, began to receive acclaim. The latter became lecturer in English in the Facolta di Magistero of the University of Rome. A notable translator, Johnson translated novels, including *Il Visconte Dimezzato* by Italo Calvino and *Peccato Originale* by Giose Rimanelli, in addition to numerous short stories. He wrote an introduction to the Modern Library Anthology, *Great Italian Stories.* Another Fisk writer was Mrs. Ariel Williams Holloway.[50]

One of the best-known black novelists is Frank Yerby, who attended Paine College and Fisk. Yerby published some interesting short stories for the *Herald,* in 1937 including "Young Man Afraid" with themes of fear and suicide. "A Date with Vera" told how being black could warp personality. After graduation from Fisk Yerby taught a few years and then during World War II began work in war plants. In 1944 his first break came with *Harper's* magazine's publication of "Health Card." The short story, written at night after working in plants during the day, won the O. Henry Memorial Award for the best first story.

Yerby's initial novel was *The Foxes of Harrow,* published in 1946. It stayed high on the best-seller lists for more than a year, and movie rights were purchased by Twentieth Century Fox. Soon Yerby became one of the most widely read novelists in the United States and he shared with Faulkner and Hemingway the honor of being the most popular American novelist in France. Yerby was the first black man to make an unqualified success in the "slick-writing" field. Readers who liked their heroes noble though rakish, their heroines sometimes rash but always faithful, and their villains properly villainous appreciated Yerby's historical romances. Plots were often straight melodrama—sometimes almost incredible. When reviewing *The Vixens,* the *New York Tribune* claimed Yerby had "balance and understanding" when portraying the South. He achieved "a detachment in dealing with the Negro characters that few writers of his race have achieved," was the judgment of historian John Hope Franklin. Some blacks may have thought Yerby was too detached. Scores of Southern racists have read Yerby's books without recognizing that he was black, even though black women in his novels are usually beautiful and irresistible. Despite some criticisms Yerby continued to publish money-making historical romances with regularity.[51]

While some Fiskites were writing for a livelihood, others were engaged in the very practical activity of social work. Especially after George Edmund Haynes and Charles S. Johnson joined the Fisk staff, there was emphasis on training social workers. Scores of students went into the work, several of them achieving distinction. Miss Birdye H. Haynes '09 became head resident of the Wendell Phillips Settlement in West Side Chicago, where she worked under the supervision of the famous Jane Addams. Later Miss Haynes moved to Lincoln House in New York City. Miss Viola Lewis was executive secretary of a child welfare and recreational center for Harlem children in the 1920s. The center provided recreation, wholesome food at cost, and health care for children over nursery school age whose mothers worked away from home.[52]

Mrs. Elizabeth Ross Haynes, wife of George Edmund Haynes, was a nationally known social worker and was considered the outstanding woman in race relations in the 1930s. Mrs. Haynes studied industrial and labor problems, taught, and was the first black to be a member of the national board of the YMCA. A member of the Harlem division of Mayor La Guardia's city planning commission, she was also on the advisory committee of the Harlem federal theater project and advisor to the Work Projects Administration household project for Harlem. In 1936 she was Democratic coleader of the Twenty-first Assembly District in Harlem. Author of two books, *Unsung Heroes* and *Negroes in Domestic Service in the United States,* Mrs. Haynes was engaged in almost every kind of activity for the uplifting of black people.[53]

Another social worker of note was Mrs. Irene McCoy Gaines, a graduate of the Normal School '10, who began her career in Chicago. During World War I she added to her duties by becoming a county organizer for the War Camp Community Services. She was president of the Illinois Federation of Republican Colored Women's Club, and she was Republican state central committeewoman. President Hoover appointed her a delegate to the President's Conference on Housing. A campaign in 1940 for a seat in the Illinois general assembly was unsuccessful.[54]

Mrs. Bernice Galloway Birch '31, a professional Red Cross worker, received national attention in 1956 for her labors during the hurricane and flood in the Waterbury, Connecticut, area. She sloshed about in mud and water, helping scores of victims to "rebuild their homes and lives." Among her duties was dispensing in excess of $50,000 in cash aid. She authorized repairs, signed dispensing orders replacing dentures, crutches, eyeglasses lost or damaged in the storm, and approved payment of medical bills for injured.[55] There are numerous other social workers whose years of patient labor trying to better the life of mankind have gone unrecorded.

The man who was perhaps the most famous Fisk alumnus, W. E. B. Dubois, falls into a special category. Historian, sociologist, novelist, teacher, agitator, editor, and social theorist, DuBois for at least a half-century was a major black leader and a force to be reckoned with on the national scene. Evaluations of him have varied from the worshipful to bitter denunciation, but few have denied his influence. Books and scores of articles have been written by and about DuBois, which makes outlining his career unnecessary.[56]

When students went out to seek success they did not break all ties with Fisk. Fisk students seemed to feel an unusually high degree of loyalty and responsibility to their alma mater. Especially during the university's early years, students owed much of their opportunity for a better life to the school. There was a loose organization of alumni almost from the beginning, an organization which gave financial support to Fisk and demonstrated an active interest in its affairs. In 1884 alumni met, selected the *Herald* as its voice, and requested an alumni member of the board of trustees. The normal school alumni organized almost as quickly. In 1890 the Non-Graduate Association of Fisk University was formed to give students who had benefited from attendance, but had been unable to graduate, an opportunity to render financial and moral support to the school. There were over 4,000 such students in 1890. After the student revolt of 1924–1925 and the formation of the general alumni association, graduates became more powerful. From that time alumni played an increasingly significant role in the university, not only in financial assistance but in determining policy.

No doubt most people included in this chapter deserve more attention than they have received and many others not mentioned warrant consideration. Nevertheless this brief treatment of alumni activities should prove conclusively that Fisk graduates have made substantial contributions to their race and their nation. Certainly their school deserves some of the credit.

Notes

CHAPTER 1

1. U.S., Department of Interior, Bureau of Education, *Survey of Negro Colleges and Universities*, Bulletin no. 7 (Washington, D.C., 1929), p. 1.

2. Francis B. Simkins, "New Viewpoints of Southern Reconstruction," *Journal of Southern History* 5 (February 1939): 59.

3. George R. Bentley, *A History of the Freedmen's Bureau* (Philadelphia, 1955), p. 70.

4. Ibid. See also Willie Lee Rose, *Rehearsal for Reconstruction: The Port Royal Experiment* (New York, 1964).

5. *Nashville Tennessean*, 20 August 1930; F. Ayers to M. E. Strieby, 2 October 1865, in American Missionary Association Archives, Amistad Research Center, Dillard University (hereafter cited as AMAA).

6. John Gate to J. Ogden, 1 December 1865, in Fiskiana Collection, Fisk University Library.

7. W. E. B. DuBois, *Black Reconstruction* (Philadelphia, 1935), p. 368.

8. Kelly Miller, "The Negro and Education," *Forum* 30 (February 1901): 695; idem, "The Past, Present and Future of the Negro College," *Journal of Negro Education* 2 (July 1933): 413; *Second Annual Report of the Western Freedmen's Aid Commission* (Cincinnati, 1865), p. 15.

9. Bentley, *History of the Freedmen's Bureau*, pp. 169–70. For reaction of abolitionists, see James M. McPherson, *The Struggle for Equality: Abolitionists and the Negro in the Civil War and Reconstruction* (Princeton, 1964).

10. E. E. White to J. Ogden, 30 April 1864, L. Merrick to J. Ogden, 14 October 1864, H. S. Dewey to J. Ogden, 16 June 1865, in Fiskiana Collection; A. O. Abbott, *Prison Life in the South* (New York, 1865), pp. 260–95.

11. Allan Johnson and Dumas Malone, eds., *Dictionary of American Biography*, 20 vols. (New York, 1930), 4: 516; "Minutes of the Board of Trustees of Fisk University," 18 April 1940, in Fisk University Library; *Nashville Banner*, 5 September 1900; *Erastus Milo Cravath* (pamphlet, n.d.), in Fisk University Library.

12. The Western Freedmen's Aid Commission had been organized on 19 January 1863 to work "for the physical relief and the mental and moral elevation" of the recently emancipated Negro. J. T. Trowbridge, *A Picture of the Desolated States; and the Work of Restoration, 1865–1868* (Hartford, 1868), p. 279; Thomas B. Alexander, *Political Reconstruction in Tennessee* (Nashville, 1950), p. 52; *Second Annual Report of the Western Freedmen's Aid Commission* (Cincinnati, 1865) p. 5.

13. E. P. Smith to M. E. Strieby, 11 October 1865, in AMAA; Ullin W. Leavell, *Philanthropy in Negro Education* (Nashville, 1930), pp. 35–36; J. B. T. Marsh, *The*

Story of the Jubilee Singers with their Songs, 3rd ed. (London, 1876), pp. 10–11; Trowbridge, *Picture of the Desolated States,* pp. 288–89; "Report of a Subcommittee of the Board of Trustees of Fisk University," 27 December 1898, in Fiskiana Collection.

14. W. E. B. DuBois, "Of the Training of Black Men," *Atlantic Monthly* 90 (September 1902): 292–93; Trowbridge, *Picture of the Desolated States,* pp. 288–89; Leavell, *Philanthropy in Negro Education,* p. 36; *American Missionary* 10 (February 1866): 41; Gustavus D. Pike, *The Singing Campaign for Ten Thousand Pounds,* rev. ed. (New York, 1875), p. vi; E. P. Smith to George W. Balloch, 25 September 1867, George Whipple to O. O. Howard, 3 March 1869, in Bureau Records, Assistant Adjutant General's Office, National Archives (hereafter cited as Bureau Records).

15. The founders of Fisk did not fight the first battle for black education in Nashville and Tennessee. This war had already been fought and partially won in Nashville by the Freedmen's Bureau and by the Reverend J. G. McKee, who had the honor of being first on the scene and bearing the brunt of white opposition. Since Fisk was free, McKee was at first fearful it would destroy his own school and he did lose many pupils to Fisk. J. G. McKee to J. B. Clark, 15 January 1866, in AMAA; *Fisk Herald,* December 1900, p. 2; G. W. Hubbard, comp., *A History of the Colored Schools of Nashville, Tennessee* (Nashville, 1874), pp. 6–9.

16. *American Missionary* 10 (March 1866): 59–60; *Nashville Daily Union and American,* 10 January 1866.

17. *Fisk Herald,* December 1900, p. 3; *American Missionary* 10 (March 1866): 59–60; *Nashville Daily Union and American,* 10 January 1866.

18. James W. Patton, *Unionism and Reconstruction in Tennessee* (Chapel Hill, 1934), p. 130; *American Missionary* 10 (March 1866): 59–60; *Nashville Daily Union and American,* 10 January 1866.

19. *Nashville Daily Union,* 11 February 1865; Alexander, *Political Reconstruction,* pp. 21, 34, 47.

20. F. Ayers to G. Whipple, 28 October 1865, F. Ayers to M. E. Strieby, 2 October 1865, E. M. Cravath to M. E. Strieby, 16 October 1865, E. P. Smith to M. E. Strieby, 11 October 1865, in AMAA; National Education Association, *Proceedings of the Conference for Education in the South, 1904* (New York, 1904), pp. 46–47; *American Missionary* 10 (March 1866): 61, 13 (October 1869): 229.

21. Joe M. Richardson, ed., "The Memphis Race Riot and its Aftermath," *Tennessee Historical Quarterly* 24 (Spring 1965): 63–64; Patton, *Unionism and Reconstruction,* pp. 163–64, 186.

22. Booker T. Washington, "A University Education for Negroes," *Independent* 68 (24 March 1910): 613.

23. Mrs. C. S. Crosby to M. E. Strieby, 1 May 1866, Miss E. A. Easter to M. E. Strieby, 12 February 1866, in AMAA.

24. E. M. Cravath to G. Whipple, 13 February 1866, C. A. Crosby to M. E. Strieby, 1 May 1866, "Monthly School Reports," January, February, and April 1866, in AMAA.

25. U.S. Commissioner of Education, *Report for the Year 1888–1889,* 2 vols. (Washington, D.C., 1891), 2: 1418; A. M. Atkinson to J. Ogden, 30 October 1868, in Fiskiana Collection.

26. *Nashville Cumberland Presbyterian,* 10 October 1895.

27. Bentley, *History of the Freedmen's Bureau,* p. 170.

28. J. Ogden to E. P. Smith, 8 May 1867, in AMAA.

29. F. Q. Blanchard, "A Quarter Century in the American Missionary Association," *Journal of Negro Education* 6 (April 1937): 155; Washington, "University
Education for Negroes," p. 614; Edward T. Ware, "Higher Education of Negroes in the United States," *Annals of the American Academy* 49 (September 1913):
210-11.

30. U.S., Department of Interior, Bureau of Education, *Negro Education, A
Study of the Private and Higher Schools for Colored People in the United States,* Bulletin
no. 38 (Washington, D.C., 1917), pp. 136, 275; U.S. Commissioner of Education,
Report for the Year 1902, 2 vols. (Washington, D.C., 1902), 1:285; Henry L. Swint,
The Northern Teacher in the South, 1862–1870 (Nashville, 1941); Clifton H.
Johnson, "The American Missionary Association, 1846–1861: A study of Chris-
tian abolitionism" (Ph.D. diss., University of North Carolina, 1959); Richard B.
Drake, "The American Missionary Association and the Southern Negro, 1861–
1888" (Ph.D. diss., Emory University, 1957).

31. The teachers were: Miss H. M. Swallow, Miss Ada C. Clapp, Miss E. A.
Easter, Miss S. S. Stevenson, Miss M. M. Spain, Miss C. M. Jones, Miss Carrie
Semple, Miss Laura Cravath, Mrs. M. Hartley, and Mrs. L. Jackson, "Monthly
Teachers Report," April 1866, in AMAA.

32. Trowbridge, *Picture of the Desolated States,* p. 287.

33. Mrs. C. S. Crosby to M. E. Strieby, 1 May 1866, T. Kennedy to J. Ogden,
17 January and 21 April 1866, in AMAA.

34. Hodding Carter, *The Angry Scar* (New York, 1959), p. 193.

35. J. Ogden to G. Whipple, 29 February 1868, E. M. Cravath to M. E. Strieby,
12 February 1866, in AMAA; *Nashville Tennessean,* 20 August 1930; E. Franklin
Frazier, *Black Bourgeoisie* (Glencoe, Illinois, 1957), pp. 71–72; Marsh, *Jubilee
Singers,* p. 13.

36. "Report of Fisk University," 8 October 1870, A. K. Spence to E. M.
Cravath, 4 October 1870, in AMAA; James N. Eaton, "The Life of Erastus Milo
Cravath, A Guiding Light in an Era of Darkness" (M.A. thesis, Fisk University,
1959), p. 89.

37. "Minutes of the General Faculty of Fisk University," 8 November 1869, in
Fisk University Library; *The Twenty-First Annual Report of the American Missionary
Association and the Proceedings at the Annual Meeting . . . October 17 and 18, 1867*
(New York, 1867), p. 4.

38. Undated account in Henrietta Matson Letter Press, Fisk University Library.

39. *American Missionary* 34 (February 1880): 50–51; *The Twenty-Fourth Annual
Report of the American Missionary Association and the Proceedings at the Annual
Meeting . . . November 9 and 10, 1870* (New York, 1870), p. 37.

40. L. Coffin to J. Ogden, 19 February 1868, J. Ogden and eight others to
American Missionary Association, 28 June 1868, in AMAA.

41. Miss E. A. Easter to M. E. Strieby, 12 February 1866, in AMAA; J. Ogden
to C. B. Fisk, 8 March 1866, in Fiskiana Collection; *First Report of the Superintendent of Public Instruction of the State of Tennessee—Ending Thursday, October 7th, 1869*
(Nashville, 1869), p. 92.

42. *Nashville Daily Union and American,* 3 and 10 January 1866.

43. Alexander, *Political Reconstruction*, pp. 94, 123–24.

44. The inspector general of the Freedmen's Bureau, F. D. Sewall, who made a Southern tour in 1866, said of Fisk: "I do not hesitate to pronounce it one of the best arranged and conducted schools for freedmen that I have seen." F. D. Sewall to O. O. Howard, 17 September 1866, in Bureau Records; E. M. Cravath to G. Whipple, 19 June 1866, in AMAA; *Nashville Tennessean*, 20 August 1930.

CHAPTER 2

1. E. P. Smith to J. Ogden, 13 May 1867, J. Ogden to E. P. Smith, 25 November 1867, in AMAA.

2. In attacking the school law, Ogden made a prophetic statement. Schools should be provided without partiality or distinction; nothing should be said about caste or color. If this were done, Ogden said, in less than fifty years needless prejudice would be dead. But legislating for prejudice, he continued, would make it respectable and provide for its continuation. Segregation and prejudice must die sometime and the sooner the legislature acted the better. If it hurt "somebody," he suggested, "let somebody get out of the way." *Nashville Daily Press and Times*, 15 November 1867; Patton, *Unionism and Reconstruction*, pp. 161–62.

3. Typed copy of Articles of Incorporation of Fisk University in Fiskiana Collection, original in Register's office, Davidson County, Tennessee, book 38, p. 339; registered 24 August 1867.

4. The first members of the board of trustees were: George Whipple, Erastus M. Cravath, Charles Crosby, John Ogden, Joseph H. Barnum, W. W. Mallory, John Lawrence, John Ruhm, and J. J. Carey. Carey was an able black man who was in charge of the Freedman's Savings Bank in Nashville. Carl R. Osthaus, *Freedmen, Philanthropy and Fraud: A History of the Freedman's Savings Bank* (Urbana, 1976), p. 107.

5. The Peabody Fund, a pioneer education foundation, was established in 1867 by George Peabody, a Massachusetts native and later a London banker. His first gift was $1,000,000, to which he added a like sum two years later to aid the South. He named sixteen Northern and Southern men of distinction to administer the fund. They in turn selected Dr. Barnas Sears as the first general agent. Funds aided both white and black education. J. Ogden to G. Whipple, 29 February 1868, in AMAA.

6. Horace Mann Bond, *The Education of the Negro in the American Social Order* (New York, 1934), p. 131.

7. J. Ogden to G. Whipple, 29 February 1868, in AMAA; *Catalog of Fisk University, 1867–1868*, p. 13; *Fisk University and Normal School* (pamphlet, 1869).

8. *Report of John M. Langston, General Inspector of Schools, Bureau of Refugees, Freedmen and Abandoned Lands* (n.p., 1869), in AMAA; *Catalog of Fisk University 1867–1868*, pp. 12–13; *Fisk University and Normal School* (pamphlet, 1869).

9. J. Ogden to E. P. Smith, 15 February 1869, in AMAA; *Twenty-Fourth Annual Report of the American Missionary Association and the Proceeding at the Annual Meeting . . . November 9 and 10, 1870* (New York, 1870), p. 4.

10. Edward King, *The Southern States of North America* (London, 1875), pp. 604–5; A. K. Spence to E. Spence, 28 March 1871, in Mary E. Spence Collection,

Fisk University Library; "Report of Fisk University," November 1872, in AMAA; U.S. Commissioner of Education, *Report for the Year 1873* (Washington, D.C., 1874), pp. 375–76; *Fisk University* (pamphlet, 1869); Tennessee, *House Journal 1875*, p. 209.

11. *Fisk University Catalog, 1871–1872*, pp. 18–20.

12. *Fisk University Catalog, 1868–1870*, pp. 20–21, *1871–1872*, p. 20.

13. "Minutes of the Union Literary Society," 31 January 1868, 1 January 1876, in Fisk University Library; J. Ogden to G. Whipple, 29 February 1868, in AMAA.

14. Henry Hugh Proctor, *Between Black and White: Autobiographical Sketches* (Boston, 1925), p. 7; *Proceedings of the Conference for Education in the South, 1904* (New York, 1904), pp. 46–47; "Report of Fisk University," November 1872, in AMAA.

15. C. Crosby to E. P. Smith, 12 January 1867, E. M. Cravath to G. L. White, 6 January 1868, in AMAA; *Twenty-Second Annual Report of the American Missionary Association and the Proceedings at the Annual Meeting . . . 1868* (New York, 1868), p. 55.

16. *Harper's Weekly* 20 (22 January 1876): 73; *Fisk University* (pamphlet, 1869); *Fisk Herald*, June 1884, p. 3; L. A. Roberts to G. L. White, 5 October 1870, in Fiskiana Collection.

17. *Rules and Regulations of Fisk University* (flyer, 1868).

18. "Minutes of the General Faculty of Fisk University," 27 December 1869, in Fisk University Library.

19. King, *Southern States*, pp. 604–5.

20. Mrs. C. A. Crosby to E. P. Smith, 31 January 1868, in AMAA; *Fisk University* (pamphlet, 1869).

21. S. L. Grant to G. L. White, 8 December 1870, in Fiskiana Collection; U.S. Commissioner of Education, *Report for the Year 1874* (Washington, D.C., 1875), p. 402.

22. M. T. Weir to E. M. Cravath, 27 April 1874, in AMAA; Sterling Brown to Mrs. A. K. Spence, 25 February 1877, in Mary E. Spence Collection; Mrs. E. Cole to J. Ogden, 16 November 1868, J. Coffey to G. L. White, 7 March 1871, J. Tillman to G. L. White, 3 April 1871, in Fiskiana Collection.

23. W. H. Bower to J. Ogden, 15 September 1868, E. M. Cravath to J. Ogden, 20 February 1868, E. O. Tade to G. L. White, 3 January 1871, in Fiskiana Collection; B. Sears to A. K. Spence, 26 December 1870, 4 March 1871, in Mary E. Spence Collection.

24. E. H. Freeman to M. E. Strieby, 3 August 1868, H. S. Bennett to M. E. Strieby, 30 August 1869, A. K. Spence to Miss D. E. Emerson, 5 September 1874, in AMAA; W. F. Carter to J. Ogden, 17 February 1868, in Fiskiana Collection; C. E. Compton, "Tennessee School Report," 31 December 1869, Bureau Records, Educational Division.

25. U.S. Commissioner of Education, *Report for the Year 1872.* (Washington, D.C., 1873), p. 324; J. Ogden to G. Whipple, 29 February 1868, H. C. Morgan to E. M. Cravath, 28 March 1871, in AMAA.

26. Nellie M. Horton to G. D. Pike, 23 October 1870, in AMAA; *Fisk University News*, October 1911, pp. 14–15.

27. Miss L. M. Stratton to E. M. Cravath, 29 October 1870, J. E. Benedict to Respected Sirs, 17 March 1871, G. L. White to E. M. Cravath, 21 August 1871, Miss A. E. Alden to E. M. Cravath, 1 December 1874, Miss A. Cahill to E. M. Cravath, 7 December 1874, in AMAA.

28. E. O. Tade to E. P. Smith, 15 May 1867, in AMAA; E. M. Cravath to G. L. White, 4 January 1868, in Fiskiana Collection.

29. Eaton, "Erastus Milo Cravath," p. 97; G. L. White to E. M. Cravath, 8 November 1870, in AMAA; *Fisk News*, June 1947, p. 2; Lucius S. Merriam, *Higher Education in Tennessee*, Bureau of Education Circular of Information, no. 5 (Washington, 1893), p. 263; *Twenty-Fourth Annual Report of the American Missionary Association, and the Proceedings at the Annual Meeting . . . November 9th and 10th, 1870* (New York, 1870), p. 40.

30. Proctor, *Between Black and White*, pp. 32–33; A. Robinson to J. D. Burrus, 26 September 1876, in America W. Robinson Letters, Fisk University Library; *Fisk Herald*, May 1900, pp. 3–5; *Greater Fisk Herald*, June 1927, pp. 24–26; *Fisk University News*, January 1924, p. 4.

31. Proctor, *Between Black and White*, p. 31; *Fisk University News*, November 1914, p. 6; *Maumee Valley* (Ohio) *News*, 30 November 1945.

32. Statement in Mary E. Spence Collection, n.d.; *Fisk Herald*, May 1904, pp. 5–6.

33. *Fisk University News*, October 1911, pp. 3–5; A. K. Spence to mother, 9 April 1872, in Mary E. Spence Collection.

34. Eaton, "Erastus Milo Cravath," p. 98; G. L. White to E. M. Cravath, 13 February 1871, S. M. Wells to E. M. Cravath, 3 January 1872, A. K. Spence to E. M. Cravath, 12 June 1874, in AMAA; A. K. Spence to Mrs. E. Spence, 14 February 1871, Mrs. E. Spence to A. K. Spence, 17 April 1872, in Mary E. Spence Collection.

35. "Minutes of the General Faculty of Fisk University," 4 January 1869; Peter Pearle to G. L. White, 24 August 1871, in Fiskiana Collection; T. C. Steward to E. M. Cravath, 25 July 1874, in AMAA.

36. "History of Fisk University," in "Minutes of the General Faculty of Fisk University," n.d.; M. E. Strieby to G. Whipple, 17 April 1869, in AMAA; *Nashville Tennessean*, 20 August 1930; Special Orders No. 122, 21 August 1869, Bureau of Refugees, Freedmen, and Abandoned Lands, in Fiskiana Collection; undated manuscript by John Ogden in AMAA; D. Burt, "Tennessee School Report," 29 June 1867, in Bureau Records, Educational Division.

37. A. K. Spence to E. M. Cravath, 24 November and 13 December 1871, in AMAA; A. K. Spence to Mrs. E. Spence, 13 December 1871, in Mary E. Spence Collection.

38. Probably the American Missionary Association would not have allowed Fisk to close, but many of the Fisk teachers thought it would. The association was in trouble financially; it was overextended. The dissolution of the Freedmen's Bureau caused a loss of approximately $30,000 per year to the missionary association. Then the Chicago fire of 1871 almost dried up Northern charity. The association began the 1870s with a retrenchment policy—a policy that included closing some of the schools. Bureau Superintendent of Education J. W. Alvord visited Fisk in 1870. The instructors worked hard, he said, "desperately—but

pull against the tide and look worn and sad." J. W. Alvord to O. O. Howard, 26 January 1870, in Bureau Records; Drake, "American Missionary Association," pp. 101–3.

CHAPTER 3

1. Marsh, *Jubilee Singers,* p. 14; Hubbard, *Colored Schools of Nashville,* p. 22.
2. J. Lawrence to E. M. Cravath, 31 March 1871, A. K. Spence to E. M. Cravath, 26 April and 8 May 1871, G. L. White to E. M. Cravath, 26 April 1871, in AMAA; E. M. Cravath to G. L. White, 24 June 1870, T. Rutling to G. L. White, 7 July 1870, M. L. Porter to G. L. White, 12 December 1870, in Fiskiana Collection; Marsh, *Jubilee Singers,* p. 14; Hubbard, *Colored Schools of Nashville,* p. 22.
3. "Minutes of the Board of Trustees of Fisk University," 21 June 1871, in Fisk University Library; G. L. White to C. B. Fisk, 3 July 1871, C. B. Fisk to G. L. White, 11 July 1871, E. M. Cravath to G. L. White, 22 August 1871, in Fiskiana Collection; U.S. Commissioner of Education, *Report for the Year 1898–1899,* 2 vols. (Washington, D.C., 1900), 2:2432–33.
4. G. L. White to E. M. Cravath, 9 and 21 September 1871, A. K. Spence to E. M. Cravath, 13 September and 1 November 1871, in AMAA; A. K. Spence to Mrs. E. Spence, 13 December 1871, in Mary E. Spence Collection; *Fisk Herald,* November 1890, pp. 1–3; *Chattanooga Times,* 1 September 1871.
5. Gustavus D. Pike, *The Jubilee Singers, and their Campaign for Twenty Thousand Dollars* (New York, 1873), pp. 54–72; Mary E. Spence, "The Jubilee of Jubilees at Fisk University," *Southern Workman* 51 (February 1922): 77; "Thomas Rutling Confession," 5 March 1870, in Fiskiana Collection.
6. *Fisk University News,* October 1911, p. 46; Marsh, *Jubilee Singers,* pp. 17–21; Pike, *Campaign for Twenty Thousand Dollars,* p. 93; A. K. Spence to E. M. Cravath, 24 November 1871, in AMAA; *Cincinnati Gazette,* 18 October 1871; *Akron Daily Beacon,* 1 December 1871; *Cleveland Herald,* 13 November 1871; *Cleveland Daily Leader,* 13 November 1871.
7. Pike, *Campaign for Twenty Thousand Dollars,* p. 100; Marsh, *Jubilee Singers,* pp. 21–25; Joseph E. Roy, *Pilgrim's Letters: Bits of Current History* (Boston, 1888), p. 178.
8. *Fisk University News,* October 1911, pp. 47–48; *Nashville Tennessean* magazine, 6 October 1946, p. 7; *Fisk News,* December 1931, p. 4; E. Sheppard to A. K. Spence, 12 November 1871, in Mary E. Spence Collection; Margaret Just Butcher, *The Negro in American Culture* (New York, 1956), p. 27; Miles Mark Fisher, *Slave Songs in the United States* (Ithaca, New York, 1953), p. 190.
9. *Fisk Herald,* November 1896, p. 13; *Fisk University News,* October 1911, p. 48; Julius Bloom, ed., *The Year in American Music: 1946–47* (New York, 1947), p. 48; *New York Times,* 30 October 1956; John G. Van Deusen, *The Black Man in White America* (Washington, D.C., 1938), pp. 226–27; H. E. Krehbiel, quoted in John A. and Alan Lomax, comp., *American Ballads and Folk Songs* (New York, 1934), p. 575.
10. Spence, "Jubilee of Jubilees," p. 73; *Fisk University News,* October 1911, p. 47.
11. G. L. White to A. K. Spence, 21 December 1871, in AMAA; Pike, *Campaign for Twenty Thousand Dollars,* pp. 108–13; *Fisk University News,* October 1911,

p. 48; *New York Tribune*, 28 December 1871; *Brooklyn Union*, 2 January 1872; *Hartford Evening Post*, 3 February 1872.

12. J. E. Smith to A. K. Spence, 6 April 1872, in Mary E. Spence Collection; *Nashville Tennessean*, 20 August 1930; Pike, *Campaign for Twenty Thousand Dollars*, pp. 113–51; *Fisk University News*, October 1911, p. 48.

13. *Fisk News*, November 1940, p. 3; E. Sheppard to A. K. Spence, 6 March 1872, T. Rutling to A. K. Spence, (n.d.) March 1872, in Mary E. Spence Collection; *Fisk University News*, October 1911, p. 48; *New National Era*, 13 February 1873.

14. Mrs. E. Spence to A. K. Spence, 22 May 1872, in Mary E. Spence Collection; Pike, *Campaign for Twenty Thousand Dollars*, pp. 145–52; "Report of a Subcommittee of the Board of Trustees of Fisk University," 27 December 1898, in Fiskiana Collection; *Fisk University News*, October 1911, p. 49; *New York Independent*, 4 March 1872; *Providence* (Rhode Island) *Herald*, 21 March 1872.

15. Mrs. E. Spence to A. K. Spence, 22 May 1872, in Mary E. Spence Collection; Marsh, *Jubilee Singers*, p. 42.

16. *Nashville Tennessean* magazine, 6 October 1946, p. 8; *Fisk University News*, October 1911, pp. 49–50; Marsh, *Jubilee Singers*, pp. 42–44; *Christian Union* 6 (3 July 1872): 23.

17. The members of the second tour included: Ella Sheppard, Maggie L. Porter, Jennie Jackson, Georgia Gordon, Minnie Tate, Thomas Rutling, Isaac Dickerson, Mabel R. Lewis, Edmund Watkins, Benjamin Holmes, and Julia Jackson. Marsh, *Jubilee Singers*, pp. 42, 45–49; *Fisk University News*, October 1911, p. 50; U.S. Commissioner of Education, *Report for the Year 1872* (Washington, D.C., 1873), p. 324.

18. Milton Meltzer, *Mark Twain Himself* (New York, 1960), p. 219; Pike, *Campaign for Twenty Thousand Dollars*, pp. 14–15.

19. Marsh, *Jubilee Singers*, pp. 53–55; *Fisk University News*, October 1911, pp. 50–51; *Nashville Tennessean*, 6 October 1928; *Times* (London), 7 May 1873; *Fisk News*, November 1940, p. 3.

20. Pike, *Ten Thousand Pounds*, pp. 77, 82; Marsh, *Jubilee Singers*, pp. 55–58; *Fisk University News*, October 1911, pp. 50–51.

21. Bernard A. Weisberger, *They Gathered at the River: The Story of the Great Revivalists and Their Impact upon Religion in America* (Boston, 1958), pp. 199–200; Pike, *Ten Thousand Pounds*, pp. 88–89, 151–54; *Rockdale Observer*, 6 December 1873; *York Telegraph*, 13 December 1873; *Leeds Post*, 18 December 1873.

22. *Glasgow* (Scotland) *Herald*, 18 August 1873; Pike, *Ten Thousand Pounds*, pp. 130–32, 137–38; *Edinburg Courier*, 23 December 1873; *Manchester Courier*, 15 and 30 January 1874; *Norfolk News*, 21 February 1874; *Norchwich Mercury*, 21 February 1874.

23. Pike, *Ten Thousand Pounds*, pp. 174–76; *Times* (London), 11 May 1874; E. Sheppard to "my dear friend," 26 April 1874, in Mary E. Spence Collection; Thomas C. Steward to E. M. Cravath, 5 May 1874, in Thomas C. Steward Letter Press, Fisk University Library; A. K. Spence to E. M. Cravath, 25 April 1874, in AMAA; M. Tate to G. D. Pike, 10 May 1874, in Fiskiana Collection; *Fisk University News*, October 1911, pp. 51–52; Marsh, *Jubilee Singers*, pp. 75–76; *Brighton Daily News*, 24 March 1874; *Bristol Daily Post*, 12 March 1874; *English Independent*, 2 April 1874.

24. Those who were members of the third company at one time or another included: Ella Sheppard, Maggie Porter, Jennie Jackson, Georgia Gordon, Julia Jackson, America Robinson, Maggie Carnes, Thomas Rutling, Hinton D. Alexander, Edmund Watkins, F. J. Loudin, Patti Malone, Lucinda Vance, Mabel Lewis, and W. B. Thomas. Ella Sheppard Diary, 10 November and 12 December 1874, in Fisk University Library; G. L. White to Fisk University Executive Committee, 11 November 1874, in Mary E. Spence Collection; *Fisk Herald,* October 1890, p. 4.

25. Ella Sheppard Diary, 24 January, 7, 11, 15, 19, and 20 February, 29 April 1875; A. W. Robinson to J. D. Burrus, 4 March 1875, in America W. Robinson Letters; *New York Times,* 2 February 1875.

26. *London Daily News,* 19 January 1925; A. W. Robinson to J. D. Burrus, 4 March and 19 May 1875, in America W. Robinson Letters; Ella Sheppard Diary, 15, 16, 20, and 31 May 1875; Marsh, *Jubilee Singers,* pp. 81–82.

27. A. W. Robinson to J. D. Burrus, 2 June and 14 July 1875, in America W. Robinson Letters; *Fisk University News,* October 1911, p. 54.

28. Ella Sheppard Diary, 23 June, 22 July, 28 September, 3 and 30 October 1875; A. W. Robinson to J. D. Burrus, 2 June, 2 July, 2 August, 18 October, and 22 November 1875, in America W. Robinson Letters.

29. Dublin *Irish Times,* 27 November 1875; Ella Sheppard Diary, 18 and 19 November 1875; A. W. Robinson to J. D. Burrus, 23 November 1875, in America W. Robinson Letters; *Lancaster Guardian,* 11 December 1875.

30. *Liverpool Daily Courier,* 31 January 1876; *Lancaster Guardian,* 11 December 1875; Ella Sheppard Diary, 6 December 1875, 25 and 26 April 1876.

31. A. W. Robinson to J. D. Burrus, 18 October 1875, 23 June and 18 September 1876, in America W. Robinson Letters; Ella Sheppard Diary, 18 November 1875.

32. *Fisk University News,* October 1911, p. 54: A. W. Robinson to J. D. Burrus, August, n.d., 19 August, 18 September and 12 October 1876, in America W. Robinson Letters; G. L. White to A. K. Spence, 14 October 1876, in Mary E. Spence Collection; Ella Sheppard Diary, 29 September 1876.

33. Ella Sheppard Diary, 28 August 1876; *Fisk University News,* October 1911, pp. 54–55.

34. A. W. Robinson to J. D. Burrus, (n.d.) February 1877, in America W. Robinson Letters; *Fisk University News,* October 1911, p. 55; M. L. Porter to Mrs. A. K. Spence, 1 May 1877, in Mary E. Spence Collection; *Times* (London), 20 October 1877.

35. Ella Sheppard Diary, 4 November 1877; *Fisk University News,* October 1911, p. 56; E. M. Cravath to A. K. Spence, 30 April 1878, in Mary E. Spence Collection.

36. Ella Sheppard Diary, 7 November and 3 December 1877, 22, 23, and 24 April 1878; A. W. Robinson to J. D. Burrus, 18 April 1877, 8 March 1878, in America W. Robinson Letters.

37. "Jubilee Day," an address by James Weldon Johnson, 7 October 1933, in James Weldon Johnson Collection, Fisk University Library; *Harper's Weekly* 20 (22 January 1876): 73; Vernon Loggins, *The Negro Author: His Development in America* (New York, 1931), pp. 255, 359; Buell G. Gallagher, *American Caste and the Negro College* (New York, 1933), p. 369; H. W. Beecher to G. L. White, n.d., in Fiskiana Collection.

Chapter 4

1. For a detailed discussion of the period from 1877 to 1900, see Rayfofd W. Logan, *The Negro in American Life and Thought: The Nadir, 1877–1901* (New York, 1954); August Meier, *Negro Thought in America, 1880–1915: Racial ideologies in the Age of Booker T. Washington* (Ann Arbor, 1963), pp. 19–21; John Hope Franklin, *From Slavery to Freedom: A History of Negro Americans*, 4th ed. rev. (New York, 1974), pp. 260–76; C. Vann Woodward, *Origins of the New South 1877–1913* (Baton Rouge, 1951), pp. 1–22.

2. *Nashville Republican Banner*, 22 October 1873; *Nashville Daily American*, 7 October 1879.

3. Mrs. C. B. Fisk to S. G. Willard, 25 August 1875, in Fiskiana Collection; *Fisk University News*, November 1915, p. 7; U.S. Commissioner of Education, *Report for the Year 1873* (Washington, D.C., 1874), p. 376; *Greater Fisk Herald*, June 1927, p. 26; Marsh, *Jubilee Singers*, p. 80.

4. *Nashville American*, 2 January 1876; *New York Times*, 2 January 1876.

5. "Minutes of the Board of Trustees of Fisk University," 23 July 1875, in Fisk University Library; A. K. Spence to M. E. Strieby, 6 January 1876, in AMAA; Statement of Frederick A. Chase, n.d., in Mary E. Spence Collection; Eaton, "Erastus Milo Cravath," p. 98.

6. Augustus Field Beard, *A Crusade of Brotherhood: A History of the American Missionary Association* (Boston, 1909), pp. 158–60; H. Matson to Mrs. A. K. Spence, 3 September 1876, in Mary E. Spence Collection; Booker T. Washington, "University Education for Negroes," p. 614; *Fisk News*, March–April 1934, p. 5; Mrs. F. A. McKenzie to "Dearest Folks," 13 November 1915, in Fayette Avery McKenzie Papers, Tennessee State Library and Archives, Nashville, Tennessee (hereafter cited as McKenzie Papers); W. E. B. DuBois, *Dusk of Dawn: An Essay Toward an Autobiography of a Race Concept* (New York, 1940), p. 31.

7. "Minutes of the Board of Trustees of Fisk University," 21 September 1875; "A Brief Statement of the Financial Relation of the American Missionary Association to Fisk University, one of its chartered Institutions, 1865–1898," 10 February 1899, in Fiskiana Collection.

8. On 8 May 1876, the faculty empowered the president to grant Miss Robinson a degree if in his judgment she had secured by experience abroad "an amount of culture equivalent to the studies in which she is behind." In Fisk records she was always listed as an 1875 graduate. "Minutes of the General Faculty of Fisk University," 8 May 1876.

9. *American Missionary* 19 (August 1875): 182; *Nashville Union and American*, 28 May 1875; Marsh, *Jubilee Singers,* p. 79; *Nashville Republican Banner,* 28 May 1875; *Fisk News,* December 1928, p. 3.

10. *A Brief Sketch of the Life and Labors of Mrs. V. W. Broughton* (pamphlet, n.d.); *Fisk Expositor* 5 (February 1882): 1; *Fisk University Catalog 1890–1891*, p. 8, *1911–1912*, p. 84; Nellie E. White, comp., *Alumni Directory of Fisk University, 1875–1930* (Nashville, 1930), p. 103.

11. For a fuller discussion of the life and career of James Dallas Burrus, see Joe M. Richardson, "A Negro Success Story: James Dallas Burrus," *Journal of Negro History* 50 (October 1965): 274–82.

12. William J. Simmons, *Men of Mark: Eminent, Progressive and Rising* (Cleve-

land, 1887), pp. 282–83; *Dartmouth Alumni Magazine,* 21 (February 1929): 257; A. W. Robinson to J. D. Burrus, 24 May 1877, in America W. Robinson Letters; *Fisk News,* December 1928, p. 3.

13. Dartmouth at that time awarded no degrees for graduate work but the faculty voted to award Burrus an honorary Master of Arts degree.

14. "Report of the State Superintendent of Public Education," in *Biennial Reports of the Departments and Benevolent Institutions of the State of Mississippi, for the years 1882–1883* (Jackson, 1884), p. 72; Mississippi *Senate Journal, 1884,* p. 27; *Nashville Tennessean,* 2 January 1929.

15. W. Milan Davis, *Pushing Forward: A History of Alcorn A. and M. College and Portraits of Some of its Successful Graduates* (Okalona, Mississippi, 1938), p. 20; Mississippi, *Senate Journal, 1884,* p. 256; Edward Mayers, *History of Education in Mississippi* (Washington, 1899), pp. 275–76.

16. *Nashville Tennessean,* 2 January 1929; *Fisk University News,* April 1916, p. 1, December 1917, p. 12; *Fisk News,* May 1929, p. 5; *Greater Fisk Herald,* November 1926, p. 25; *Report of the President of Fisk University, 1930–1931,* p. 33, Fiskiana Collection; *New York Times,* 3 January 1929; *Nashville Banner,* 4 January 1929.

17. *Fisk University Catalog, 1877,* pp. 8–10, *1878,* p. 16, *1883,* p. 15; U.S. Commissioner of Education, *Report for the Year 1884–1885* (Washington, D.C., 1886), p. 680, *Report for the Year 1897–1898,* 2: 2494–95.

18. *Fisk University Catalog, 1880–1881,* p. 8; *Fisk Herald,* July 1893, pp. 4, 14; *Fisk University News,* April 1922, pp. 2–3.

19. "Minutes of the General Faculty of Fisk University," 4 February 1878; *Fisk University Catalog, 1879,* p. 35 *1879–1880,* p. 31, *1880–1881,* p. 31; *Fisk Herald,* March 1887, p. 6, April 1890, p. 6.

20. "House Joint Resolution No. 38," in *Acts of the State of Tennessee 1879,* p. 374; *Fisk University Catalog, 1879,* p. 28; A. K. Spence to M. E. Strieby, 28 February 1876, in AMAA.

21. Quoted in *Fisk Herald,* March 1886, p. 4; *Nashville Daily American,* 4 January 1885, 25 May 1886.

22. Fisk University Visitors Register, 21 January 1877–1941, in Fisk University Library; Mrs. Mary E. Barnes to General and Mrs. C. B. Fisk, 9 April 1884, quoted in *Fisk Herald,* July 1884, p. 6.

23. "Fisk University," *Southern Workman* 39 (May 1910): 259; Franklin, *From Slavery to Freedom,* p. 377.

24. DuBois, *Dusk of Dawn,* p. 97; *Fisk Herald,* June 1883, p. 5; October 1883, p. 4; June 1884, p. 1; January 1889, p. 9; February 1889, p. 8; March 1889, p. 12; July 1891, p. 9; November 1891, p. 9; June 1897, p. 5; May 1899, p. 1.

25. "Minutes of the General Faculty of Fisk University," 22 November 1875, 18 May 1876, 19 February 1877, 15 May 1878, 27 September 1881; *Washington* (D.C.) *People's Advocate,* 24 July 1880.

26. Arna Bontemps, "Why I Returned," *Harper's* 230 (April 1965): 181; *Nashville Daily American,* 4 January 1885; Drake, "The American Missionary Association," p. 169: James M. McPherson, *The Abolitionist Legacy: From Reconstruction to the NAACP* (Princeton, 1975), p. 15.

27. DuBois, *Dusk of Dawn,* pp. 30–31; W. E. B. DuBois, "My Evolving Program for Negro Freedom," in *What the Negro Wants,* ed. Rayford W. Logan (Chapel Hill, 1944), pp. 36–39; Francis L. Broderick, *W. E. B. DuBois: Negro*

Leader in a Time of Crisis (Stanford, 1959), pp. 7–9; *Fisk Herald,* July 1886, p. 6, October 1886, pp. 6–7, December 1886, p. 10.

28. One misfit did turn up at Fisk in 1875. Much to the dismay of the faculty it was discovered that an instructor of reading, hired just that fall, was an inveterate shoplifter. A search warrant was procured by Professor Frederick Chase to investigate her room. Officials found 108 books, mostly stolen from the Fisk Library, and several packages of silver. Nashville merchants kept watch for her arrival but none had reported her activities to Fisk officials. Mrs. Julia Chase to Mrs. A. K. Spence, 4 September 1875, in Mary E. Spence Collection.

29. A. K. Spence to M. E. Strieby, 16 May 1876, in AMAA; J. Chase to mother, 3 and 12 June 1876, H. C. Morgan to A. K. Spence, 1 January 1879, in Mary E. Spence Collection; DuBois, "My Evolving Program," p. 36; U.S. Commissioner of Education, *Report for the Year 1902*, 2 vols. (Washington, D.C., 1903), 1: 290; McPherson, *Abolitionist Legacy,* p. 161.

30. *Fisk University Catalog, 1890–1891,* p. 56.

31. A. K. Spence to E. M. Cravath, 13 September 1871, in AMAA; *Alumni Directory of Fisk University, 1875–1930*, pp. 12–28.

32. A. K. Spence to Mrs. A. K. Spence, 16 June 1876, G. D. Pike to A. K. Spence, 21 September 1878, in Mary E. Spence Collection; *American Missionary* 51 (June 1897): 199–200; "Minutes of the Board of Trustees of Fisk University," 13 June 1878, in Fisk University Library; U.S. Commissioner of Education, *Report for the Year 1888–1889,* 2 vols. (Washington, D.C., 1891), 2: 1137.

33. "Minutes of the Board of Trustees of Fisk University," 16 February 1885, 4 June 1894; "Report of a Subcommittee of the Board of Trustees of Fisk University," 27 December 1898, in Fiskiana Collection.

34. *Alumni Directory of Fisk University, 1875–1930,* p. 6.

35. State of Tennessee, *Annual Report of the State Superintendent of Public Instruction for the Scholastic Year ending June 30, 1900,* pp. 305–6; U.S. Commissioner of Education, *Report for the Year 1899–1900,* 2 vols. (Washington, D.C., 1901), 2: 1421; J. N. Hill, "The Negro College Faces Desegregation," *College and University* 31 (Spring 1956): 293–94; *Fisk University Catalog, 1890–1891,* pp. 8–13.

36. C. Perkins to A. K. Spence, 26 March 1878, in Mary E. Spence Collection; *Fisk Herald,* November 1883, p. 2; Roy, *Pilgrim's Letters,* pp. 179–80; H. Paul Douglass, *Christian Reconstruction in the South* (Boston, 1909), pp. 214–15.

CHAPTER 5

1. Lawrence Cremin, *The Transformation of the School: Progressivism in American Education, 1876–1957* (New York, 1961), pp. 27–29; Meier, *Negro Thought in America*, p. 85.

2. Meier, *Negro Thought in America*, pp. 42, 87, 98–99; Carter G. Woodson, "Twenty-Five Years of Higher Education Among Negroes," in *Higher Education Among Negroes,* ed. Theophilus E. McKinney (Charlotte, North Carolina, 1932), pp. 17–18.

3. DuBois, *Dusk of Dawn,* p. 74; Meier, *Negro Thought in America,* p. 99; Frazier, *Black Bourgeoisie*, p. 68.

4. Booker T. Washington, *The Future of the American Negro* (Boston, 1907), pp. 3–4, 38, 49–50, 57, 77, 80–87; Samuel R. Spencer, Jr., *Booker T. Washington and*

the Negro's Place in American Life (Boston, 1955), p. 155; DuBois, *Dusk of Dawn*, p. 74.

5. Donald Young, *American Minority Peoples: A Study in Racial and Cultural Conflicts in the United States* (New York, 1932), pp. 454–56; *Proceedings of the Fourth Conference for Education in the South . . . 1901* (Harrisburg, Pennsylvania, 1901), p. 107; *Proceedings . . . 1903*, p. 213.

6. Woodson, "Twenty-Five Years of Higher Education," p. 19; Douglass, *Christian Reconstruction*, pp. 289–92; DuBois, "Training of Black Men," p. 295; Woodward, *Origins of the New South*, p. 367.

7. Miller, "The Negro and Education," p. 700; *Fisk Herald*, April 1895, p. 9.

8. Frazier, *Black Bourgeoisie*, p. 68; Dubois, *Dusk of Dawn*, p. 76; Woodward, *Origins of the New South*, p. 365; G. A. Gates to B. T. Washington, 31 January 1910, H. L. Simmons to B. T. Washington, 21 October 1911, in Booker T. Washington Papers, Library of Congress; "State Papers as Governor and President, 1899–1909," in *The Works of Theodore Roosevelt*, 22 vols. (New York, 1926), 11: 354–55.

9. J. Ogden to E. P. Smith, 11 April 1868, in AMAA; *New York Times*, 22 January 1933; Meier, *Negro Thought in America*, p. 88.

10. *Fisk Herald*, November 1883, p. 3, February 1884, p. 3, April 1885, p. 9.

11. *Fisk Herald*, January 1884, p. 6, May 1884, p. 2; "Minutes of the Executive Committee of Fisk University," 7 January 1884; *American Missionary* 36 (December 1882): 371; Drake, "American Missionary Association," pp. 210–11.

12. *Fisk University Catalog, 1885–1886*, p. 37; *Fisk Herald*, February 1889, p. 1.

13. U.S. Commissioner of Education, *Report for the Year 1888–1889*, 2 vols. (Washington, D.C., 1891), 2: 1427; Louis D. Rubin, Jr., ed., *Teach the Freeman: The Correspondence of Rutherford B. Hayes and the Slater Fund for Negro Education, 1881–1893*, 2 vols. (Baton Rouge, 1959), 1:167, 2:90.

14. "Minutes of the Board of Trustees of Fisk University," 2 December 1898, 21 July 1902; *Scranton* (Pennsylvania) *Truth*, 8 October 1890; *Fisk University Catalog, 1890–1891*, pp. 48–49; U.S. Commissioner of Education, *Report for the Year 1892–1893*, 2 vols. (Washington, D.C., 1895), 2:1561.

15. J. G. Merrill to Editor, *Boston Evening Transcript*, 7 February 1900; "Minutes of the Board of Trustees of Fisk University," 26 June 1903, 17 June 1904; *Fisk Herald*, June 1900, p. 9.

16. "Minutes of the Board of Trustees of Fisk University," 26 June 1903, 17 June 1904, 8 March 1905, 22 June 1906; McPherson, *Abolitionist Legacy*, pp. 216–17.

17. "Report of the President to the Trustees of Fisk University," (n.d.) 1900, in Fiskiana Collection; "Minutes of the Board of Trustees of Fisk University," 23 November 1900, 21 June 1901; *Dictionary of American Biography*, 12:561–62.

18. *Fisk University Catalog, 1908–1909*, pp. 53–55; "Minutes of the Board of Trustees of Fisk University," 21 July 1902.

19. "Minutes of the Board of Trustees of Fisk University," 25 June 1908, 6 October 1909; J. G. Merrill to B. T. Washington, 29 July and 25 October 1908, in Booker T. Washington Papers; *Southern Workman* 39 (May 1910):260; *Fisk University News*, November 1912, p. 1.

20. P. D. Cravath to B. T. Washington, 28 October 1909, in Booker T.

Washington Papers; Isabel Smith Gates, *The Life of George Augustus Gates* (New York, 1915), pp. 12, 54.

21. *Fisk University News*, November 1912, p. 7; *Fisk University: Forty-Five Years, 1866-1911* (brochure, 1911).

22. *South African Christian Recorder*, quoted in *Fisk News*, November 1930, p. 20; Mary White Ovington, *The Walls Came Tumbling Down* (New York, 1947), p. 112; Franklin, *From Slavery to Freedom*, p. 441; Cremin, *Transformation of the School*, p. 98; *Fisk University News*, September 1912, p. 5; Mrs. R. W. MacDonald to G. E. Haynes, (n.d.) 1911, in George E. Haynes Letters, Fisk University Library; Benjamin Brawley, *A Short History of the American Negro* (New York, 1931), p. 142.

23. *Journal of the Proceedings and Addresses of the Nineteenth Annual Session of the Southern Educational Association . . . 1908* (Chattanooga, 1908), p. 127; *Nashville Globe*, 5 July 1907; *Fisk Herald*, March 1908, p. 11; Miller, "The Negro and Education," p. 703; E. G. Murphy to W. Buttrick, 14 November 1907, in Booker T. Washington Papers; *New York Times*, 4 August 1903; Meier, *Negro Thought in America*, pp. 161–62; Franklin, *From Slavery to Freedom*, pp. 431–36.

24. "Minutes of the Board of Trustees of Fisk University," 26 June 1903, 29 June 1904, 6 January 1913; *Nashville Globe*, 25 January 1907; "President's Report to the Board of Trustees," 29 June 1905, in Fiskiana Collection; Willard Range, *The Rise and Progress of Negro Colleges in Georgia, 1867-1949* (Athens, Georgia, 1951), p. 165; J. G. Merrill to W. Buttrick, 29 March 1902, quoted in Raymond B. Fosdick, *Adventures in Giving: The Story of the General Education Board* (New York, 1962), p. 190.

25. M. Murray to M. E. Spence, 3 November 1889, in Mary E. Spence Collection; *Fisk Herald*, December 1899, p. 2; Spencer, *Booker T. Washington*, pp. 88–89.

26. B. T. Washington to J. G. Merrill, 10 January, 25 February, 7 March, and 2 July 1908, J. G. Merrill to B. T. Washington, 2 July 1908, in Booker T. Washington Papers; "Minutes of the Board of Trustees of Fisk University," 8 May 1905, 25 June 1909; *Fisk News*, February 1956, p. 5.

27. Meier, *Negro Thought in America*, p. 114; E. L. Parks to B. T. Washington, 22 January and 4 February 1908, P. D. Cravath to B. T. Washington, 28 October and 13 November 1909, B. T. Washington to P. D. Cravath, 16 November 1909, B. T. Washington to G. A. Gates, 21 May 1910, in Booker T. Washington Papers; *Fisk University News*, February 1910, p. 2.

28. B. T. Washington to G. A. Gates, 12 April and 21 May 1910, to Andrew Carnegie, 18 October 1910, to W. G. Waterman, 18 November 1910, W. G. Waterman to B. T. Washington, 27 October 1910, J. E. Bertram to B. T. Washington, (n.d.) 1910, in Booker T. Washington Papers.

29. *New York Times*, 2 January and 28 June 1913; H. L. Simmons to B. T. Washington, 13 and 27 January and 11 November 1911, B. T. Washington to H. L. Simmons, 16 January and 20 November 1911, B. T. Washington to A. Carnegie, 18 October 1910, Margaret Washington to A. Carnegie, 18 and 25 November 1910, in Booker T. Washington Papers.

30. Gates, *Life of George Gates*, pp. 55–57; "Minutes of the Board of Trustees of Fisk University," 13 September 1912; M. E. Spence to M. Chase, 14 September 1925, in Mary E. Spence Collection.

31. Washington, "University Education for Negroes," pp. 614-17; B. W.

Hooper to W. Bartlett, 30 April 1912, Cornelius W. Morrow to I. Seligman, (n.d.) 1913, in Fiskiana Collection; Gates, *Life of George Gates,* p. 51; Beard, *Crusade of Brotherhood,* p. 274.

32. McPherson, *Abolitionist Legacy,* pp. 176, 391; Lester C. Lamon, "The Black Community in Nashville and the Fisk University Student Strike of 1924-1925," *Journal of Southern History* 40 (May 1974): 226-31.

CHAPTER 6

1. The school was governed primarily by Dean Herbert H. Wright in 1912-1913 and by Dean Cornelius W. Morrow in 1913-1914. They were assisted by Treasurer James T. Fairchild.

2. U.S., Department of Interior, *Negro Education* (prepared in cooperation with the Phelps-Stokes Fund under the direction of Thomas Jesse Jones), pp. 64, 76, 80, 320; Charles S. Johnson, *The Negro in American Civilization* (New York, 1930), p. 288; Board of Trustees of Fisk University to the Carnegie Foundation, (n.d.) 1916, in McKenzie Papers; *Fisk University News,* October 1921, p. 8; *Crisis* 34 (August 1927):185.

3. Previously the board had selected Thomas Jesse Jones, the U.S. Bureau of Education's specialist on black education, but Jones declined the honor.

4. W. O. Thompson to Gov. M. G. Brumbaugh, 21 January 1916, biographical note in McKenzie Papers; G. E. Haynes to L. H. Wood, 23 October 1915, in George E. Haynes Letters; "Minutes of the Board of Trustees," 10 July 1914, 8 February 1915.

5. "Ideals of Fisk," inaugural address of Fayette Avery McKenzie, 9 November 1915, Mrs. F. A. McKenzie to "Dearest Folks," 13 November 1915, in McKenzie Papers.

6. U.S., Department of Interior, *Negro Education,* pp. 536-37; Joseph A. Pierce, *Negro Business and Business Education* (New York, 1947), p. 236; *Fisk University Catalog, 1924-1925,* pp. 44-81.

7. Cornelius W. Morrow, *The Fisk of Today* (brochure, 1920); M. Echols to "Dear Mr. President and Factures," (n.d.) 1921, W. L. Allen to Principal, 28 June 1923, O. Nevils to "Proffeser," 17 October 1923, C. Turner to F. A. McKenzie, 1 September 1924, in Fiskiana Collection.

8. *New York Times,* 20 July 1924; F. A. McKenzie to Kelly Miller, 19 December 1921, to Miss C. Ada, 27 December 1922, in Faculty and Staff Letters, Fisk University Library (hereafter cited as F & S Letters). "Minutes of the Board of Trustees of Fisk University," 16 November 1922; State of Tennessee, *Biennial Report of the State Superintendent of Public Instruction for the Scholastic Year ending June 30, 1920* (Nashville, 1921), pp. 30-32; Isaac Fisher, "An Appraisal of the Work Done by President Fayette A. McKenzie at Fisk University," in McKenzie Papers.

9. F. A. McKenzie to G. F. Peabody, 7 December 1921, in F & S Letters; "Minutes of the Board of Trustees of Fisk University," 10 May 1919; *Fisk University News,* March 1918.

10. G. E. Haynes to L. H. Wood, 23 October 1915, to J. H. Dillard, 29 April 1916, to Mrs. N. C. Henderson, 1 May 1917, to E. F. Goin, 22 October 1917, in George E. Haynes Letters; *Greater Fisk Herald,* December 1927, p. 12; Lamon, "Black Community in Nashville," p. 231.

11. F. A. McKenzie to Miss D. A. Scribner, 27 June 1918, in F & S Letters; "Minutes of the Prudential Committee of Fisk University," 22 September 1917; *Fisk University News*, October 1917, p. 21, November 1917, p. 35, December 1917, p. 24, September 1918, pp. 3–4; Langston Hughes, *Fight for Freedom: The Story of the NAACP* (New York, 1962), p. 38; Franklin, *From Slavery to Freedom*, p. 465.

12. Franklin, *From Slavery to Freedom*, pp. 466–77; G. F. Peabody to F. A. McKenzie, 23 October 1917, in Administrative Papers, Fisk University Library; *Fisk University News*, October 1918, pp. 1–8.

13. F. A. McKenzie to W. W. Newell, 28 June 1920, to G. Smith, 17 February 1922, to L. J. Loventhal, 22 June 1922, to W. F. McClure, 7 December 1922, I. Fisher to R. E. Gill, 31 January 1922, in F & S Letters; *Fisk University News*, October 1921, p. 2, December 1922, pp. 1–3, March 1923, p. 3; B. T. Washington to J. Rosenwald, 9 March 1915, I. Fisher to W. C. Graves, 22 April 1925, in Julius Rosenwald Fund Papers, Amistad Research Center, Dillard University (hereafter cited as Rosenwald Fund Papers); Lamon; "Black Community in Nashville," p. 231.

14. Lance G. E. Jones, *Negro Schools in the Southern States* (Oxford, England, 1928), pp. 12–15; Frazier, *Black Bourgeoisie*, p. 78.

15. The average salary in small Southern colleges in 1915 was around $1,340. Naturally it was higher in the rest of the country. Trevor Arnett, *Teachers' Salaries in Certain Endowed Colleges and Universities in the United States* (New York, 1921), p. 19; Board of Trustees of Fisk University to Carnegie Foundation, (n.d.) 1916, in McKenzie Papers; J. A. Robinson to F. A. McKenzie, 12 July 1917, in F & S Letters; *Fisk University News*, September 1919, p. 22, January 1923, p. 1, February 1924, p. 1; F. A. McKenzie to General Education Board, 1 March 1915, quoted in Fosdick, *Adventures in Giving*, p. 191.

16. Estimate based on figures collected by Isaac Fisher, editor of the *Fisk University News*.

17. From 1910, with an expenditure of $61,487.14, the budget had slowly declined to a low of $50,934.33 in 1912–1913. Expenditures began to rise during McKenzie's first year—$70,135.68—until by 1922 more than $153,000 was expended by Fisk; G. E. Haynes to R. Davis, 21 March 1917, in George E. Haynes Letters; W. C. Graves to F. A. McKenzie, 29 May 1919, in F & S Letters; *Fisk University News*, January 1920, pp. 2, 13, October 1920, p. 19, January 1921, p. 3.

18. *New York Tribune*, 8 August 1880; H. B. Stowe to G. L. White, 23 June 1882, in Mary E. Spence Collection; *New York Times*, 24 December 1885; C. Schurz to C. B. Fisk, 2 May 1881, in Fiskiana Collection; *Sheffield and Rotherham* (England) *Independent*, 24, 26, and 27 March 1885.

19. They were Paul L. LaCour, Thomas W. Talley, Alice M. Vassor, Fannie E. Snow, Lincolnia Hynes, J. W. Holloway, and Maria A. Crump.

20. *Fisk University Catalog, 1890–1891*, p. 64; *Fisk Herald*, February 1890, p. 1, November 1890, p. 7; "Minutes of the Board of Trustees of Fisk University," 21 June 1901, 26 June 1903.

21. *Washington Times*, 9 March 1916; *Washington Evening Star*, 9 March 1916; *Nashville Tennessean*, 10 March 1916.

22. *New York Times*, 18 January 1923, 20 July 1924; *Nashville Morning Tennessean*, 21 March 1922; *Nashville Evening Tennessean*, 22 March 1922; J. T. Fairchild to Miss A. G. Chandler, 27 July 1925, in F & S Letters.

23. *Nashville Banner*, 14 April 1924; "Minutes of the Executive Committee of

the Board of Trustees of Fisk University," 2 May 1921; *Southern Workman* 49 (April 1920): 149; "Minutes of the Board of Trustees of Fisk University," 17 November 1919; Fosdick, *Adventures in Giving*, pp. 190–92.

24. J. C. Olden to F. A. McKenzie, 11 January 1923, F. A. McKenzie to J. C. Olden, 24 January 1923, in F & S Letters; "Minutes of the Executive Committee of the Board of Trustees of Fisk University," 17 August 1923.

25. *Southern Workman* 53 (September 1924):389–90; *New York Times*, 20 July 1924; *School and Society* 20 (2 August 1924):144.

26. "Minutes of the Board of Trustees of Fisk University," 20 April 1925; F. A. McKenzie to Mrs. A. J. Henry, 27 January 1925, L. H. Wood to C. F. Dale, 27 October 1925, in F & S Letters; *School and Society* 17 (17 March 1923):293.

CHAPTER 7

1. John Davis, "Unrest in the Negro Colleges," *New Student* 8 (January 1929):13–14; Jones, *Negro Schools in Southern States*, p. 34; Douglass, *Christian Reconstruction*, pp. 244–45.

2. "Minutes of the Prudential Committee of Fisk University," 27 September and 13 and 15 December 1909; "Minutes of the Board of Trustees of Fisk University," 25 June 1908; *Fisk News*, June 1947, p. 16.

3. "Minutes of the Prudential Committee of Fisk University," 24 October 1910, 14 October 1912, 25 January 1915; "Minutes of the General Faculty of Fisk University, 26 February 1912.

4. F. A. McKenzie to C. A. Hodges, 31 March 1918 to D. A. Scribner, 27 June 1918, in F & S Letters; Raymond Wolters, *The New Negro on Campus: Black College Rebellions of the 1920s* (Princeton, 1975), p. 31.

5. A. F. Shaw to F. A. McKenzie, 20 November 1918, Memorandum of Miss Belle R. Paramenter, 16 September 1921, F. A. McKenzie to Mrs. L. B. Murphey, 18 October 1922, in F & S Letters; *Fisk University Catalog, 1917–1918*, p. 23.

6. F. A. McKenzie to Mrs. L. B. Murphey, 26 March 1923, in F & S Letters; "Minutes of the Prudential Committee," 10 January 1917, 21 and 26 January 1918, 2 April 1918, 22 October 1923.

7. "Minutes of the Prudential Committee," 24 October 1917, 28 October 1918, 13 January 1925; Letters from parents in Fiskiana Collection.

8. Langston Hughes, "Cowards from the Colleges," *Crisis* 41 (August 1934):226; Jones, *Negro Schools in Southern States*, p. 34; Davis, "Unrest in Negro Colleges," pp. 13–14.

9. "Minutes of the Board of Trustees of Fisk University," 9 November 1915; "Minutes of the Prudential Committee," 3 January 1917; *Fisk University Catalog, 1920–1921*, p. 21; *Fisk University News*, January 1920, p. 8.

10. F. A. McKenzie to J. L. Peacock, 16 December 1921, to Dr. R. F. Scholz, 24 January 1922, in F & S Letters; "Minutes of the Prudential Committee," 5 April 1917; *Fisk University News*, January 1921, p. 6, January 1922, p. 7.

11. T. E. Jones to L. H. Wood, 20 September 1926, F. A. McKenzie to F. M. Poindexter, 29 June 1920, to A. D. Philippse, 7 April 1924, to R. H. Nicol, 25 May 1924, to Mrs. A. W. Partch, 6 May 1924, P. F. Laubenstein to F. A. McKenzie, 1 September 1921, in F & S Letters; Lamon, "The Black Community in Nashville," pp. 233–34.

12. For a more thorough discussion of the revolution in manners and morals, see Frederick Lewis Allen, *Only Yesterday: An Informal History of the Nineteen-Twenties* (New York, 1931).

13. Isaac Fisher claimed that the "incendiary utterances" of some of Fisk's *"most militant graduates"* stirred students "to disgraceful conduct. . . ." Isaac Fisher to J. Rosenwald, 21 March 1925, in Rosenwald Fund Papers; C. W. Kelly to F. A. McKenzie, 7 March 1923, in F & S Letters; W. E. B. DuBois, "The Dilemma of the Negro," *American Mercury* 3 (October 1924):183-84; "John Work: Martyr and Singer," *Crisis* 32 (May 1926):33; Davis, "Unrest in Negro Colleges," pp. 13-14.

14. Hughes, "Cowards from Colleges," pp. 226-28; Davis, "Unrest in Negro Colleges," pp. 13-14; P. L. Julian to Miss M. M. Kern, 29 April 1922, in F & S Letters; Wolters, *New Negro on Campus*, pp. 33-34.

15. There had been no black college faculty members until James Burrus joined the staff in 1875. One of the Burruses (James or John) was on the faculty until 1882, but there were no blacks from 1882 to 1888. Starting in 1891, except for five years, there were at least two blacks on the staff. Beginning with the McKenzie administration, the number increased rapidly. Most of the black faculty during McKenzie's administration were Fiskites. From 1918 to the 1930s blacks accounted for about one-fourth to one-third of the faculty.

16. *New York Amsterdam News*, 17 March 1924; "Minutes of the Executive Committee of the Board of Trustees of Fisk University," 22 October 1924; Wolters, *New Negro on Campus*, pp. 33, 35; *Crisis* 28 (September 1924): 199-203.

17. Copy in "Minutes of the Board of Trustees of Fisk University," 17 November 1924; "Minutes of the Executive Committee of the Board of Trustees of Fisk University," 22 October 1924.

18. "Minutes of the Executive Committee of the Board of Trustees of Fisk University," 22 October 1924.

19. *Crisis*, 28 (October 1924):251-52; Wolters, *New Negro on Campus*, p. 38.

20. Copy in "Minutes of the Board of Trustees of Fisk University," 17 November 1924.

21. *New York Times*, 28 January and 25 February 1925; *Crisis* 29 (April 1925):247-48.

22. McKenzie publicly announced that the board agreed with his policies, but he apparently felt insecure in his job. After the November board meeting the president "talked very frankly" to Isaac Fisher about the uncertainties of the situation and gave Fisher permission quietly to look for another job because McKenzie's tenure might be ended. I. Fisher to J. Rosenwald, 21 March 1925, in Rosenwald Fund Papers.

23. Copy of chapel talk in Mary E. Spence Collection; *Crisis* 29 (April 1925):248.

24. *New York Times*, 5 February 1925; "Minutes of the Prudential Committee," 5 February 1925; Form letter from Miss D. A. Scribner to alumni, 14 February 1925, in Mary E. Spence Collection; F. A. McKenzie to T. H. Jones, 19 February 1925, in McKenzie Papers; Wolters, *New Negro on Campus*, pp. 48, 50.

25. Lamon, "The Black Community in Nashville," p. 239; Wolters, *New Negro on Campus*, p. 60.

26. *Nation*, 120 (18 March 1925):283; *Crisis*, 29 (April 1925):250; *New York*

Times, 8 February 1925; Hughes, *Fight for Freedom,* p. 87; Streator quoted in Wolters, *New Negro on Campus,* p. 60.

27. M. E. Spence to M. Chase, 26 February and 14 September 1925, in Mary E. Spence Collection; F. A. McKenzie to Louis (?), 1 March 1925, to E. O. Fisk, 11 May 1925, in McKenzie Papers; DuBois, *Dusk of Dawn,* p. 282; Wolters, *New Negro on Campus,* pp. 57–58; Lamon, "The Black Community in Nashville," p. 283.

28. G. N. White to F. A. McKenzie, 13 February 1925, A. W. Davis to F. A. McKenzie, 12 February 1925, Statement of R. Augustus Lawson, (n.d.) 1925, in Mary E. Spence Collection; *Crisis,* 34 (December 1927):348.

29. Copy of alumni committee's report in "Minutes of the Board of Trustees of Fisk University," 20 April 1925.

30. "Minutes of the Board of Trustees of Fisk University," 20 April 1925; H. A. Miller to G. W. Streator, 30 May 1925, in Mary E. Spence Collection.

31. DuBois, *Dusk of Dawn,* p. 282; A. Flexner to F. A. McKenzie, 8 May 1925, B. R. Payne to F. A. McKenzie, 11 May 1925, T. J. Jones to P. D. Cravath, 9 January 1924, in McKenzie Papers; T. J. Jones to T. E. Jones, 16 December 1929, in Letters of the Board of Trustees of Fisk University.

CHAPTER 8

1. The trustees had alienated the alumni by their automatic support of McKenzie. Alumni distrust was not caused just by Southern white trustees; most of the trustees were from the Northeast. The first board was composed of Fisk teachers, American Missionary Association officials and former United States Army officers or Freedmen's Bureau agents in Nashville. By the mid-1870s most of the trustees were from New York City and were ordinarily American Missionary Association officers. Occasionally someone like John Eaton, Jr., U.S. commissioner of education, was appointed. Usually if trustees were not missionary association officers they were rich men from the East who could help the university financially but were uninterested in the day-to-day operation of the school. Booker T. Washington was appointed to the board in 1909 to help raise money. When he died, Robert R. Moton took his place. Both were naturally more concerned about Tuskegee than Fisk. George W. Moore was a Fisk alumnus but was never a strong voice on the board. Only William N. DeBerry, appointed in 1915, came close to representing alumni opinion. Most of the trustees were concerned about black education, but they were patronizing. Only after Thomas E. Jones became president were many white Southerners elected to the board. In 1928 five white Nashville businessmen became trustees.

2. A. F. Shaw to P. D. Cravath, 9 October 1925, in Letters of the Trustees; Mrs. A..B. Edmiston to F. A. McKenzie, 11 February 1926, O. A. Boatright to McKenzie, 23 June 1924, in McKenzie Papers; Miss C. C. Fisher to T. E. Jones, 3 December 1926, in Administrative Papers; C. W. Wesley to M. E. Spence, 16 October 1925, in Mary E. Spence Collection.

3. "Minutes of the Prudential Committee," 4 March, 3 September and 30 November 1925; A. F. Shaw to L. H. Wood, 15 November 1925, L. H. Wood to A. F. Shaw, 23 November 1925, P. D. Cravath to A. F. Shaw, 16 and 27 November 1925, A. F. Shaw to P. D. Cravath, 2 December 1925, in Letters of the Trustees.

4. "Minutes of the Executive Committee of the Board of Trustees of Fisk University," 17 May 1925; A. F. Shaw to L. H. Wood, 6 April and 13 May 1926, in Letters of the Trustees.

5. Biographical sketch of Thomas E. Jones in Administrative Papers; "Minutes of the Board of Trustees of Fisk University," 15 February 1926; *New York Times*, 19 February 1926; *Nashville Tennessean*, 4 September 1926; James Weldon Johnson, *Along This Way* (New York, 1938), p. 407.

6. *Fisk Herald*, November 1902, p. 12; *Greater Fisk Herald*, December 1927, p. 11; *Alumni Directory of Fisk University*," pp. 64–65.

7. "Minutes of the Board of Trustees of Fisk University," 14 June 1917, 13 July 1926, 6 December 1927.

8. The alumni secretaries were: Andrew J. Allison '13, 1927–1943, Randall L. Tyus '32, 1944–1947, Mrs. Helen Howard Davis '35, 1947–1950, W. Dickerson Donnelly '31, 1951–1968. Thomas M. Brumfield '09 served as acting secretary between each administration.

9. Paul D. Cravath, who had been associated with Fisk since he was a small boy, said that "at no time within my memory has there been so much enthusiasm and hope among all concerned in the future of Fisk. . . ." P. D. Cravath to J. Rosenwald, 29 April 1929, in Rosenwald Fund Papers; *Crisis* 34 (March 1927):33; "Minutes of the Board of Trustees of Fisk University," 13 July 1926; M. E. Spence to M. Chase, 15 November 1927, in Mary E. Spence Collection.

10. *Nashville Banner*, 5 June 1928; P. D. Cravath to T. E. Jones, 4 December 1928, in Letters of the Trustees; Robert T. Swaine, *The Cravath Firm and Its Predecessors*, 3 vols. (New York, 1946), 1:585–88, 2:256–57; T. E. Jones to H. V. Nichol, 15 December 1927, in Administrative Papers; T. E. Jones to E. R. Embree, 2 January 1928, in Rosenwald Fund Papers.

11. T. E. Jones to L. J. Loventhal, 25 November 1930, to L. H. Wood, 29 November 1930, in Letters of the Trustees; T. E. Jones to Miss G. Webb, 16 December 1935, in Administrative Papers.

12. "Minutes of the Board of Trustees of Fisk University," 6 December 1926.

13. *Greater Fisk Herald*, March 1927, p. 24; *Fisk University Catalog, 1926–1927*, p. 21; T. E. Jones to Miss R. V. Routt, 14 February 1928, in Administrative Papers: T. E. Jones to P. D. Cravath, 28 March 1928, in Letters of the Trustees; A. A. Taylor to T. E. Jones, 13 March 1928, in F & S Letters.

14. T. E. Jones to A. F. Shaw, 11 February 1927, to L. H. Wood, 11 February 1927, in Letters of the Trustees; T. E. Jones to Miss G. Webb, 16 December 1935, in Administrative Papers.

15. *Fisk University Catalog, 1927–1928*, p. 24; "Minutes of the Board of Trustees of Fisk University," 6 December 1926; *Report of the President of Fisk University, 1929–1930*, p. 4.

16. The fraternities were: Eta Psi chapter of Omega Psi Phi, Alpha Chi chapter of Alpha Phi Alpha, Alpha Delta chapter of Kappa Alpha Psi, and Alpha Gamma chapter of Phi Beta Sigma. The sororities were Pi chapter of Alpha Kappa Alpha and Alpha Beta chapter of Delta Sigma Theta.

17. A. F. Shaw to L. H. Wood, 5 November 1925, G. L. White to P. D. Cravath, 30 August 1934, in Letters of the Trustees; M. E. Spence to M. Chase, 15 November 1927, in Mary E. Spence Collection; T. E. Jones to A. A. Taylor, 12 September 1928, in F & S Letters; *Fisk Herald*, April 1930, p. 8.

18. *Greater Fisk Herald*, April 1926, p. 21 and February 1927, pp. 7–8; *Fisk*

Herald, October 1934, p. 20; Mrs. H. J. Foster to L. H. Wood, 15 June 1931, P. D. Cravath to T. E. Jones, 12 July 1934, in Letters of the Trustees.

CHAPTER 9

1. *Nashville Tennessean,* 18 August 1929; J. R. Aust to L. H. Wood, 23 April 1936, in Fiskiana Collection; Miss L. J. Bowles to L. H. Wood, 18 March 1931, in Letters of the Trustees.
2. *New York Times,* 2 June 1926, 6 December 1926, 2 July 1927; T. E. Jones to L. Foster, 29 October 1926, to M. U. Foster, 15 July 1927, in Administrative Papers.
3. For example, in 1928 the Rosenwald Fund gave Fisk $75,000 for current expenses. In 1931 the Rosenwald Fund made an additional $15,000 appropriation for current expenses and in 1930 gave Fisk $10,000 for student loans. The Rosenwald Fund granted $20,000 for current expenses in 1936-1937. An additional $25,000 was added for 1937-1938. "Minutes of the Trustees of the Julius Rosenwald Fund," 4 November 1928, D. A. Elvidge to T. E. Jones, 5 January and 13 April 1937, E. R. Embree to T. E. Jones, 5 November 1928, in Rosenwald Fund Papers; *Report of the President of Fisk University, 1930-1931,* p. 6; Charles H. Thompson, "The Socio-Economic Status of Negro College Students," *Journal of Negro Education* 2 (January 1933): 26; Woodson, "Twenty-Five Years of Higher Education," pp. 15-16; U.S., Department of Interior, *Survey of Negro Colleges* p. 735; U.S., Department of Interior, Office of Education, *Statistics of the Education of Negroes, 1929-30 and 1931-32,* Bulletin no. 13 (Washington, D.C., 1935), p. 40.
4. *New York Times,* 7 June 1928; *Pittsburgh Courier,* 16 November 1929; *Report of the President of Fisk University, 1941-1942,* p. 11; *Fisk News,* November-December 1934, p. 9; *St. Louis Argus,* 2 September 1934; T. E. Jones to C. S. Stilwell, 29 October 1928, in Administrative Papers.
5. *Toronto Evening Telegram,* 21 April 1926; *Chicago Tribune,* 10 and 14 November 1926; *New York Herald,* 11 November 1926, 21 February 1927; *Nashville Banner,* 5 January and 15 June 1929, *Detroit News,* 6 January 1929; *New York Times,* 9 and 27 October 1926, 11 November 1926, 20 February 1927, 6 March 1927, 7 December 1929.
6. *New York Amsterdam News,* 3 December 1930; *Nashville Banner,* 18 December 1928; *Libraries* 34 (February 1929): 61; T. E. Jones to Board of Trustees, 1 October 1929, in Fiskiana Collection.
7. Ethel B. Gilbert, "Fisk's New Library," *Southern Workman* 60 (February 1931):64; L. S. Shores to C. H. Milam, 20 August 1930, to College Administrators and City Librarians, 2 October 1930, to "Dear Alumnus," 15 November 1930, in Fiskiana Collection.
8. Fred McCuistion, *Higher Education of Negroes* (Nashville, 1933), p. 36; "Report of the Librarian, 1935-1936," in Administrative Papers; *Fisk University Catalog, 1929-1930,* p. 26.
9. *Indianapolis News,* 8 September 1928; *Alumni Directory of Fisk University, 1875-1930,* pp. 66-70.
10. "Minutes of the Board of Trustees of Fisk University," 10 December 1931; *Kansas City* (Missouri) *Call,* 13 November 1931; *Atlanta World,* 11 November

1931; *Report of the Commission on Interracial Cooperation Regarding the Automobile Accident in Dalton, Ga., November 6* (pamphlet, 1931).

11. T. E. Jones to L. H. Wood, 5 March 1928, 23 September 1930, J. T. Caruthers to Board of Trustees, 24 April 1930, in Letters of the Trustees; *Greater Fisk Herald*, November 1927, p. 25; *Alumni Directory of Fisk University, 1875–1930*, pp. 65–71; *Report of the President of Fisk University 1929–1930*, p. 11; T. E. Jones to J. W. Johnson, 11 October 1934, in James Weldon Johnson Collection, Fisk University; E. R. Embree to T. E. Jones, 1 May 1934, T. E. Jones to E. R. Embree, 7 May 1934, D. L. Jones to A. K. Stern, 6 December 1928, in Rosenwald Fund Papers.

12. T. E. Jones to Miss D. A. Scribner, 25 June 1928, to Miss J. J. Saddler, 21 August 1933, in F & S Letters; "Statement of Faculty Salaries for 1933-1934," in Fiskiana Collection.

13. *Fisk University Catalog, 1889–1890*, p. 57, *1913–1914*, p. 25; Fred McCuistion, *Graduate Instruction for Negroes* (Nashville, 1939), pp. 112–13.

14. McCuistion, *Graduate Instruction for Negroes*, pp. 38, 119; U.S., Department of Interior, *Survey of Negro Colleges*, p. 744; *Fisk University Catalog, 1929–1930*, pp. 55–57; Lawrence C. Bryant, "Graduate Training in Negro Colleges," *Journal of Negro Education* 30 (Winter 1961): 69; Walter Clinton Jackson, "The Future College for the Higher Education of Negroes," in *Higher Education Among Negroes*, ed. Theophilus E. McKinney (Charlotte, North Carolina 1932), p. 69.

15. *New York Times*, 7 June 1928; "Report of the Registrar," April 1952, in Fiskiana Collection; E. Franklin Frazier, "Graduate Education in Negro Colleges and Universities," *Journal of Negro Education* 2 (July 1933):337.

16. L. Hadley to T. E. Jones, 9 August 1939, in F & S Letters; "Graduate Enrollment at Fisk," mimeographed table in Fiskiana Collection; McCuistion, *Graduate Instruction for Negroes*, p. 47; *Fisk News*, May-June 1939, pp. 10–11.

17. Harry W. Greene, "The Negro College and Social Change," *Opportunity* 14 (August 1936):235; *Fisk News*, November–December 1933, p. 5; McCuistion, *Graduate Instruction for Negroes*, p. 29; *New York Times*, 25 February 1934; Van Deusen, *Black Man in White America*, p. 184.

18. E. R. Embree to P. D. Cravath, 29 November 1937, in Letters of the Trustees; Edwin R. Embree, "The Educational Opportunity of the American Negro," address given in St. Louis, Missouri, 31 March 1939, in Fiskiana Collection; James Weldon Johnson, "Jubilee Day," address given at Fisk University, 7 October 1933, in Fiskiana Collection; *New York Times*, 9 December 1926, 28 April 1933.

19. *Report of the President of Fisk University, 1929–1930*, pp. 6–7; T. E. Jones to P. D. Cravath, 28 March 1928, in Letters of the Trustees.

20. Thomas E. Davis, "A Study of Fisk University Freshmen from 1928 to 1930," *Journal of Negro Education* 2 (October 1933):479; Bond, *Education of the Negro*, pp. 323–34; F. B. O'Rear and T. L. Hungate, "Some Present Problems at Fisk University: A Report of the Nashville Members of the Board of Trustees of Fisk University," 4 October 1940, in Letters of the Trustees.

21. *Fisk University Catalog, 1935–1936*, p. 49.

22. Thomas E. Davis, "Some Racial Attitudes of Negro College and Grade School Students," *Journal of Negro Education* 6 (April 1937):160-61; *Fisk Herald*, February 1930, p. 7.

23. *Report of the President of Fisk University, 1932–1933,* pp. 2–3; Hughes, "Cowards from Colleges," p. 227.

Chapter 10

1. Franklin, *From Slavery to Freedom,* p. 536.

2. T. E. Jones to L. H. Wood, 18 August 1930, T. E. Jones to P. D. Cravath, 2 January 1940, in Letters of the Trustees; *Fisk News,* December 1932, p. 4; "Report of the Registrar," 1932 and 1934, in Administrative Papers; H. D. Schmidt to A. A. Taylor, (n.d.) 1938, in F & S Letters; O'Rear and Hungate, "Some Present Problems at Fisk," in Letters of the Trustees.

3. T. E. Jones to J. W. Johnson, 29 October 1932, in James Weldon Johnson Memorial Collection, Yale University; P. D. Cravath to T. E. Jones, 20 December 1932, T. E. Jones to L. H. Wood, 12 October 1932, in Letters of the Trustees; T. E. Jones to F. A. Stewart, 6 December 1933, in Fiskiana Collection; *Fisk News,* October 1932, pp. 2–3; "Report of the President to the Board of Trustees for the Year ending June 30, 1934," Fiskiana Collection.

4. T. E. Jones to J. F. Beals, 12 April 1934, 19 August 1935, J. F. Beals to T. E. Jones, 4, 7, and 10 March 1933, to "Dear Friend," 11 November 1935, to O. Boatright, 14 November 1935, T. E. Jones to J. F. Beals, 18 November 1935, in F & S Letters; T. E. Jones to J. W. Johnson, 18 July 1934, in James Weldon Johnson Collection, Fisk University.

5. L. H. Wood to T. E. Jones, 14 November 1939, T. E. Jones to L. H. Wood, 29 November 1943, to C. E. Haydock, 14 March 1944, in Letters of the Trustees; *Report of the President of Fisk University, 1941–1942,* p. 5; "Minutes of the Subcommittee of the Board of Trustees of Meharry Medical College," 1 March 1944, in Fiskiana Collection.

6. *Fisk News,* December 1943, p. 2; O'Rear and Hungate, "Some Present Problems at Fisk," in Letters of the Trustees; Range, *Progress of Negro Colleges,* pp. 196–97.

7. *New York Times,* 18 January 1936, 18 November 1937; *Fisk News,* November–December 1937, p. 5; McCuiston, *Graduate Instruction for Negroes,* p. 41; E. R. Embree to T. E. Jones, 15 November 1937, P. D. Cravath to E. R. Embree, 23 November 1937, in Rosenwald Fund Papers.

8. L. H. Wood to New York Trustees of Fisk University, 17 September 1940, in Letters of the Trustees; *Fisk News,* June 1940, p. 8, June 1953, p. 11; "Report of the President to the Board of Trustees, 1910, 1920, 1930, 1940."

9. W. J. Trent, Jr., "Private Negro Colleges Since the Gaines Decision," *Journal of Educational Sociology* 32 (February 1959): 273; *New York Times,* 27 May 1944, 27 April 1946.

10. *Fisk News,* October 1930, p. 9, December 1932, pp. 23–24; *Fisk Herald,* February 1937, p. 2; *Dayton* (Ohio) *Forum,* 21 November 1930; *Chicago Whip,* 4 October 1930; *Nashville Tennessean,* 21 December 1930.

11. *Fisk News,* November–December 1937, p. 11; *Fisk Herald,* April 1940, p. 14; *Nashville Tennessean,* 28 December 1930, 14 October 1940, 20 October 1946; *Nashville Defender,* 13 and 27 October 1939.

12. T. E. Jones to L. J. Loventhal, 13 August 1933, in Letters of the Trustees; *Fisk News,* January–February 1934, pp. 10, 12.

13. T. E. Jones to J. A. Kingsbury, 9 May 1933, in James Weldon Johnson Memorial Collection, Yale University; *Fisk University and Negro Health* (pamphlet, n.d.).

14. *Report of the President of Fisk University, 1934–1935*, pp. 7–8; *Pittsburgh Courier*, 1 June 1935.

15. T. E. Jones to C. E. Van Horn, 9 October 1934, to J. Balderston, 23 December 1942, in F & S Letters; T. E. Jones to L. H. Wood, 5 January 1943, in Letters of the Trustees; C. S. Johnson to J. W. Johnson, n.d., in James Weldon Johnson Memorial Collection, Yale University; *The Fisk Rural Life Program: A Plan for the Development of Negro Leaders for the Rural South* (pamphlet, 1945).

16. T. E. Jones to M. L. Crosthwaite, 14 February 1933, M. L. Crosthwaite to T. E. Jones, 5 May and 8 June 1933, in Letters of the Trustees; T. E. Jones to A. A. Taylor, 15 April and 15 May 1933, in F & S Letters; *Baltimore Afro-American*, 17 March 1934.

17. "Youth Exhibits a New Spirit," *Crisis* 43 (August 1936): 237+; T. E. Jones to L. H. Wood, 26 December 1933, to M. L. Crosthwaite, 26 January 1934, in Letters of the Trustees; A. E. Barnett to Walter White, 11 March 1946, in F & S Letters.

18. *Fisk News*, November–December 1934, p. 3; *Iowa* (Des Moines) *Bystander*, 30 November 1934; Henry McRaven, *Nashville: "Athens of the South"* (Chapel Hill, 1949), p. 217.

19. T. E. Jones to L. H. Wood, 26 February 1934, in Letters of the Trustees; *New York Amsterdam News*, 17 March 1934.

20. *New York Amsterdam News*, 17 March 1934; *Chicago Defender*, 24 March 1934; *Baltimore Afro-American*, 17 March 1934; T. E. Jones to L. H. Wood, 26 February 1934, in Letters to the Trustees; "Minutes of the Board of Trustees of Fisk University," 20 April 1934; Hughes, "Cowards from Colleges," p. 227; *Crisis*, "Youth Exhibits New Spirit," p. 238.

21. *Chicago Defender*, 24 March 1934; "Report of Personnel Officer to Board of Trustees," 12 December 1934, in Fiskiana Collection; T. E. Jones to L. H. Wood, 26 December 1933, in Letters of the Trustees.

22. *Fisk Herald*, March 1937, p. 5, October 1937, p. 7; C. Bell to Board of Trustees, 6 December 1937, in Fiskiana Collection; "Minutes of the Board of Trustees of Fisk University," 11 February 1938; "University Minister's Report of Religious Activities, 1936–1937," in Administrative Papers.

23. "Resume of Minutes of the Executive Committee of Fisk University, October 2–November 13, 1939," in Administrative Papers; H. A. Johnson to T. E. Jones, 23 January 1934, in F & S Letters; T. E. Jones to L. H. Wood, 11 March 1935, in Letters of the Trustees.

24. "Report of the Registrar," April 1952, in Fiskiana Collection; T. E. Jones to Board of Trustees, (n.d.) October 1941, in Letters of the Trustees.

25. Copy of undated resignation in Administrative Papers; T. E. Jones to A. A. Taylor, 14 January, 13 June, and 29 July 1941, in F & S Letters.

26. L. H. Wood to T. E. Jones, 17 and 22 April 1941, T. E. Jones to L. H. Wood, 2 February 1942, in Letters of the Trustees.

27. Special alumni committee on the present and future status of Fisk (signed by thirty-six alumni) to Board of Trustees, 26 April 1941, in Fiskiana Collection; "Minutes of the Board of Trustees of Fisk University," 2 May 1941.

28. T. E. Jones to L. H. Wood, 10 January 1942, in Letters of the Trustees; A. J. Allison to T. E. Jones, 5 May 1943, in F & S Letters; "Report of the Faculty War Policy Committee," n.d., in Administrative Papers; *Fisk News*, February 1943, p. 1.

29. *Atlanta World*, 20 May 1945; *Chicago Bee*, 1 April 1945; *New York Times*, 4 May 1945; *New York Age*, 14 April 1945; *Nashville Globe*, 2 March 1945; *Fisk News*, December 1943, p. 9, May 1944, pp. 7, 11, December 1944, pp. 7, 14, May 1945, p. 13, April 1946, pp. 7, 14.

30. *New York Times*, 22 April 1945; *Norfolk* (Virginia) *Journal and Guide*, 28 April 1945; *Richmond* (Virginia) *Afro-American*, 28 April 1945; Alumni Office Weekly News Letter, 22 September 1945; *Fisk News*, December 1944, p. 1; *Nashville Tennessean*, 28 September 1944; A. Bontemps to L. Hughes, 14 September 1943, in James Weldon Johnson Memorial Collection, Yale University.

31. C. H. Wesley to L. H. Wood, 16 March 1943, T. E. Jones to L. H. Wood, 22 April 1943, B. Fensterwald to T. E. Jones, 26 December 1945, in Letters of the Trustees; "Minutes of the Board of Trustees of Fisk University," 26 February and 25 March 1943, 27 April 1945.

32. J. E. Stamps to Board of Trustees, 27 April 1945, in Fiskiana Collection; *New York Times*, 26 April 1946.

33. T. M. Brumfield to T. E. Jones, 25 March 1946, in Administrative Papers; "To Command Respect," *Time* 48 (15 July 1946): 69-70; *Fisk University Catalog, 1952-1953*, p. 7.

34. *New York Times*, 26 and 28 April 1946, 30 October 1946.

35. *Nashville Tennessean*, 7 November 1947; *New York Herald Tribune*, 4 May 1947; Anson Phelps Stokes, et al., *Negro Status and Race Relations in the United States, 1911-1946* (New York, 1948), p. 46; C. Van Vechten to A. Bontemps, 28 January 1944, in Carl Van Vechten Collection, Yale University Library.

CHAPTER 11

1. U.S., Department of Interior, Office of Education, *Education of Negro Teachers*, Bulletin no. 10 (Washington, D.C., 1933), p. 113.

2. Edwin R. Embree, *Brown America* (New York, 1931) p. 101; V. V. Oak, "Some Outstanding Defects in Institutions of Higher Learning for Negroes," *School and Society* 46 (18 September 1937):358-59; Charles W. Florence, "Critical Evaluation of Present Policies and Practices of Negro Institutions of Higher Learning," in *Higher Education Among Negroes*, ed. Theophilus E. McKinney (Charlotte, North Carolina, 1932), p. 50.

3. *New York Times*, 22 January 1933; McCuistion, *Graduate Instruction for Negroes*, p. 100; Van Deusen, *Black Man in White America*, p. 181; *Fisk News*, May-June 1934, p. 4, January-February 1939, pp. 3-6, May-June 1939, p. 3, April 1946, p. 5.

4. The teaching of social science declined after George Edmund Haynes went to Washington, D.C., during World War I. Even while Haynes was at Fisk he was interested primarily in training social workers. Edwin R. Embree, *13 Against the Odds* (New York, 1944), pp. 58-61; Van Deusen, *Black Man in White America*, p. 212; *Opportunity* 25 (Winter 1947):26.

5. *New York Times*, 2 July 1927, 28 and 30 October 1956; W. F. Ogburn to

T. E. Jones, 31 August 1929, C. S. Johnson to T. E. Jones, 16 October 1929, in F & S Letters.

6. In 1934 Edwin R. Embree said, "The work of Dr. Charles S. Johnson's department of the social sciences is one of the outstanding achievements of any university in recent years." In his 1967 presidential address to the Southern Historical Association, Dewey W. Grantham, Jr., said Johnson "was the leader in making Fisk University the major Negro center for social research in the South and one of the outstanding research institutions in the entire field of race relations." E. R. Embree to T. E. Jones, 21 March 1934, in Rosenwald Fund Papers; Dewey W. Grantham, Jr., "The Regional Imagination: Social Scientists and the American South," *Journal of Southern History* 34 (February 1968):13; Edgar T. Thompson, "Sociology and Sociological Research in the South," *Social Forces* 23 (March 1945):364–65; D. D. Jones, "Cultural Obligations of the Faculty in a Negro Liberal Arts College," *Association of American Colleges Bulletin* 25 (March 1939):67; Stokes et al., *Negro Status and Race Relations*, p. 53; *Des Moines* (Iowa) *Bystander*, 27 July 1934; L. H. Wood to T. E. Jones, 7 February 1937, in Letters of the Trustees.

7. *Fisk News*, November 1930, p. 13, November–December 1934, p. 17, January–February 1937, p. 15; *Philadelphia Independent*, 22 July 1934; *St. Louis Call*, 12 April 1940.

8. *New York Times*, 5 February 1944, 1 April 1955; *Fisk News*, January–February 1934, p. 9; T. E. Jones to C. S. Johnson, 28 June 1935, in F & S Letters.

9. *Fisk University Catalog, 1949–1950*, p. 17; *Christian Science Monitor*, 8 July 1950; *New York Times*, 9 July 1949, 3 July 1951, 11 July 1954; Bontemps, "Why I Returned," p. 181; *Advance* (National Journal of Congregational Christian Churches), May 1945, p. 22.

10. "The Johnson Family," *Negro History Bulletin* 12 (November 1948):27; Merl R. Eppse, *The Negro Too, in American History* (Nashville, 1943), p. 377; *New York Times*, 27 June 1938.

11. "The Johnson Family," p. 27; Franklin, *From Slavery to Freedom*, pp. 493–94.

12. T. E. Jones to J. W. Johnson, 7 June 1932, G. F. Peabody to J. W. Johnson, 12 January 1932, in James Weldon Johnson Memorial Collection, Yale University; T. D. Mabry to T. E. Jones, 11 May 1932, in James Weldon Johnson Collection, Fisk University; J. W. Johnson, *Along This Way*, pp. 407–9; Arthur D. Spingarn et al., *James Weldon Johnson* (pamphlet, n.d.).

13. Charles S. Johnson, *Exercises Marking the Opening of the James Weldon Johnson Memorial Collection of Negro Arts & Letters* (pamphlet, 1950): Van Deusen, *Black Man in White America*, p. 254; *Fisk News*, January–February 1934, p. 9.

14. Poppy Cannon, *A Gentle Knight: My Husband, Walter White* (New York, 1956), p. 24; Spingarn et al., *James Weldon Johnson; Fisk News*, April 1933, p. 16, January–February 1934, p. 10; Knoxville *East Tennessee News*, 25 February 1932.

15. *NAACP Bulletin* (January 1944):1; Spingarn et al., *James Weldon Johnson;* L. V. Miller to M. S. Loventhal, 27 June 1938, in James Weldon Johnson Collection, Fisk University.

16. Franklin, *From Slavery to Freedom*, pp. 503–6; Earl E. Thorpe, *The Mind of the Negro: An Intellectual History of Afro-Americans* (Baton Rouge, 1961), pp. 468–69, 471; *New York Amsterdam News*, 24 February 1945; Jessie P. Guzman, ed.,

Negro Year Book: A Review of Events Affecting Negro Life, 1941–1946 (Tuskegee, 1947), p. 444.

17. Bontemps, "Why I Returned," pp. 177–82.

18. Guzman, *Negro Year Book,* pp. 467, 470; *Negro Digest* 15 (June 1966): 39–47.

19. T. E. Jones to L. H. Wood, 21 June 1928, in Letters of the Trustees; *Nashville Banner,* 5 June 1928, 20 April 1929.

20. *New York Times,* 13 September 1931; *Oakland* (California) *Tribune,* 19 April 1931; C. S. Johnson to T. E. Jones, 24 February 1933, in F & S Letters.

21. Guzman, *Negro Year Book,* p. 418.

22. *Fisk University Catalog, 1949–1950,* p. 24; Bill Woolsey, "An Afternoon With Art," *Nashville Tennessean Magazine,* 18 December 1949, p. 18; "Catalogue of the Alfred Stieglitz Collection for Fisk University," Fisk University Library.

23. *New York Times,* 22 January 1952; *Fisk University Catalog, 1949–1950,* p. 24.

24. *Nashville Banner,* 24 May 1929; *New York Herald Tribune,* 4 May 1947; *The Story of Music at Fisk University* (pamphlet, n.d.), p. 21.

25. *Nashville American,* 25 March 1899; *The Story of Music at Fisk University;* "Minutes of the Executive Committee of Fisk University," 15 December 1884.

26. *The Story of Music at Fisk University; Fisk University News,* October 1923; M. E. Spence to M. Chase, 14 September 1925, in Mary E. Spence Collection; *Nashville Banner,* 7 September 1925; "John W. Work: Martyr and Singer," *Crisis* 32 (May 1926):32–34.

27. *New York Times,* 26 April 1946; *New York Herald Tribune,* 4 May 1947; *Nashville Banner,* 2 October 1957.

28. *Nashville Tennessean,* 27 April 1923, 27 September 1928; *Nashville Banner,* 27 April 1923, 6 June 1928; *Fisk University Catalog, 1935–1936,* pp. 15–16; *Report of the President of Fisk University, 1929–1930,* p. 23.

29. *Musical Leader,* 2 February 1933; *Boston Transcript,* 25 January 1933; *Boston Globe,* 25 January 1933; *New York Evening Sun,* 3 January 1933; *Cincinnati Times Star,* 14 January 1933; *Boston Herald,* 8 January 1933; *New York Times,* 8 and 27 January 1933; *The Prompter* 3 (January 1933):12; Casimir V. Kiczuk to Station WNAC, New York City, 15 February 1932, in Fiskiana Collection; "Fisk University," *Southern Workman* 61 (March 1932):129.

30. J. F. Ohl to C. Van Vechten, 11 May 1948, in Carl Van Vechten Collection; *New York Times,* 4 November 1945; *Nashville Tennessean,* 23 October 1947; *Nashville Banner,* 7 November 1939.

31. A. Bontemps to C. Van Vechten, 22 October and 22 December 1943, 12 January, 30 March, 14 April, 11 December, and 14 December 1944, C. Van Vechten to A. Bontemps, 10 January and 3 March 1944, in Carl Van Vechten Collection.

CHAPTER 12

1. Frederick Rudolph, *The American College and University: A History* (New York, 1962), pp. 136–37.

2. *Fisk Herald,* November 1937, p. 5; *Fisk University Catalog, 1882–1883,* p. 24.

3. *American Missionary* 44 (April 1890):118; "Minutes of the White Cross League," 15 February, 7 March 1894, 15 April 1894; *Nashville Globe,* 1 February 1907.

4. *Fisk University News*, March 1916, pp. 16–18, April 1916, pp. 29–30.

5. *Nashville Globe*, 1 February 1907; H. Berolzheimer to T. E. Jones, 2 April 1928, T. E. Jones to H. Berolzheimer, 27 March 1928, in Administrative Papers.

6. *Fisk News*, January–February 1936, p. 3, June 1940, p. 5, June 1955, p. 5; *Nashville Tennessean*, 9 January 1940; *Nashville Banner*, 15 March 1958; A. Bontemps to L. Hughes, 18 June 1943, in James Weldon Johnson Memorial Collection, Yale University.

7. Rudolph, *American College and University*, p. 145.

8. *Fisk University Catalog, 1889–1890*, pp. 49–50.

9. Foster Rhea Dulles, *America Learns to Play: A History of Popular Recreation, 1607–1940* (New York, 1940), pp. 197–98; *Fisk Herald*, November 1897, p. 16; *Fisk News*, March–April 1939, p. 6, February 1940, pp. 12–13, June 1947, p. 17, November 1950, p. 13; L. Moore to A. J. Allison, 20 May 1935, in Fiskiana Collection.

10. *Fisk University News*, February 1916, p. 23, March 1916, p. 13; *Nashville Globe*, 1 November 1907; H. H. Wright to W. G. Waterman, 4 November 1908, in F & S Letters.

11. "Minutes of the Prudential Committee of Fisk University," 5 April 1917; *Fisk University News*, November 1919, p. 45, December 1919, p. 32, January 1922, p. 7; F. A. McKenzie to J. L. Peacock, 16 December 1921, J. L. Peacock to F. A. McKenzie, 12 December 1921, in Administrative Papers.

12. *Atlanta World*, 27 January 1931; *Chicago Bee*, 14 December 1930; *New York Age*, 1 November 1930; T. E. Jones to H. A. Johnson, 2 July 1928, H. A. Johnson to T. E. Jones, 28 March 1929, in F & S Letters.

13. *New York Age*, 1 November 1930; G. Streator to A. J. Allison, 10 October 1930, in F & S Letters; *Chicago Defender*, 14 October 1929; *Timely Digest* (October, 1931):5; *Fisk News*, November 1930, p. 16.

14. *Fisk Herald*, October 1934, p. 18.

15. T. E. Jones to Board of Trustees, (n.d.) October 1941, T. E. Jones to H. A. Johnson, 10 December 1934, 18 August 1937, in F & S Letters.

16. *Nashville Tennessean*, 8 October 1946; *Nashville Banner*, 11 October 1948; *Fisk News*, January 1952, p. 2.

17. *Fisk Herald*, May 1935, p. 5.

CHAPTER 13

1. This chapter on alumni deals primarily with those who graduated by the end of World War II. No attempt has been made to discuss more recent distinguished alumni such as Nikki Giovanni. Statistics supplied by former Fisk Alumni Secretary, the late W. Dickerson Donnelly.

2. State of Tennessee, *Annual Report of the Superintendent of Public Instruction for the Scholastic Year Ending June 30, 1900*, pp. 305–6; U.S. Commissioner of Education, *Report for the Year 1899–1900*, 2 vols. (Washington, D.C., 1901), 2:1421; Board of Trustees of Fisk University to the Carnegie Foundation, (n.d.) 1916, in McKenzie Papers; *Report of the President of Fisk University, 1929–1930*.

3. U.S. Commissioner of Education, *Report for the Year 1899–1900*, 2:1421; *Fisk Herald*, March 1884, p. 4, April 1884, p. 6, December 1900, p. 12; *Fisk News*, November 1930, p. 21, April 1932, p. 30, January–February 1934, p. 13, June 1957, p. 5, Summer 1964, p. 21, and Spring 1965, p. 28.

4. McCuistion, *Graduate Instruction for Negroes*, p. 28; U.S., Department of Interior, *Education of Negro Teachers*, p. 46; *Fisk Herald*, May 1899, p. 15.

5. Franklin has also written *The Free Negro in North Carolina, 1790–1860; The Militant South; The Emancipation Proclamation; Racial Equality in America;* and *A Southern Odyssey: Travelers in the Antebellum North,* and he has edited *The Civil War Diary of J. T. Ayers.*

6. *New York Times*, 15 January 1948, 15 February 1956; *Fisk News*, November–December 1936, p. 14; Harry Washington Greene, *Holders of Doctorates Among American Negroes* (Boston, 1946), p. 68.

7. *Fisk Herald*, July 1886, p. 6, December 1899, pp. 2–3; *Fisk News*, October 1930, pp. 44–45, January 1931, p. 7, May–June 1936, p. 15.

8. *Christian Science Monitor*, 1 July 1953; *The United Presbyterian* 100 (23 November 1942):13; *Fisk News*, February 1943, p. 8, Spring 1961, p. 3.

9. Other college presidents include Dr. John Q. Taylor King '41, Huston-Tillotson College; Dr. Rufus B. Atwood '20, Kentucky State College at Frankfort; Dr. Samuel P. Massie, M.A. '40, North Carolina College, Durham; Dr. Maynard P. Turner, Jr., '34, Western Baptist Seminary, Kansas City, Missouri, and American Baptist Theological Seminary, Nashville, Tennessee; Lucius H. Pitts, M.A. '36, Jarvis Christian College, Hawkins, Texas; and Thomas Inborden '91, Brick Junior College. Inborden was president of Brick for thirty-one years, during which time he also served for eight years as president of the North Carolina Farmers Congress. Later he became president of the Eagle Life Insurance Company in Raleigh, North Carolina. Information supplied by the Fisk alumni secretary; *Louisville Leader*, 3 February 1930; "Report of the President to the Board of Trustees of Fisk University, 1955–1956"; *Fisk University News*, March 1916, p. 30, November 1922, p. 25; *Fisk News*, November 1929, p. 5, January 1931, pp. 22–23, August 1931, p. 20, March 1959, p. 5.

10. L. O. Bartow to E. M. Cravath, 19 May 1894, quoted in *Fisk Herald*, August 1894.

11. Douglass, *Christian Reconstruction*, pp. 163, 165; Franklin, *From Slavery to Freedom*, p. 399; *Fisk University News*, November 1910, pp. 8–9; Charles Howard Hopkins, *The Rise of the Social Gospel in American Protestantism, 1865–1915* (New Haven, 1940), pp. 1–4, 53; "Fisk Men After Graduation," in Mary E. Spence Collection; Proctor, *Between Black and White*, pp. 93–95, 109–10.

12. Proctor, *Between Black and White*, pp. 98–112, 157–58; Franklin, *From Slavery to Freedom*, p. 459; Ray Stannard Baker, *Following the Color Line: An Account of Negro Citizenship in the American Democracy* (New York, 1908), pp. 20–21; *Southern News* 3 (June 1926):3; *New York Herald Tribune*, 19 December 1926.

13. W. N. DeBerry to T. E. Jones, 20 March 1928, T. E. Jones to W. N. DeBerry, 25 March 1928, in Letters of the Trustees; Franklin, *From Slavery to Freedom*, p. 399; *Nashville Tennessean*, 21 January 1948; Benjamin Brawley, *Negro Builders and Heroes* (Chapel Hill, 1937), p. 210; *Fisk University News*, May 1916, p. 18.

14. *Fisk News*, December 1931, pp. 9–10, November–December 1933, p. 15, June 1944, p. 5; *Fisk University Catalog, 1900–1901*, p. 76.

15. U.S., Department of Interior, *Survey of Negro Colleges*, p. 745; *American Missionary* 54 (July–September 1900):108; Allen A. Wesley, *The Spanish-American*

War as Seen by the Military Surgeon (pamphlet, 1900), pp. 1–16; *Fisk Herald*, May 1900, p. 1, March 1902, p. 15.

16. T. F. Sublett to Editor, 26 June 1888, in *Fisk Herald*, June 1888, p. 5, June 1897, pp. 12–13, December 1900, p. 12; *Fisk University News*, July 1923, p. 11.

17. *Fisk Herald*, January 1899, p. 5, March 1902, p. 14; *Fisk News*, January 1928, p. 2.

18. *Chicago Bee*, 20 October 1928; *Pittsburgh Courier*, 22 September 1928; *Nashville Globe*, 14 November 1930.

19. Statement about Dr. George Sheppard Moore in Mary E. Spence Collection; *Fisk News*, November–December 1936, p. 8.

20. Numerous other Fiskites became prosperous physicians. H. E. Hampton, '23 was appointed Medical Director of Hospital No. 2 in St. Louis, Missouri. H. H. Weathers '23 was surgeon-in-chief at St. Mary's Infirmary, St. Louis. Homer P. Cooper '11 became chairman of the Division of Surgery of the New Provident Hospital in Chicago. The first black member of the City Hospital Staff, Newark, New Jersey, was Dr. E. Mae McCarroll, a Fiskite. Walter Grant '15 became Senior Attending Urologist, Provident Hospital, Chicago and Attending Urologist, Michigan Avenue Hospital in Chicago. William Moses Jones '22 was appointed ophthalmologist of the University of Chicago. Internationally known for his research on liver disease, Carroll Moton Leevy '41 taught at Seton Hall College of Medicine, Jersey City, New Jersey. William Grant '26 and Guerney D. Holloway '23 both taught at Meharry. Many other Fiskites performed valuable services to their race as physicians. Many Fisk graduates also became pharmacists including a husband and wife team. M. V. '08 and Etnah Rochon Boutte '28 and a mother and son team, Mabel Chadwell '02 and E. L. Price, Jr. Information supplied by the Fisk Alumni Association; *Fisk Herald*, October 1893, pp. 10–11; *Fisk University News*, June 1922, p. 32; *Fisk News*, November 1930, p. 13, January–February 1934, p. 13, March–April 1934, p. 13, April 1946, p. 15.

21. *Fisk Herald*, November 1884, p. 5, April 1890, pp. 3–4.

22. Statement about James B. Cashin in Letters of the Trustees; *Fisk News*, January–February 1934, p. 6, January–February 1936, p. 8, December 1939, p. 17, May 1945, p. 6.

23. *Springfield* (Massachusetts) *Union and Republican*, 20 May 1928; *Fisk News*, January 1955, p. 16, March 1955, p. 19, March 1958, p. 15, Fall 1961, p. 10, Fall 1963, p. 16; *Fisk Herald*, December 1937, p. 10.

24. Other lawyers in important positions were: Charles M. May '50, assistant state's attorney for Cook County, Illinois; Harry Schell '27, city attorney, Gary, Indiana; Barton W. Morris, former student, assistant United States attorney, Detroit, Michigan; Alpha Montgomery '41, member, San Diego, California, city council commissioners; Frederick Work '56, assistant city attorney, Gary, Indiana.

25. *Tallahassee Democrat*, 26 January 1966; *Fisk News*, January 1955, p. 18.

26. *Pittsburgh Courier*, 14 September 1934; *Fisk News*, January–February 1934, p. 13, December 1959, p. 14, Winter 1963, p. 16, Spring 1964, p. 29.

27. Simmons, *Men of Mark*, pp. 498–505; Franklin, *From Slavery to Freedom*, p. 338; C. Vann Woodward, *The Strange Career of Jim Crow* (New York, 1957), p. 25;

Fisk Herald, April 1885, p. 7, December 1886, p. 9, October 1888, pp. 15–16, December 1901, p. 11; *Fisk University Catalog, 1883–1884,* p. 5.

28. *New York Times,* 24 October 1956; Statement about Dr. John Edward Porter in Mary E. Spence Collection; *Fisk News,* October 1957, p. 15, Fall 1961, p. 11.

29. *Chicago Bee,* 27 May 1945; *Christian Science Monitor,* 1 July 1953; *Biographical Directory of the American Congress, 1774–1961* (Washington, D.C., 1961), pp. 790, 812; *Fisk News,* February 1943, p. 8, November 1952, p. 16; Franklin, *From Slavery to Freedom,* pp. 596–97.

30. *New York Amsterdam News,* 28 February 1934; *Indianapolis Recorder,* 23 July 1932; *Fisk News,* November–December 1933, p. 12, March–April 1939, p. 21, November 1940, p. 9; T. E. Jones to A. J. Allison, 12 September 1932, in F & S Letters.

31. Information about Franck Legendre supplied by the Fisk alumni association; *Nashville Tennessean,* 5 September 1956; *New York Times,* 4 May 1945.

32. *Fisk News,* January 1931, p. 21.

33. *Atlanta World,* 20 May 1945; *Fisk University News,* October 1921, p. 15; *Fisk News,* January 1931, pp. 18–19, 22–27, November 1939, p. 16, December 1939, p. 17, March 1952, p. 15, June 1952, p. 3, November 1955, p. 10, June 1956, p. 16.

34. Information supplied by Fisk alumni association; *Fisk University News,* November 1910, p. 9.

35. *Chicago Banker, Merchant and Manufacturer,* quoted in *Fisk University News,* October 1919, p. 37, December 1919, p. 28.

36. *Fisk News,* March–April 1934, p. 13, December 1945, p. 17.

37. *Nashville Tennessean,* 24 April 1958; L. H. Wood to Board of Trustees, 27 March 1942, in Letters of the Trustees; *Fisk News,* April 1946, p. 3.

38. *Chicago Defender,* 1 June 1935; *Washington Tribune,* 26 January 1924; Guzman, *Negro Year Book,* p. 425.

39. Other concert pianists who studied at Fisk include Thomasina Talley Greene '29, C. Warner Lawson '26, Grace Price Goens '27, Andrades Lindsay Brown '19, and Sonoma Talley Hadley '20. *Fisk News,* January 1930, pp. 4–5, October 1930, p. 20; Program of a performance by Lawson at Fisk Memorial Chapel, 30 December 1898, in Fiskiana Collection.

40. Among well-known concert singers from Fisk were Lenora Lafayette '47, Marthra Flowers '47, Catherine Van Buren '31, and Leverne Hutcherson, former student.

41. W. J. Henderson, "The Rise of Roland Hayes," *Mentor* 14 (May 1926):46–47; *Greater Fisk Herald,* April–May 1927, p. 23; G. A. Gates to B. T. Washington, 9 May 1911, in Booker T. Washington Papers; *New York Times,* 4 October 1925, 24 April 1932, 4 November 1948; *Nashville Tennessean,* 6 December 1930; *Nashville Banner,* 11 March 1932; "Minutes of the Board of Trustees of Fisk University," 10 December 1931.

42. *Pittsburgh Courier,* 19 May 1934; *Kansas City Call,* 12 January 1940; Marshall W. Stearns, *The Story of Jazz, With an Expanded Bibliography and a Syllabus of Fifteen Lectures on the History of Jazz* (New York, 1958), pp. 134–36; *Fisk News,* March–April 1934, pp. 9–13, January–February 1937, p. 15.

43. *Savannah Journal,* 6 February 1932; *Chicago Tribune,* 6 February 1965; Stearns, *Story of Jazz,* p. 118.

44. Other Fisk performers were Anne Gamble Kennedy '41 and Matthew Kennedy '47. The latter was acclaimed for his debut in Carnegie Hall in 1957. *Chicago Bee*, 18 February 1945; *Chicago Defender*, 24 February 1945; *Nashville Banner*, 18 February 1928; *Fisk News*, March 1958, p. 15.

45. *Fisk University Catalog, 1887–1888*, p. 9; *Fisk Herald*, September 1883, p. 4, September 1886, p. 6, August 1890, p. 15.

46. *Chicago Defender*, quoted in *Fisk University News*, July 1923, pp. 5–6; *Fisk News*, April 1929, pp. 8–9.

47. *Fisk News*, June 1931, p. 10, December 1931, p. 26, April 1932, p. 13, November–December 1934, p. 18.

48. Knoxville *East Tennessee News*, 24 November 1934; *Fisk News*, May–June 1934, p. 13.

49. *Fisk News*, April 1929, pp. 8–9, January–February 1934, p. 13, November–December 1936, p. 17, May–June 1939, p. 15.

50. Guzman, *Negro Year Book*, p. 461; *Fisk News*, January–February 1934, p. 13, November–December 1934, p. 13, March 1958, p. 16.

51. *New York Times*, 4 May 1946, 17 May 1947; *Christian Science Monitor*, 1 March 1948; *New York Tribune*, 4 May 1947; Franklin, *From Slavery to Freedom*, p. 507; C. Van Vechten to A. Bontemps, 20 May 1946, in Carl Van Vechten Papers; *Fisk Herald*, October 1937, pp. 10, 16–17; *Fisk News*, April 1946, p. 7.

52. *New York World*, 5 December 1926; *Fisk University News*, May 1923, p. 23.

53. *Manchester Guardian*, 21 March 1936; *Fisk News*, January–February 1937, p. 6.

54. *Negro History Bulletin* 17 (May 1954):175–76.

55. *Ebony*, January 1956, p. 85.

56. For detailed studies of DuBois, see: Francis L. Broderick, *W. E. B. DuBois: Negro Leader in a Time of Crisis* (Stanford, California, 1959); Elliott M. Rudwick, *W. E. B. DuBois: A Study of Minority Group Leadership* (Philadelphia, 1960); Arna Bontemps, *100 Years of Negro Freedom* (New York, 1962); Saunders Redding, *The Lonesome Road: The Story of the Negro's Part in America* (New York, 1958); Embree, *13 Against the Odds*.

Selected Bibliography

MANUSCRIPTS

American Missionary Association Archives, 1861–1879, Amistad Research Center, Dillard University, New Orleans, Louisiana.

Bureau of Refugees, Freedmen, and Abandoned Lands, Educational Division, National Archives, Washington, D.C.

Fisk University, Faculty and Staff Letters, Fisk University Library.

Fisk University, Letters of the Board of Trustees, Fisk University Library.

Fisk University, Minutes of the Board of Trustees, 24 August 1867–April 1947, Fisk University Library.

Fisk University, Minutes of the Executive Committee, 1875–1890, Fisk University Library.

Fisk University, Minutes of the Faculty of the Department of Music, 7 September 1885–25 October 1906.

Fisk University, Minutes of the General Faculty, 4 January 1869–17 October 1881, Fisk University Library.

Fisk University, Minutes of the General Faculty, 23 October 1881–26 May 1920, Fisk University Library.

Fisk University, Minutes of the General Faculty, 7 February 1924–14 August 1924, Fisk University Library.

Fisk University, Minutes of the Prudential Committee, 29 September 1909–2 January 1917, Fisk University Library.

Fisk University, Minutes of the Prudential Committee, 2 January 1917–6 June 1927, Fisk University Library.

Fisk University, Minutes of the Union Church, 1868–1908, Fisk University Library.

Fisk University, Minutes of the Union Literary Society, 31 January 1868–19 March 1875.

Fisk University, Minutes of the Union Literary Society, 1 January 1876–20 April 1883, Fisk University Library.

Fisk University Letter Book, 6 September 1869–2 June 1873, Fisk University Library.

Fisk University Visitors Register, 21 January 1877–1941, Fisk University Library.

Fiskiana Collection, includes manuscript, pamphlets, brochures, pictures, scrapbooks, and newspaper clippings, Fisk University Library.

O. O. Howard Papers, Hawthorne-Longfellow Library, Bowdoin College, Brunswick, Maine.

George E. Haynes Letters, 1915–1922, Fisk University Library.

Charles S. Johnson Papers, Amistad Research Center, Dillard University, New Orleans, Louisiana.

James Weldon Johnson Memorial Collection, Beinecke Library, Yale University, New Haven, Connecticut.

Thomas E. Jones Administrative Papers, Fisk University Library.

Thomas E. Jones Letters 1926-1934, Fisk University Library.

Jubilee Singers, Letters concerning, Fisk University Library.

Fayette Avery McKenzie Papers, Tennessee State Library and Archives, Nashville.

Fayette Avery McKenzie Administrative Papers, Fisk University Library.

Henrietta Matson Letter Press, January 1873-March 1876, Fisk University Library.

James G. Merrill Administrative Papers, Fisk University Library.

James Carroll Napier Papers, 1868-1939, Fisk University Library.

America Robinson Letters, 4 March 1875-4 August 1878, Fisk University Library.

Julius Rosenwald Fund Papers, Fisk University Library.

Ella Sheppard Diary, 7 November 1874-14 November 1876, Fisk University Library.

Ella Sheppard Diary, 19 October 1877-15 July 1878, Fisk University Library.

Mary E. Spence Collection, Fisk University Library.

Thomas C. Steward Letter Press, November 1872-October 1874, Fisk University Library.

Tappan Papers, 1825-1871, Library of Congress, Washington, D.C.

Carl Van Vechten Papers, Beinecke Library, Yale University, New Haven, Connecticut.

Booker T. Washington Papers, Library of Congress, Washington, D.C.

George L. White Letter Press, September 1869-September 1871, Fisk University Library.

SCRAPBOOKS

Herbert H. Wright Scrapbook, 1892-1895, Fisk University Library.

Herbert H. Wright Scrapbook, 1895-1901, Fisk University Library.

Henry S. Bennett Scrapbook, 1874-1875, Fisk University Library.

Henry S. Bennett Scrapbook, 1892-1895, Fisk University Library.

Fisk University Scrapbook, 1870-1876, Fisk University Library.

Fisk University Scrapbook, 1886-1891, Fisk University Library.

George L. White Scrapbook, 1867-1872, Fisk University Library.

George L. White Scrapbook, 1873-1874, Fisk University Library.

PAMPHLETS AND BROCHURES

Beard, A. F. *After Forty Years: Discourse at the Fortieth Anniversary of Fisk University.* Nashville, n.d.

Beard, A. F. et al. *Erastus Milo Cravath*. N.p.n.d.

Catalogue of the Alfred Stieglitz Collection for Fisk University. N.p.n.d.

Charles Spurgeon Johnson: A Bibliography. Nashville, 1947.

Exercises Marking the Opening of the James Weldon Johnson Memorial Collection of Negro Arts and Letters. New Haven, 1950.

Fisk: After Seventy Years. Nashville, n.d.

Fisk and the Race's Future. Nashville, n.d.

The Fisk Rural Life Program: A Plan for the Development of Negro Leaders for the Rural South. Nashville, 1945.

Fisk University. N.p.n.d.

Fisk University and Negro Health. Nashville, n.d.

Fisk University in 1911. Nashville, 1911.

Fisk University: Forty-Five Years, 1866-1911. Nashville, 1911.

Fisk University: History, Building and Site, and Services of Dedication, at Nashville, Tennessee, January 1st, 1876, New York, 1876.

A Milestone in Negro Education: Announcing the Jubilee and Founders' Day Exercises November 16-17, 1924. Nashville, 1924.

Moore, Ella Sheppard. *Before Emancipation.* New York, n.d.

Morrow, Cornelius W. *The Fisk of Today.* Nashville, 1920.

Requiescat in Pace: Charles Spurgeon Johnson 1893-1956. N.p.n.d.

Spence, Adam K. *After Twenty-Five Years in Negro Education.* N.p., 1895.

Spingarn, Arthur D. et al. *James Weldon Johnson.* N.p.n.d.

The Story of Music at Fisk University. Nashville, n.d.

Wesley, Allen A. *The Spanish-American War as Seen By The Military Surgeon.* Chicago, 1890.

NEWSPAPERS

Baltimore *Afro-American.*

Chicago *Defender.*

Nashville *American.*

Nashville *Colored Tennessean.*

Nashville *Daily Press and Times.*

Nashville *Daily Union.*

Nashville *Daily Union and American.*

Nashville *Republican Banner.*

Nashville *Tennessean.*

New York *Amsterdam News.*

New York *Times.*

New York *Tribune.*

Pittsburgh *Courier.*

Times (London), 1873, 1874, 1877.

Washington, D.C. *People's Advocate.*

JOURNALS

Advance, 1873-1879.
American Freedman, 1866-1869.
American Missionary, 1866-1900.
Crisis, 1923-1927.
Christian Union, 1871-1875.
Fisk Expositor, 1878-1882.
Fisk Herald, 1878-1905.
Fisk News, 1927-1960.
Fisk University News, 1910-1927.
The Freedman, 1864-1869.
Freedmen's Record, 1865-1868.
National Freedman, 1865-1866.
Pennsylvania Freedman's Bulletin, 1865-1867.

CATALOGUES

Catalog of Fisk University, 1867-1950.
Catalogue of the Officers and Students of Alcorn A. and M. College, 1884-1885.

REPORTS AND PROCEEDINGS

Association of Colleges and Secondary Schools for Negroes. *Proceedings of.* N.p. 1934.
National Educational Association, *Journal of Proceedings, and Addresses . . . 1889.* Topeka, 1889.
Proceedings of the Conference For Education in the South, 1903. New York, 1903.
Proceedings of the Conference For Education in the South, 1904. New York, 1904.
Proceedings of the Fifth Conference For Education in the South, Held at Athens, Georgia, April 24, 25 and 26, 1902. Knoxville, 1902.
Proceedings of the Fourth Conference For Education in the South, Held at Winston-Salem, North Carolina, April 18, 19, and 20, 1901. Harrisburg, Pennsylvania, 1901.
Report of the Trustees and Faculty of the Alcorn A. & M. College to the Legislature of Mississippi for the Years 1884-85. Jackson, Mississippi, 1885.
Reports of the President of Fisk University, 1929-1942.
Southern Educational Association. *Journal of Proceedings and Addresses of the Nineteenth Annual Session Held at Atlanta, Georgia, December 29-31, 1908.* Chattanooga, 1908.
Twenty-Second Annual Report of the American Missionary Association and the Proceedings at the Annual Meeting . . . 1868. New York, 1868.
Twenty-Fourth Annual Report of the American Missionary Association and the Proceedings at the Annual Meeting . . . 1870. New York, 1870.

Western Freedmen's Aid Commission. *Annual Reports 1865–1866*. Cincinnati, 1865–1866.

GOVERNMENT DOCUMENTS

Tennessee. *Biennial Report of the State Superintendent of Public Instruction for the Scholastic Years ending June 30, 1919–1920*, Nashville, 1921.
Tennessee. *Reports of the State Superintendent of Public Instruction, 1878–1922*.
United States, Bureau of Education. *Statistics of Education of the Negro Race, 1924–1926*, Bulletin, No. 19: 1–42, 1928.
U.S. Commissioner of Education. *Reports 1884–1902*. Washington, 1888–1903.
U.S. Department of Interior, Office of Education. *Education of Negro Teachers*. Bulletin No. 10, Vol. IV, 1933, Prepared under Direction of Ambrose Caliver, Washington, 1933.
U.S. Department of Interior, Office of Education. *Statistics of the Education of Negroes, 1929–30 and 1931–32*. Bulletin No. 13, 1938. Prepared under Direction of David T. Blose and Ambrose Caliver, Washington, 1936.
U.S. Department of Interior. Office of Education. *Statistics of the Education of Negroes 1933–34 and 1935–36*. Bulletin No. 13, 1935. Prepared under Direction of David T. Blose and Ambrose Caliver. Washington, 1939.
U.S. Department of Interior, Bureau of Education. *Survey of Negro Colleges and Universities*. Bulletin No. 7, 1928. Prepared under Direction of Arthur J. Klein, Washington, 1929.

BOOKS

Abbott, A. O. *Prison Life in the South*. New York, 1865.
Alexander, William T. *History of the Colored Race in America*. New Orleans, 1887.
Alvord, John W. *Letters From the South, Relating to the Freedmen, Addressed to Major General O. O. Howard*. Washington, D.C., 1870.
Aptheker, Herbert, ed. *The Correspondence of W. E. B. DuBois: Selections, 1877–1934*. Vol. I, Amherst, 1973.
Armstrong, Byron K. *Factors in the Formulation of Collegiate Programs for Negroes*. Ann Arbor, 1939.
Arnett, Trevor. *Teachers' Salaries in Certain Endowed and State Supported Colleges and Universities in the United States, with Special Reference to Colleges of Arts, Literature and Science 1926–1927*. New York, 1928.
——. *Teachers' Salaries in Certain Endowed Colleges and Universities in the United States*. New York, 1921.
Atkins, Gaius G. and Fagley, Fred L. *History of American Congregationalism*. Boston, 1942.
Bailey, Thomas P. *Race Orthodoxy in the South, and other Aspects of the Negro Question*. New York, 1914.

Baker, Ray Stannard. *Following the Color Line: An Account of Negro Citizenship in the American Democracy.* New York, 1908.

Beard, Augustus Field. *A Crusade of Brotherhood: A History of the American Missionary Association.* Boston, 1909.

Bentley, George R. *A History of the Freedmen's Bureau.* Philadelphia, 1955.

Bloom, Julius, ed. *The Year in American Music: 1946–47.* New York, 1947.

Bond, Horace Mann. *The Education of the Negro in the American Social Order.* New York, 1934.

Bontemps, Arna. *100 Years of Negro Freedom.* New York, 1962.

Brawley, Benjamin. *A Short History of the American Negro.* New York, 1931.

———. *A Social History of the American Negro.* New York, 1921.

———. *Negro Builders and Heroes.* Chapel Hill, 1937.

Broderick, Francis L. *W. E. B. DuBois: Negro Leader in a Time of Crisis.* Stanford, 1959.

Brownlee, Fred L. *New Day Ascending.* Boston, 1946.

Bullock, Henry Allen. *A History of Negro Education in the South from 1619 to the Present.* Cambridge, 1967.

Butcher, Margaret Just. *The Negro in American Culture.* New York, 1956.

Campbell, Sir George. *White and Black, The Outcome of a Visit to the United States.* London, 1879.

Cannon, Poppy. *A Gentle Knight: My Husband, Walter White.* New York, 1956.

Carnegie Foundation for the Advancement of Teaching. *The Financial Status of the Professor in America and in Germany.* New York, 1908.

Carpenter, John A. *Sword and Olive Branch.* Pittsburgh, 1964.

Carter, Hodding. *The Angry Scar.* New York, 1959.

Clayton, W. W. *History of Davidson County, Tennessee.* Philadelphia, 1880.

Cremin, Lawrence. *The Transformation of the School: Progressivism in American Education 1876–1957.* New York, 1961.

Curry, J. L. M. *Education of the Negroes Since 1860.* Baltimore, 1894.

Dabney, Charles William. *Universal Education in the South.* 2 vols. Chapel Hill, 1936.

Davis, W. Milan. *Pushing Forward; a History of Alcorn A. and M. College and Portraits of Some of its Successful Graduates.* Okolona, Mississippi, 1938.

Derbigny, Irving Antony. *General Education in the Negro College.* Stanford, 1947.

Donald, Henderson H. *The Negro Freedman.* New York, 1952.

Douglass, Harlan Paul. *Christian Reconstruction in the South.* Boston, 1909.

DuBois, W. E. B. *The Autobiography of W. E. B. DuBois: A Soliloquy on Viewing My Life From the Last Decade of its First Century.* New York, 1968.

———. *Dusk of Dawn: An Essay Toward an Autobiography of a Race Concept.* New York, 1940.

———. *The Souls of Black Folk.* New York, 1903.

Dulles, Foster Rhea. *America Learns to Play: A History of Popular Recreation 1607–1940.* New York, 1940.

Embree, Edwin R. *American Negroes: A Handbook.* New York, 1942.

———. *Brown America.* New York, 1931.

———. *13 Against the Odds.* New York, 1944.

Eppse, Merl R. *The Negro, Too, in American History.* Nashville, 1943.

Evans, Maurice S. *Black and White in the Southern States: A Study of the Race Problem in the United States From a South African Point of View.* London and New York, 1915.

Fertig, James Walter. *The Secession and Reconstruction of Tennessee.* Chicago, 1898.

Fisher, Miles Mark. *Slave Songs in the United States.* Ithaca, New York, 1953.

Fosdick, Raymond B. *Adventures in Giving: The Story of the General Education Board.* New York, 1962.

Franklin, John Hope. *From Slavery to Freedom: A History of Negro Americans.* 4th ed. rev. New York, 1974.

Frazier, E. Franklin. *Black Bourgeoisie.* Glencoe, 1957.

Freeman, Edward A. *Some Impressions of the United States.* New York, 1883.

Gallagher, Buell G. *American Caste and the Negro College.* New York, 1933.

Gates, Isabel Smith. *The Life of George Augustus Gates.* New York, 1915.

Greene, Henry Washington. *Holders of Doctorates Among American Negroes.* Boston, 1946.

Haley, James T., comp. *Afro-American Encyclopedia or, the Thoughts, Doings and Sayings of the Race.* Nashville, 1896.

Harlan, Louis R. *Separate and Unequal.* Chapel Hill, 1958.

History of Nashville, Tennessee. Nashville, 1890.

History of the American Missionary Association; Its Churches and Educational Institutions Among the Freedmen, Indians, and Chinese. New York, 1874.

Holmes, Dwight O. W. *The Evolution of the Negro College.* New York, 1934.

Hopkins, Alphonso A. *The Life of Clinton Bowen Fisk.* New York, 1890.

Hopkins, Charles Howard. *The Rise of the Social Gospel in American Protestantism 1865-1915.* New Haven, 1940.

Hubbard, G. W., comp. *A History of the Colored Schools of Nashville, Tennessee.* Nashville, 1874.

Hughes, Langston. *Fight For Freedom: The Story of the NAACP.* New York, 1962.

Jessen, Mrs. Maude Weidner. *Nashville, Then and Now.* Nashville, 1930.

Johnson, Charles S. *The Negro College Graduate.* Chapel Hill, 1938.

――――. *The Negro in American Civilization.* New York, 1930.

Johnson, Charles S., et al. *Into the Main Stream: A Survey of Best Practices in Race Relations in the South.* Chapel Hill, 1947.

Johnson, James Weldon. *Along This Way.* New York, 1938.

Jones, Lance G. E. *Negro Schools in the Southern States.* Oxford, England, 1928.

King, Edward. *The Southern States of North America.* London, 1875.

Krehbiel, Henry E. *Afro-American Folksongs: A Study in Racial and National Music.* New York, 1914.

Leavell, Ullin W. *Philanthropy in Negro Education.* Nashville, 1930.

Locke, Alain, ed. *The New Negro.* New York, 1925.

Logan, Rayford W. *The Negro in American Life and Thought: The Nadir, 1877-1901.* New York, 1954.

――――. *What the Negro Wants.* Chapel Hill, 1944.

Loggins, Vernon. *The Negro Author: His Development in America.* New York, 1931.

Lomax, John A. and Alan, comp. *American Ballads and Folk Songs.* New York, 1934.

McCuistion, Fred. *The South's Negro Teaching Force.* Nashville, 1931.

McKinney, Richard I. *Religion in Higher Education Among Negroes.* New Haven, 1945.
McKinney, Theophilus E., ed. *Higher Education Among Negroes.* Charlotte, N.C., 1932.
McPherson, James M. *The Abolitionist Legacy: From Reconstruction to the NAACP.* Princeton, 1975.
―――. *The Struggle for Equality: Abolitionists and the Negro in the Civil War and Reconstruction.* Princeton, 1964.
Macrae, David. *The Americans at Home: Pen and ink sketches of American men, manners, and Institutions.* Glasgow, 1875.
McRaven, Henry. *Nashville: "Athens of the South."* Chapel Hill, 1949.
Marsh, J. B. T. *The Story of the Jubilee Singers with Their Songs.* 3rd. ed. London, 1876.
Mayers, Edward. *History of Education in Mississippi.* Washington, 1899.
Meier, August. *Negro Thought in America, 1880–1914: Racial ideologies in the Age of Booker T. Washington.* Ann Arbor, 1963.
Meltzer, Milton. *Mark Twain Himself.* New York, 1960.
Merriam, Lucius S. *Higher Education in Tennessee.* Washington, 1893.
Merrill, James G. "Fisk University," in *From Servitude to Service.* Boston, 1905.
Mims, Edwin. *Chancellor Kirkland of Vanderbilt.* Nashville, 1940.
Murphy, Edgar Gardner. *The Basis of Ascendancy.* New York, 1909.
Myrdal, Gunnar. *An American Dilemma: The Negro Problem and Modern Democracy.* New York, 1944.
Nolen, Claude H. *The Negro's Image in the South: The Anatomy of White Supremacy.* Lexington, 1967.
Ovington, Mary White. *The Walls Came Tumbling Down.* New York, 1947.
Pierce, Joseph A. *Negro Business and Business Education.* New York, 1947.
Pike, Gustavus D. *The Jubilee Singers, and their Campaign for Twenty Thousand Dollars.* New York, 1873.
―――. *The Singing Campaign for Ten Thousand Pounds; or The Jubilee Singers in Great Britain.* rev. ed. New York, 1875.
Proctor, Henry Hugh. *Between Black and White: Autobiographical Sketches.* Boston, 1925.
Range, Willard. *The Rise and Progress of Negro Colleges in Georgia 1865–1949.* Athens, Georgia, 1951.
Robert, Charles Edwin. *Negro Civilization in the South; Educational, Social and Religious Advancement of the Colored People.* Nashville, 1880.
Rose, Willie Lee. *Rehearsal for Reconstruction: The Port Royal Experiment.* New York, 1964.
Roy, Joseph E. *Pilgrim's Letters: Bits of Current History.* Boston, 1888.
Rubin, Louis D., ed. *Teach the Freeman: the Correspondence of Rutherford B. Hayes and the Slater Fund for Negro Education, 1881–1893.* 2 vols. Baton Rouge, 1959.
Rudolph, Frederick. *The American College and University: A History.* New York, 1962.
Simmons, William J. *Men of Mark: Eminent, Progressive and Rising.* Cleveland, Ohio, 1887.
Somers, Robert. *The Southern States Since the War, 1870–1871.* London, 1871.

Spencer, Samuel R., Jr. *Booker T. Washington and the Negro's Place in American Life.* Boston, 1955.

Stearns, Marshall W. *The Story of Jazz, with an Expanded Bibliography and a Syllabus of Fifteen Lectures on the History of Jazz.* New York, 1958.

Stowell, J. S. *Methodist Adventures in Negro Education.* New York, 1922.

Swaine, Robert T. *The Cravath Firm and Its Predecessors 1819–1947.* 3 vols. New York, 1948.

Swint, Henry L. *The Northern Teacher in the South, 1862–1870.* Nashville, 1941.

Thomas, William Hannibal. *The American Negro.* New York, 1901.

Thompson, Seymour D. and Steger, Thomas M. *A Compilation of the Statute Laws of the State of Tennessee.* 2 vols. St. Louis, 1873.

Thorpe, Earl E. *The Mind of the Negro: An Intellectual History of Afro-Americans.* Baton Rouge, 1961.

Trowbridge, J. T. *A Picture of the Desolated States; and the Work of Restoration 1865–1868.* Hartford, Connecticut, 1868.

Van Deusen, John G. *The Black Man in White America.* Washington, D.C., 1938.

Vaughan, William Preston. *Schools For All: The Blacks and Public Education in the South, 1865–1877.* Lexington, 1974.

Washington, Booker T. *The Future of the American Negro.* Boston, 1907.

Weidner, Maude. *Nashville Then and Now 1780–1930.* Nashville, 1930.

Weisberger, Bernard A. *They Gathered at the River: The Story of the Great Revivalists and Their Impact Upon Religion in America.* Boston, 1958.

White, Walter. *A Man Called White.* New York, 1948.

Williams, George W. *History of the Negro Race in America from 1619 to 1880.* 2 vols. New York, 1883.

Wolters, Raymond. *The New Negro on Campus: Black College Rebellions of the 1920's.* Princeton, 1975.

Woodson, Carter G. *The Negro in Our History.* Washington, D.C., 1931.

Woodward, C. Vann. *Origins of the New South 1877–1913.* Baton Rouge, 1951.

————. *The Strange Career of Jim Crow.* New York, 1957.

Wyatt-Brown, Bertram. *Lewis Tappan and the Evangelical War Against Slavery.* Cleveland, 1969.

PERIODICALS

Armstrong, Warren B. "Union Chaplains and the Education of the Freedmen," *Journal of Negro History,* 52 (April 1967), 104–15.

Bent, M. J. and Green, Ellen F. "An Experiment in Health Education," *The Journal of Health and Physical Education,* 7 (October 1936), 486–88.

Blanchard, F. Q. "A Quarter Century in the American Missionary Association," *Journal of Negro Education,* 6 (April 1937), 152–56.

Bontemps, Arna. "Why I Returned," *Harper's,* 230 (April 1965), 177–82.

Chivers, W. R. "Religion in Negro Colleges," *Journal of Negro Education,* 9 (January 1940), 5–12.

Clark, E. R. "Music Education in Negro Schools and Colleges," *Journal of Negro Education,* 9 (October 1940), 580–90.

Cox, O. C. "Vested Interests Involved in the Integration of Schools for Negroes," *Journal of Negro Education,* 20 (Winter 1951), 112–14.

Crooks, K. B. M. "Entrance Examinations for Negro Colleges," *Journal of Negro Education*, 3 (October 1934), 593-97.

_____. "Is Negro Education Failing?" *Journal of Negro Education*, 8 (January 1939), 19-25.

Dartmouth Alumni Magazine, 21 (February 1929), 257.

Davis, Arthur P. "The Negro Professor," *Crisis*, 43 (April 1936), 103-04.

Davis, E. P. "The Negro Liberal Arts College," *Journal of Negro Education*, 2 (July 1933), 299-311.

Davis, John. "Unrest in the Negro Colleges," *New Student*, 8 (January 1929), 13-14.

Davis, Thomas E. "A Study of Fisk University Freshmen from 1928 to 1930," *Journal of Negro Education*, 2 (October 1933), 477-83.

_____. "Some Racial Attitudes of Negro College and Grade School Students," *Journal of Negro Education*, 6 (April 1937), 157-65.

Decker, P. "A Study of 'White' Teachers in Selected 'Negro' Colleges," *Journal of Negro Education*, 24 (Fall 1955), 501-05.

DuBois, W. E. Burghardt. "A Crisis at Fisk," *Nation*, 163 (7 September 1946), 267-70.

_____. "The Dilemma of the Negro," *American Mercury*, 3 (October 1924), 179-85.

_____. "Does the Negro Need Separate Schools?" *Journal of Negro Education*, 4 (July 1935), 328-35.

_____. "Negroes in College," *Nation*, 122 (3 March 1926), 228-30.

_____. "Of the Training of Black Men," *Atlantic Monthly*, 90 (September 1902), 289-97.

"The Fight at Fisk," *The Independent*, 114 (9 May 1925), 513-14.

"The Fisk Drive," *The Southern Workman*, 49 (April 1920), 149.

"The Fisk Endowment," *The Southern Workman*, 53 (September 1924), 388-90.

"Fisk University," *The Southern Workman*, 39 (May 1910), 259.

"Fisk University," *The Southern Workman*, 61 (March 1932), 129-30.

Frazier, E. Franklin. "Graduate Education in Negro Colleges and Universities," *Journal of Negro Education*, 2 (July 1933), 329-41.

Gallagher, B. G. "Reorganize the College to Discharge its Social Function," *Journal of Negro Education*, 5 (July 1936), 464-73.

Gilbert, Ethel B. "Fisk's New Library," *The Southern Workman*, 60 (February 1931), 61-67.

Grantham, Dewey, W., Jr. "The Regional Imagination: Social Scientists and the American South," *The Journal of Southern History*, 34 (February 1968), 3-32.

Greene, Harry W. "Crucial Problems in the Higher Education of Negroes," *School and Society*, 46 (21 August 1937), 245-46.

_____. "The Negro College and Social Change," *Opportunity*, 14 (August 1936), 235-38.

_____. "The Ph.D. and the Negro," *Opportunity*, 6 (September 1928), 267-69.

Harper's Weekly, 20 (22 January 1976), 73.

Hill, J. N. "The Negro College Faces Desegregation," *College and University*, 31 (Spring 1956), 291-97.

Henderson, W. J. "The Rise of Roland Hayes," *The Mentor*, 14, (May 1926), 46-47.

Himes, J. S., Jr., "Development and Status of Sociology in Negro Colleges," *Journal of Educational Sociology,* 23 (September 1949), 17–32.

——. "The Teacher of Sociology in the Negro College," *Social Forces,* 29 (March 1951), 302–05.

Holmes, D. O. W. "Beginnings of the Negro College," *Journal of Negro Education,* 3 (April 1934), 168–93.

——. "The Future Possibilities of Graduate Work in Negro Colleges and Universities," *Journal of Negro Education,* 7 (January 1938), 5–11.

——. "The Negro College Faces the Depression," *Journal of Negro Education,* 2 (January 1933), 16–25.

Jenkins, Martin D. "Enrollment in Negro Colleges and Universities: 1937–38," *Journal of Negro Education,* 7 (April 1938), 118–23.

——. "Graduate Work in Negro Institutions of Higher Education," *Journal of Higher Education,* 18 (June 1947), 300–06.

Johnson, G. B. "Desegregation and the Future of the Negro College; a Critical Summary," *Journal of Negro Education,* 28 (Summer 1958), 430–35.

"The Johnson Family," *The Negro History Bulletin,* 12 (November 1948), 27–28.

"John Work: Martyr and Singer," *Crisis,* 32 (May 1926), 32–34.

Jones, D. D. "Cultural Obligations of the Faculty in a Negro Liberal Arts College," *Association of American Colleges Bulletin,* 25 (March 1939), 62–65.

Lamon, Lester C. "The Black Community in Nashville and the Fisk University Student Strike of 1924–1925," *Journal of Southern History,* 40 (May 1974), 224–44.

Libraries, 34 (February 1929), 61.

Libraries, 34 (November 1929), 431–32.

Library Journal, 56 (February 1931), 107–10.

Lloyd, R. G. "Loyalty Oaths and Communistic Influences in Negro Colleges and Universities," *School and Society,* 75 (5 January 1952), 8–9.

McCulloch, M. C. "Function of the Negro Cultural College," *Journal of Negro Education,* 6 (October 1937), 617–22.

McPheeters, A. A. "Departments of Education in Seventeen Small Negro Liberal Arts Colleges," *Journal of Negro Education,* 7 (April 1938), 160–64.

McPherson, James M. "White Liberals and Black Power in Negro Education, 1865–1915," *American Historical Review,* 75 (June 1970), 1357–79.

Mays, Benjamin E. "Does Integration Doom Negro Colleges," *Negro Digest,* 11 (May 1962), 3–6.

Meier, August. "Toward a Reinterpretation of Booker T. Washington," *The Journal of Southern History,* 23 (May 1957), 220–27.

Miller, Kelly. "The Negro and Education," *Forum,* 30 (February 1901), 693–705.

——. "Reorganization of the Higher Education of the Negro in light of Changing Conditions," *Journal of Negro Education,* 5 (July 1936), 484–94.

——. "The Past, Present and Future of the Negro College," *Journal of Negro Education,* 2 (July 1933), 411–22.

"The Modern University with a Heritage: An Introduction to Fisk University," *Fisk University Bulletin,* 32 (December 1957), 1–29.

Myers, A. F. "The Colleges for Negroes," *Survey,* 86 (May 1950), 233–39.

Nabrit, S. M. "Desegregation and the Future of Graduate and Professional Education in Negro Institutions," *Journal of Negro Education*, 27 (Summer 1958), 414-18.

Negro Digest, 11 (September 1962), 3-5.

"Negro Universities and Colleges," *School and Society*, 17 (31 March 1923), 350-51.

Oak, Vishnu V. "Higher Education and the Negro," *Education* 53 (November 1932), 176-81.

_____. "Some Outstanding Defects in Institutions of Higher Learning for Negroes," *School and Society*, 46 (18 September 1937), 357-62.

Opportunity, 25 (Winter 1947), 26.

The Outlook, 99 (23 December 1911), 935.

The Outlook, 111 (24 November 1915), 700.

Patterson, F. D. "The Private Negro College in A Racially-Integrated System of Higher Education," *Journal of Negro Education*, 21 (Summer 1952), 363-69.

Payne, J. A., Jr. "The Role of the Negro College in the Light of Integrative Trends," *Journal of Negro Education*, 22 (Winter 1953), 80-83.

Rand, E. W. "The Negro Private and Church College at Mid-Century," *Journal of Negro Education*, 22 (Winter 1953), 77-79.

Redd, G. N. "Present Status of Negro Higher and Professional Education; Critical Summary," *Journal of Negro Education*, 17 (Summer 1948), 400-09.

Richardson, Joe M. "A Negro Success Story: James Dallas Burrus," *Journal of Negro History*, 50 (October 1965), 274-82.

_____. "The Early Years of Fisk University," *Tennessee Historical Quarterly*, 29 (April 1970), 21-41.

Roberts, S. O. "Negro Higher and Professional Education in Tennessee," *Journal of Negro Education*, 17 (Summer 1948), 361-72.

Ross, Mary, "The Leaven and the Loaf," *Survey*, 62 (1 May 1929), 171-75.

School and Society, 17 (17 March 1923), 293-94.

School and Society, 20 (2 August 1924), 144.

School and Society, 54 (30 August 1941), 136-37.

Smythe, H. H. "Effects of the War on the Negro College," *Journal of Higher Education*, 16 (February 1945), 98-100.

Spence, Mary E. "The Jubilee of Jubilees at Fisk University," *The Southern Workman*, 51 (February 1922), 73-80.

Stewart, Ollie. "Too Much of Nothing," *Southern Workman*, 61 (August 1932), 333-37.

Strider, R. H. "Negro's Contribution to Music Education," *Music Educators Journal*, 39 (February 1953), 27-28.

"A Student Revolution," *Nation*, 120 (18 March 1925), 283.

Sumner, F. C. "Morale and the Negro College," *Educational Review*, 73 (March 1927), 168-72.

Taylor, A. A. "Fisk University and the Nashville Community, 1866-1900," *Journal of Negro History*, 39 (April 1954), 111-26.

Thompson, Charles H. "Administrators of Negro Colleges and the Color Line in Higher Education in the South," *Journal of Negro Education*, 17 (Fall 1948), 437-45.

_____. "The Education of the Negro in the United States," *School and Society*, 42 (9 November 1935), 625-33.

――――. "Are There Too Many Negro Colleges?" *Journal of Negro Education*, 3 (April 1934), 159-67.

――――. "The Socio-Economic Status of Negro College Students," *Journal of Negro Education*, 2 (January 1933), 26-37.

――――. "The Critical Situation in Negro Higher and Professional Education," *Journal of Negro Education*, 15 (Fall 1946), 579-84.

Thompson, Edgar T. "Sociology and Sociological Research in the South," *Social Forces*, 23 (March 1945), 356-65.

"To Command Respect," *Time*, 48 (15 July 1946), 69-70.

Trent, W. J., Jr. "Private Negro Colleges Since the Gaines Decision," *Journal of Educational Sociology*, 32 (February 1959), 267-74.

――――. "The Problems of Financing Private Negro Colleges," *Journal of Negro Education*, 18 (Spring 1949), 114-22.

Ware, Edward T. "Higher Education of Negroes in the United States," *Annals of American Academy*, 49 (September 1913), 209-18.

Washington, Booker T. "A University Education for Negroes," *The Independent*, 68 (24 March 1910), 613-18.

Wilson, Dwight H. "John H. Burrus and His Family," *The Negro History Bulletin*, 12 (October 1948), 3, 15, 23.

Wilson, R. D. "Negro Colleges of Liberal Arts," *American Scholar*, 19 (October 1950), 461-70.

"Youth Exhibits a New Spirit," *Crisis*, 43 (August 1936), 237+.

                                   UNPUBLISHED MATERIALS

Brownlee, Fred. "A Memorandum Concerning Fisk University Growing Out of Personal Conversations Between Certain Members of the Staff and Fred Brownlee Together with On-The-Campus Diagnostic Observations." Typescript, Fiskiana Collection, 1951, Fisk University Library.

Drake, Richard B. "The American Missionary Association and the Southern Negro, 1861-1888," Ph.D. dissertation, Emory University, 1957.

Eaton, James N. "The Life of Erastus Milo Cravath; A Guiding Light in an Era of Darkness," M.A. Thesis, Fisk University, 1959.

Imes, Mabel Lewis. "Autobiography," Typescript, Fiskiana Collection, Fisk University Library.

Johnson, Clifton H. "The American Missionary Association, 1846-1861: A Study of Christian Abolitionism," Ph.D. dissertation, University of North Carolina, 1959.

Index